Haiti's Literary Legacies

Haiti's Literary Legacies

Romanticism and the Unthinkable Revolution

*Edited by Kir Kuiken and
Deborah Elise White*

BLOOMSBURY ACADEMIC
NEW YORK · LONDON · OXFORD · NEW DELHI · SYDNEY

BLOOMSBURY ACADEMIC
Bloomsbury Publishing Inc
1385 Broadway, New York, NY 10018, USA
50 Bedford Square, London, WC1B 3DP, UK
29 Earlsfort Terrace, Dublin 2, Ireland

BLOOMSBURY, BLOOMSBURY ACADEMIC and the Diana logo are trademarks
of Bloomsbury Publishing Plc

First published in the United States of America 2022
This paperback edition published 2023

Volume Editor's Part of the Work © Kir Kuiken and Deborah Elise White, 2022
Chapters 1–7 © of Contributors "Revolutionary Shattering:
Emerson on the Haitian Revolution" by Branka Arsić © *Telos*, 2015

For legal purposes the Acknowledgments on p. vii constitute an extension
of this copyright page.

Cover design: Eleanor Rose
Cover image: *The Life of Toussaint L'Ouverture: Contemplation*, 1993.
Jacob Lawrence (American, 1917–2000). Silkscreen on paper; sheet: 81.3 x 55.9 cm (32 x 22 in.).
The Cleveland Museum of Art, Gift of Agnes Gund in honor of Gordon Gund 2019.79.10.
©The Jacob and Gwendolyn Knight Lawrence Foundation, Seattle/Artists Rights
Society (ARS), New York

All rights reserved. No part of this publication may be reproduced or transmitted
in any form or by any means, electronic or mechanical, including photocopying,
recording, or any information storage or retrieval system, without prior
permission in writing from the publishers.

Bloomsbury Publishing Inc does not have any control over, or responsibility for, any
third-party websites referred to or in this book. All internet addresses given in this book were correct at
the time of going to press. The author and publisher regret any inconvenience caused if addresses have
changed or sites have ceased to exist, but can accept no responsibility for any such changes.

Library of Congress Cataloging-in-Publication Data
Names: Kuiken, Kir, editor. | White, Deborah Elise, editor.
Title: Haiti's literary legacies : Romanticism and the unthinkable
revolution / edited by Kir Kuiken and Deborah Elise White.
Description: New York : Bloomsbury Academic, 2021. |
Includes bibliographical references and index.
Identifiers: LCCN 2021021766 (print) | LCCN 2021021767 (ebook) |
ISBN 9781501366352 (hardback) | ISBN 9781501366338 (eBook) |
ISBN 9781501366345 (ePDF) | ISBN 9781501366321
Subjects: LCSH: Haiti–In literature. | Haiti–History–Revolution, 1791–1804–Literature
and the revolution. | Romanticism. | LCGFT: Literary criticism. | Essays.
Classification: LCC PN56.3.H35 H35 2021 (print) | LCC PN56.3.H35 (ebook) |
DDC 809/.93358729403–dc23
LC record available at https://lccn.loc.gov/2021021766
LC ebook record available at https://lccn.loc.gov/2021021767

ISBN: HB: 978-1-5013-6635-2
PB: 978-1-5013-7604-7
ePDF: 978-1-5013-6634-5
eBook: 978-1-5013-6633-8

Typeset by Newgen KnowledgeWorks Pvt. Ltd., Chennai, India

To find out more about our authors and books visit www.bloomsbury.com
and sign up for our newsletters.

CONTENTS

Acknowledgments vii

Introduction 1
Kir Kuiken and Deborah Elise White

1 The Shadow of Voltaire: Early Haitian Literature and the Claims of Intertextuality 25
Chris Bongie

2 Romantic Fevers: Calenture and Calenda in the Americas 49
Mary Grace Albanese

3 Toussaint Louverture: Creating a Public Romantic Subject 71
Theresa M. Kelley

4 Seeing into the Very Bones: C. L. R. James and William Wordsworth on Figure, Personhood, and Revolutionary Discourse 95
Brian McGrath

5 Unavowed Community in Kleist's *Betrothal in San Domingo* 117
Kir Kuiken

6 "Despair Begins with Stupefaction": Unthinkable Agencies in Hugo's *Bug-Jargal* 141
Deborah Elise White

CONTENTS

7 Revolutionary Resonances in Frances Watkins Harper's "Triumph of Freedom" 163
Brigitte Fielder

8 Revolutionary Shattering: Emerson on the Haitian Revolution 185
Branka Arsić

Notes on Contributors 207
Index 209

ACKNOWLEDGMENTS

This volume was aided and abetted by a number of scholars and friends whom the editors would like to thank. As the project first took shape, the early support of Colin Dayan, Marlene Daut, David Lloyd, and Grégory Pierrot was instrumental in helping it get underway. We are also grateful to Branka Arsić, Valérie Loichot, Elissa Marder, Zita Nunes, José Quiroga, Orrin Wang, and Priscilla Wald for their generous advice on multiple occasions; this project has benefited profoundly from their fund of knowledge in Caribbean, Transatlantic, and Romantic Studies. Katherine De Chant at Bloomsbury Academic guided us through the initial proposal stage, and Amy Martin and Haaris Naqvi offered valuable editorial support and guidance throughout the publication process. Thanks as well to our cover designer Eleanor Rose and to the anonymous readers for the press. The editors would especially like to thank our contributors for their patience, their persistence, and their remarkable work. Chapter Eight appeared previously in *Telos* 170 (Spring 2015) and we are grateful to Telos Press for granting permission to reprint. And, finally, we thank our families, Andrew Altman and Miles and Vesna Kuiken, who filled a difficult pandemic year with joy and love.

Note to the reader: Across the book, block quotations where the translation has a source are not enclosed within square brackets; translations enclosed in brackets are the author's.

Introduction

Kir Kuiken and Deborah Elise White

Michel-Rolph Trouillot's remark in *Silencing the Past: Power and the Production of History* that the Haitian revolution "entered history with the peculiar characteristic of being unthinkable even as it happened" speaks directly to the challenge the revolution poses to the interpretation and theorization of Romanticism.[1] But what exactly is that challenge? Romantic-era writers can scarcely be said to have nothing to say about the revolution, and his claim that it underwent a kind of silencing at its very inception has been contested by a number of historians. In the words of Ada Ferrer "at the time, as news of the slaves' actions erupted onto the world stage, everyone seemed to be thinking and speaking about events in Saint-Domingue ... If this was silence, it was a thunderous one indeed."[2] One may add that thinking and speaking about events in Saint-Domingue continued long after the revolution was over. In a recent issue of *Studies in Romanticism* edited by Paul Youngquist and devoted to "Black Romanticism," Marlene Daut notes that "for well over 100 years, the Haitian Revolution haunted Romantic fictions on both sides of the Atlantic."[3] Yet Trouillot's intervention retains its force. Indeed Ferrer herself writes that "it compels us to try to understand more deeply the ways in which ... silences (and mentions) [of the Revolution] were constructed, sustained, and challenged, and the ways particular kinds of historical knowledge and narratives became ascendant."[4] The wager of *Haiti's Literary Legacies* is that the very unthinkability of the revolution that arose in colonial Saint-Domingue, which is to say its resistance to pre-given categories, generated Ferrer's paradoxically thunderous silence and, for that very reason, demanded distinctively *literary* responses. That is, it demanded responses that drew on the figurative and fictive resources of language testing itself against events that at least seemed to be without precedent. "Romanticism" played a double-edged role in this dynamic since, at the very moment when Romantic literature was laying claim to an unprecedented idea of its own freedom from precedent, it found itself confronted with the challenge of representing and responding to events that had at once exposed the limits, and compelled the reimagining, of the scope and meaning of that freedom. The essays collected in *Haiti's Literary Legacies* address that encounter from a range of historical and theoretical perspectives—Haitian and North American as well as European.

In what follows, we fill out some of these claims at least briefly, offering background on the historical context and specific achievement of the Revolution as well as further reflection on the contested concept of "the unthinkable" as well as on the almost equally vexed literary-historical term "Romanticism." The issues we raise are far from settled, and our aim is not to resolve them; it is, rather, to unsettle, in turn, inherited literary histories that have not fully come to terms with the impact of the Revolution's achievement on their own trajectories. The essays that follow take up this project in distinct and manifold ways that, joined together, begin to suggest the intricate and overlapping networks that make up the Romantic afterlife of Haiti's literary legacies.

"The Only Successful Slave Revolt in History"

C. L. R. James's famous claim about the Haitian Revolution's uniqueness as "the only successful slave revolt in history" emerged out of an intellectual context that had either systematically neglected this event or relegated it to a footnote of the French Revolution. But it has worn the test of time well.[5] To be sure, the Haitian Revolution did not emerge out of a vacuum. As Carolyn Fick notes, it had its precedents, including four other armed insurrections on the island of Saint-Domingue between the years of 1679 and 1704.[6] What differentiates such early slave insurrections from the revolts of the later eighteenth and nineteenth centuries is marronage, a phenomenon Fick identifies as key to the possibility of full-scale revolution. And as Eugene Genovese shows, though marronage began as an attempt to seek individual freedom from the horrors of the slave system, it had become an increasingly widespread collective enterprise by the time of revolution.[7] Maroon societies consisted of escaped slaves living in the mountains or in otherwise sparsely populated areas, and they ranged from small groups to larger long-established communities. They interacted with slaves who were still confined to the plantation, and this in turn created not only the possibility of a physical space outside the plantation system in which former slaves could operate freely, but also enabled a form of communication between different slave communities across the island. Elsewhere in the Caribbean where the

INTRODUCTION

Maroons engaged in extended and successful guerilla warfare against the authorities, their influence on resistance among plantation slaves came to be limited once treaties with local governments guaranteed them (relative) freedom in exchange for their agreeing to help return fugitive slaves to plantations rather than accepting them as new members.[8] However, in Saint-Domingue, as Fick describes, "a contingent relationship necessarily developed between the fugitives and their plantation counterparts, who often sheltered them, gave them food, helped them steal for provisions, and aware of the goings-on in the master's house, could advise and warn them."[9] Without the fact of marronage, and the form its development took in Saint-Domingue, the broader Haitian Revolution of 1791 and thereafter, which involved a variety of different slave communities jointly coordinating attacks, could not have taken place.

The complex interrelationship between Maroon and plantation communities is not by itself sufficient to explain how and why forms of resistance that were at first individual, then more collective, transitioned from attempts to escape the plantation system to a movement that sought that system's complete and total destruction. A number of different acts of resistance that preceded the revolution could be viewed as part of the context for it—from widespread acts of suicide or infanticide, to individual slaves poisoning their masters. These acts were direct forms of resistance, striking as they did at the economic foundation of slavery, but they did not yet constitute the massive collective endeavor that would seek not just to deprive slaveholders of their "property," or to end an individual slave-owner's life, but to destroy the vast system that perpetuated slavery as an institution.

A key facet in the transition from collective forms of resistance like marronage to the total collective enterprise of full-scale revolution was the role of Vodou. A hybrid mixture of Catholicism and traditional "animist" religions, including Yoruba, Kongo, and Taino religious practices, Vodou acted as a kind of social "glue" permitting slaves from vastly different backgrounds to coalesce around a set of common cosmological, philosophical, and political structures. As Eduardo Grüner insists, "Vodou became the first and oldest form of resistance, a force that was not only 'cultural' in the narrow sense, but also ideological and political."[10] While it had a definite practical effect in Maroon societies, as Carolyn Fick suggests, facilitating secret meetings, providing a common "language" for slaves of diverse backgrounds, and securing "the pledge of solidarity and secrecy of those involved in plots against their masters,"[11] it also acted as an alternative cosmology or ontology to the one that had relegated slaves and Africans to the bottom of the racial hierarchy the master class naturalized as the great chain of Being. Dahomeyan Vodou in particular, as Eduardo Grüner insists, "offered the slave in Saint-Domingue a cultural 'infrastructure' capable of sustaining linguistic, ethnic, and of course mythical and religious traditions, as well as folkloric and literary forms."[12] In other words, it provided not only a common language, a shared set of beliefs and practices, but a surrogate discourse and practice that could mobilize large numbers of disparate slaves and provide them with a means of contesting the religious, metaphysical, and ideological structures that had underwritten their brutalization. All of this, of course, was possible only in the condition of marronage, since the practice of Vodou was outlawed, and widely feared by plantation owners precisely for those reasons.

This context of transcultural religious practice, marronage, and other acts of resistance, including prior slave revolts, which were decisive elements in the development of the revolution, modifies significantly the way the Haitian Revolution has until recently been understood—namely, as a tributary of the French Revolution. Even the title of C. L. R. James's classic study (*The Black Jacobins*), which firmly established the Haitian Revolution's historical importance, demonstrates the long shadow the French Revolution has cast over its Haitian counterpart. While no account of the Haitian Revolution can dispense with its relation to the French Revolution, especially given that the latter's outbreak was probably the single most important factor in the white owners', and sometimes in the free mulattoes' decisions to side with one or another colonial power vying for control of the island, the two revolutions' aims were far from commensurate. Compelled by events in Saint-Domingue, the Convention abolished slavery in the colonies in 1794, but the changing dynamics of the French Revolution made that decree at once strategic (enlisting by fiat all rebelling slaves against the Spanish and British who had yet to abolish slavery in their own colonies) and short-lived. With the rise of Napoleon it would be only a matter of time before the détente between the inheritors of the French Revolution and the revolutionaries of the Haitian Revolution once again collapsed.

When the French Revolution was devolving as Wordsworth writes in the *Prelude*, into a "gewgaw, a machine," the Haitian Revolution was the site where the limits of its ideals were most severely tested, and consequently where another vision of them became possible. In Nick Nesbitt's words: "no society had ever been constructed in accord with the axiom of universal emancipation. The construction of a society without slavery, one of a *universal* and *unqualified* right to freedom, properly stands as Haiti's unique contribution to humanity."[13] Developing a similar vein of thought, Eduardo Grüner writes that the slaves "demonstrated that the supposed 'universalism' of the French Revolution was in fact a *particularism* that, having become hegemonic for the new dominant class—that is, for only a *part* of white society, could now illusorily claim to be 'universal.'"[14] Insisting that the Haitian Revolution enacts a "counter-modernity" that borrows from the dominant European conception while challenging and surpassing it, Grüner locates this counter-modernity in the syncretic cultural practices that combined African and European religious practices, in forms of postcolonial solidarity

INTRODUCTION

that could hardly be termed "nationalist," and finally in the construction of the first Haitian Constitution, the most important and remarkable aspect of which—article fourteen—acts as an almost direct counterpoint to the abstract "rights of Man" that forms the preamble to the French revolutionary constitution. Article fourteen proclaims that all Haitian citizens, including the Germans and Poles who had been granted Haitian citizenship when they defected from the forces sent by Napoleon to restore slavery to the island, were "Black." This remarkable proclamation—in effect, "we are all black"—strikes at the heart of the system of racial classifications that had underpinned the slave system, and it does so not only by denaturalizing the category "Black" as a racial designation, but also by actively challenging the French Revolution's homogenizing abstract, albeit heavily gendered universal—"Man"—from within. The new category—Black—functions *as if* its excluded particularity were the universal. It therefore points, as Grüner concludes, to "the limits of Western juridical realism, its silence in the face of a reality that is *unrepresentable* in Eurocentric universalism."[15]

In short, the Haitian Revolution constitutes a profoundly historical "event" in Badiou's sense of the term: it does not merely realize a possibility—it creates one.[16] More than just a consequence of the French Revolution, and more than a return to traditional African culture and forms of life, it represents an interruption in an ostensibly determined movement of history, allowing for something unprecedented to come into existence. The fact that, ever since, Haitians have been forced to pay a terrible price for this event, even as it has served as a model for other slave revolts and independence movements, only highlights its fundamentally radical and far-reaching nature. The legacy of its historical singularity has not faded, though it continues to be the object of a historical amnesia and/or of the calculated simulacrum of one. As Laurent Dubois insists: "we should remember how this story began, and what the ancestors of today's Haitians accomplished two hundred years ago. In the midst of a brutal plantation system, they imagined a different order, one based on freedom, equality, and autonomy. But they did more than imagine it. They built it out of nothing—with fury, solidarity, and determination."[17]

Thinking the Unthinkable

Whatever the unprecedented character of the Haitian Revolution, the explosion of recent scholarship on it—some already referred to above—may seem to date Trouillot's intervention when it comes to the historiographic record.[18] We choose to retain his word, "unthinkable," not least because of *its* revolutionary force. For, the silence to which Trouillot refers does not merely amount to the historical amnesias that seemed to envelop the Revolution in the nineteenth century—as when hegemonic forces in France, the United States, and other colonial centers immediately mobilized, in Christopher Miller's words, to "forget Haiti."[19] That kind of silence may be corrected or, at least it is correctable and can be filled in by research that seeks to redress absences from the historical record. In the case of Haiti, a great deal of such research has taken place in recent decades.[20] And yet, despite such academic trends, one should not dismiss how often varieties of this kind of correctable silence continue to shape discourse on Haiti. Trouillot remarks that the public celebrations held to commemorate the bicentennial of the French Revolution in 1989 continued to perpetrate a silence about Haiti that fostered profound historical amnesia concerning the intertwining of France's revolutionary and colonial legacies, and that silence is still at work. As we are drafting this introduction in December 2020 Lauren Collins has just published an article in *The New Yorker* on the continued absence of the Haitian Revolution from most standard French Lycée curricula: "France has not seen [Toussaint Louverture] and his fight as elements of its national narrative. 'It's thought of as a minor story, not *la grande histoire*,' Elisabeth Landi, a history professor in Martinique, said."[21]

However, by marking the unprecedented nature of the revolution, we also refer to a more complex kind of silence—more complex because it is inherent *to* the event itself, a feature of its very occurrence. In its unprecedented character, the substance and meaning of the Revolution necessarily surpassed any discourse that might venture to represent it. In other words, the silence Trouillot alerts us to is created by the fact that the discursive formations available at the advent of the Haitian Revolution were simply incapable of measuring up to its inherent singularity.[22] The issue is thus not whether or not people "thought" or spoke or wrote about what was happening in Saint-Domingue between 1791–1804 and after (as self-evidently, they did) nor whether the actors and sufferers of those events were themselves thinking beings (as, self-evidently, they were) but how the categories and concepts that shaped discursivities in the Atlantic world fundamentally distorted or otherwise fell short of much that gave the revolution its singular importance and made it an event of planetary import.[23] Since this form of "silence" was inseparable from what made the event properly historical— an inaugural event that required a new way of speaking and thinking to do it justice— it occurred not only retrospectively but also co-terminously with the event's very unfolding. This is why for Trouillot, the silence generated by the Revolution's uniqueness rendered it "unthinkable" as it happened.

This silence inherent to the event itself inevitably provokes responses, multiple ways in which it is transmitted or reinforced by the idioms that address or perpetuate it. To fully grasp the way in which the revolution was "unthinkable as it happened," therefore, requires a shift to the conceptual and linguistic registers, where its unthinkability becomes a structural feature of its very occurrence. While Trouillot frames the problem in relation to historical narratives, posing the question of how one can record a "plot"

INTRODUCTION 7

that is "unthinkable in the world within which the narrative takes place," his commentary on European Enlightenment as the framework through which the Haitian Revolution was initially understood hints at another aspect of its status as unthinkable: *The events that shook up Saint-Domingue from 1791 to 1804 constituted a sequence for which not even the extreme political left in France or in England had a conceptual frame of reference.* They were 'unthinkable' facts in the framework of Western thought."[24] The broader point is clear even if we refrain from subscribing to the monolith of "Western thought": the language and the conceptual matrices by which the Haitian Revolution could be fully comprehended in all its radicality were not yet in place, or rather, were being invented *alongside* the creation of the revolution itself. The event therefore took place not just "on the ground" and in the mountains of Haiti, but also in relation to the conceptual frameworks underpinning other democratic revolutions of the period. Haiti was not only the site of a new language—Creole—that amalgamated European, Taino, and African languages, it also engendered a necessary revision of European conceptual lexicons, from the meaning of "liberty, equality and fraternity," to the definition of "we the people."

Several of the essays in our collection explore precisely this discursive aspect of the revolution's unthinkability: if the success of the revolution irrevocably altered not just Caribbean but also European and ultimately "world" history, then the literary domain offers a privileged point of entry for tracing the revolutionary shock of this upheaval. Though not always escaping the same blind spots as other forms of discourse, literary language has at its disposal a set of resources capable of registering the unthinkable in other ways. Fiction or, indeed "romance," is often positioned at the border between the possible and the impossible, the believable and the unbelievable, and so it becomes a crucial site for *thinking* the unthinkable, whether explicitly or not—whether intentionally or not. As the Haitian Revolution was not just a political revolution in the traditional sense, but also a linguistic and ontological one, registering its unthinkability involved experimentation—with images of revolution, with traditional ontological coordinates and presuppositions, with diverse literary traditions and their supposed distinction from each other and, finally, with language itself. Such experimentation was increasingly though not exclusively the domain of literature at this time—more precisely, of an imaginative literature that had begun to set itself apart from other kinds of "letters" even as borders between genres remained porous. However, as Deborah Jenson has shown, Toussaint Louverture and Dessalines are also literary figures in the sense we intend, literary "in the degree to which they harnessed poetics" in the service of the "political construction of themselves and their constituencies."[25] "Poetics" marks the inventive, *literary* supplement that makes their writings more than historical records—and that puts those writings in relation to literary Romanticism.[26]

We have already discussed another example of the inventiveness that yokes the revolutionary to the literary in the Haitian constitution of 1805. The unthinkable nature of the revolution was structured into Article Fourteen of the constitution itself, which declares all Haitians, regardless of ethnic background, to be "Black." As Grüner and others have discussed, the article, in effect, wrenches the term "Black" away from its position within the system of racial classifications that gave it a meaning or value at the bottom of a racial hierarchy, and that justified an economic system predicated on slavery. In thus collapsing the whole classificatory system, the performative or perlocutionary dimension of the term "Black" doesn't simply reverse the value of existing terms, making "Black" function in a similar way to "white" in the existing structure of racial hierarchies. Instead, the term's redeployment points precisely to what remains unthinkable in that structure: the fact that "Black" and the meanings or values associated with it are *nothing but* performative, dependent on an act of linguistic creation that is not founded on any natural category.[27] By no means are such acts without what may be called a bodily or *material* impact. On the contrary, part of the material violence they impose comes from the confusion they create and exploit between linguistic and phenomenal experience. To evoke the performative character of the term "Black" is to underline its historical effects *along with* its historicity and to open the possibility of turning it—or troping it—toward other histories.

Such terminological overwriting further points to something unthinkable within the present: to suggest that the term "Black" could function as a new concept of universal humanity, or at least a principle of citizenship, is to point out the impossibility of that very gesture—both then and now. As Grüner suggests, to act *as if* the category that had been systematically excluded from the European Enlightenment's conception of universal humanity were in fact the universal itself, is to allow the term to mutate from a fiction (an "as if") to a new mode of speaking or writing whereby the term becomes "a metaphor or synecdoche for the incommensurable, the incomparable, the inassimilable."[28] In short, Article 14 exposes at once the injustice of the present, but also the promise of what to that point (the inclusion of the term "Black" within the universal) had been impossible, indeed literally unthinkable. The unprecedented fact of Haiti, registered in the exceptional document that helped found it, moves from a fictional "as if" to a promissory "not yet" that still graces the contours of the unthinkable up to the present.

One caveat may be worth underlining. In "The Odd and the Ordinary: Haiti, the Caribbean, and the World," Trouillot himself warns against allowing Haiti's uniqueness (a uniqueness it shares, so to speak, with other nations) to become a fetish. He warns, in other words, against falling into a certain Haitian exceptionalism—as if Haitian history were simply *inexplicable* and thus not amenable to any but the most patronizing and

INTRODUCTION 9

colonial of analyses and interventions. The unthinkable, as he formulates it, and as we understand it here, is not "exceptional" in the sense of something that escapes rational analysis or eludes historical interpretation.[29] To be unthinkable is not to be cast off into an abject reality outside the limits of thought and language. It registers, rather, in the friction it generates *within* thought and language. The shock of the new thus mutates the language that, in its very breakdowns and often in spite of itself, nevertheless transmits it—a mutation for which literature (or the literary) is one name.

Rethinking Romanticism

The need to rethink literary-historical boundaries when studying the Haitian Revolution has previously been remarked—especially the need for comparative work that crosses national and linguistic borders. In *Modernity Disavowed: Haiti and the Cultures of Slavery in the Age of Revolution*, Sibylle Fischer argues that critical scholarship should cut across the disciplinary fragmentation that has divided the study of Haiti and of "radical anti-slavery" in the Atlantic world and notes, for example, that a focus on homogeneous national and linguistic areas of study serves to silence histories of radical, transnational struggle in favor of state histories that privilege ameliorist abolitionism.[30] In *Tropics of Haiti: Race and the Literary History of the Haitian Revolution in the Atlantic World 1789–1865*, a magisterial study that offers "the most comprehensive literary history of the Haitian Revolution to date," Marlene Daut also emphasizes the need for comparatist work on Haiti and underlines how much remains to be done, adding that "the reach of the Haitian Revolution was so wide that it may never be possible to uncover everything that has been written and preserved about these events."[31] As these comments suggest, and despite important work that has been done in recent years, greater scholarly—and specifically comparative—attention is needed to the impact of the Haitian Revolution on Romanticism's imaginative, linguistic, and ideological investments.[32] While the French Revolution's impact on Romantic writing has generated an enormous amount of debate and discussion, the Haitian Revolution often remains (even now) something of an afterthought for romanticists. What, then, does it mean—or, better, what does it *do*—to read Haiti and Romanticism together, to rethink Romanticism's relation to revolution beyond the familiar horizon of the French Revolution in particular, and to take up Haiti's literary legacies not just as a topic or theme but as an *event* for the history of Romanticism itself?

The name and figure of Romanticism is far from innocent in this context. As Emily Apter has discussed, the deployment of European literary periodizations as more or less transparent and translatable norms of comparative literary history is all too often used to override "discrepant temporal orders" across the planet in the service of a unified, unidirectional, and Eurocentric timeline. Moreover, literary period terms "tend to naturalize parameters of comparison that exclude certain kinds of cultural production from the realm of 'art.' "[33] However, at the present time, simply giving up on the name "Romanticism" would perhaps risk keeping its presuppositions and effects in place under cover of a new nomenclature.[34] The essays in this volume have been brought together, rather, with the aim of re-constellating a "Romanticism" sensitive to its own artificial and imposed character. As a period term, Romanticism has always implied a certain conceptual specificity beyond its rough historical association with literary and cultural texts of the mid-eighteenth through mid-to-late-nineteenth centuries. Yet what that specificity *is* has eluded stable characterization– so much so that the difficulty of defining Romanticism has now become a hallmark of its definition.[35] From interpretations of "Romanticism" as individualistic and subject-centered, to interpretations of it as politically charged and historically engaged, Romanticism seems to exceed its categorization. Or, rather, Romanticism proliferates categories in heterogeneous and contradictory ways—it is somehow revolutionary *and* reactionary, traditional *and* avant-garde. Nor are these problems ultimately solved by separating out different national traditions or by creating more subtly differentiated timelines. Instead they seem to proliferate within each newly delimited "sub" romanticism.

Romanticism's specificity for our project is thus partly pragmatic—a matter of thematic and interpretive contexts that have long been construed as crucial to its self-understanding: revolution, democracy, colonialism, slavery, abolition, and war. But it is not solely pragmatic. The unresolved dialectic of Romanticism and revolution—whether Romanticism is the excited herald of revolution or rather its melancholic eulogist—takes on distinct difficulties in relation to Haiti. The liberty claimed by so much European Romantic writing, its "right to say everything," encounters in Haiti something like a limit case or, rather, it encounters its own limits both as free utterance and as an utterance about freedom.[36] To take an example closely associated with Romanticism's revolutionary drive, Percy Shelley's *Defense of Poetry* consecrates poets as "the unacknowledged legislators of the world"—which is to say as forces for historical and political change.[37] In Shelley's words, "the most unfailing herald, companion, and follower of the awakening of a great people to work a beneficial change in opinion or institution is Poetry."[38] Poetry here signifies a newly militant understanding of literature as inseparable from discourses of "freedom" and "democracy." Such a claim for literature allies Romanticism with currents of the radical Enlightenment that the Haitian Revolution at once fulfilled and (by fulfilling) exploded *even when*, as Shelley acknowledges may be the case, individual poets themselves have conservative or reactionary intent.[39] Yet the "Defense" has itself seemed to many readers more wishful than legislative. Our argument here is that Romantic claims to "legislate" freedom whether for the world or,

INTRODUCTION 11

more modestly, for itself need to be read anew in relation to Haiti's founding of a society based on the "*universal* and *unqualified* right to freedom."[40]

Orrin Wang once suggested that the relevance of "Romanticism" finally depends on its ability to stress precisely those forces that put it into motion— that turn it into something other than what it is or what it *was* understood to be: "only such an emphasis—one that increasingly includes not only Romanticism's transhistorical but also its cross-cultural transmissions— will expose the naturalizing, totalizing tendencies within Romanticism's significations."[41] Re-constellating the traditions of Romantic studies in relation to the Haitian Revolution and, indeed, to Haitian literary history, speaks to just such "transhistorical' and "cross-cultural transmissions." It thus cannot and does not mean bringing various conceptions of "Romanticism" under one master narrative. Over seventy years ago, Lovejoy considered the deployment of the *one* name for a range of northern European movements and texts a "scandal of literary history and criticism."[42] Looking back, one might rather argue that its deployment was not nearly scandalous enough. For it is as a scandal of literary history and an impetus for cross-cultural transmissions—and not as a fixed conceptual field or textual canon—that Romanticism has its most consequent afterlives.

Literary Histories to Come

The contributors to this volume are not alone, of course, in taking on the task of re-constellating Romanticism in relation to the Haitian Revolution. The explosion of recent historical work on the revolution alluded to above has not left literary and cultural studies untouched. Some of this work has served as compensatory, recovering a missing piece of a larger story. If, as Susan Buck-Morss suggests in her groundbreaking essay "Hegel and Haiti," "events in Saint-Domingue were central to contemporary attempts to make sense out of the reality of the French Revolution and its aftermath," then the relative lack of attention to the many ways writers of the Romantic era thought (or failed to think) those events obviously has called for redress and renewed attention.[43] But the work of literary scholars who have begun the task of engaging with the Haitian Revolution in the context of a Romantic studies that has mostly paid it too little heed has been something more than compensatory; it has been transformative.[44] To echo Joel Pace's arguments concerning "Black Romanticism" in the same issue of *Studies in Romanticism* cited at the beginning of our introduction, a further expansion and enrichment of the field of Romantic studies through an engagement with Haiti might prove little better than a sophisticated mode of (neo)colonial appropriation absent the imaginative dynamism through which terms like "Romanticism"—or even "revolution"—have come to be debated and displaced in the course of that expansion.[45] As suggested above, sounding the resonance of the Haitian Revolution across world literatures of the Romantic era inevitably uncovers new tonalities in those literatures. It was not simply "Romanticism" that challenged existing literary categories beginning in the eighteenth century, but events in Haiti that made a new kind of literature essential and that today must bring about new reconfigurations of literary–historical scholarship.

The contributors to this volume by no means share a monolithic view of what those reconfigurations will be. But fresh historical and cultural understanding can only emerge from the cross-hatching of multiple Romanticisms and multiple interpretations of Romanticism. Through juxtapositions, overlaps, and clashes, one becomes able to think the unthinkable and to read its operations where for too long they have been invisible and inaudible. In this way, Romanticism becomes at once witness and disseminator for the "unthinkability" of the Haitian Revolution, and its testimony will continue to resonate in twenty-first century attempts to address the relation of the Revolution to what *remains* unthinkable in the histories of a receding present. The word "unthinkable" is, after all, finally an invitation to thought. Attention to the singularity of the Haitian Revolution's planetary impact and, more narrowly, to its participation in the larger literary-historical configuration of transnational Romanticism is crucial to articulating a critical relation to Haiti's literary *legacies* that can ultimately speak to our contemporary moment—a moment that includes, in the United States today, a resurgence of the #BlackLivesMatter movement in the wake of the May 2020 murder of George Floyd by Minneapolis police and the underscoring of gross social and racial inequalities by the advent of SARS-CoV-2.

The essays themselves have been organized to draw out the cross currents flowing between them. The opening two essays address direct encounters—and missed encounters—between Haitian and European literary and cultural texts. Chris Bongie's essay "The Shadow of Voltaire: Early Haitian Literature and the Claims of Intertextuality" opens the volume by examining the way Voltaire helped to inform the political imaginary of the leaders of the "free colored" movement of 1791 (a group of mixed race citizens who had obtained limited rights). Focusing on references to Voltaire's tragedies in Juste Chanlatte's writing, including Chanlatte's hand in crafting the proclamation of April 28, 1804, Bongie examines the troubled history of the struggle for recognition and the crucial limitations on the scope of political emancipation imagined by that group of insurrectionists to which Chanlatte belonged. Uncovering the literary legacy of what he calls "(the other) 1791," Bongie charts the historical and genealogical links between that moment and the emergence of independent Haitian literature in the wake of the 1804 proclamation. Though the proclamation insists on the irrevocable union of the two classes (slaves and "free persons of color") who had become temporary allies, Bongie reads the proclamation's references to

INTRODUCTION

Voltaire in terms of the earlier moment of 1791, when the reference served different political ends. At that time references to Voltaire acted not just as an affirmation of a shared humanity and literary culture with French colonists, but as a source of identification for those intent on having their rights recognized as fellow citizens. However, as Bongie demonstrates, this sense of identification carried with it a fundamentally restrictive sense of equality that, in identifying itself with Voltaire, was reserved for those who could own property. In short, Voltaire functions in the (other) 1791 as a reference to "free persons" who had rights and equality, but only insofar as those rights necessarily excluded non-free slaves. Bongie then reads Chanlatte's return to Voltaire in the 1804 proclamation as a double-edged sword, suggesting at once Chanlatte's turn toward a more encompassing notion of freedom and yet also an indication that the moment of the (other) 1791 remained alive and well. Charting the legacy of this genealogy, Bongie connects the rights-based struggle for recognition in the (other) 1791 to the structural problems connected with the politics of recognition in the present.

In "Romantic Fevers: Calenture and Calenda in the Americas," Mary Grace Albanese traces the mutual imbrication of calenda, a Caribbean dance important in Vodou practice, and calenture, a hallucinatory experience that involves a vision of land superimposed on a seascape, and which was often reported by white mariners in the Atlantic world, becoming an important recurring trope in Romantic literature. Charting the ways in which these two phenomena overlap in terms of the ontological fluidities they suggest—between sea and land, or between different genders—Albanese articulates the way calenda, as a Black peasant tradition, opened up a cultural practice that dislodged white colonial assumptions regarding the stability of personhood. It thus challenged and complicated what was already at stake in the Romantic era's fascination with calenture: a conceptual mobility between solid and fluid that was, nevertheless, always limited to the perspective of the white male gaze, which thereby controlled the very contagion that fascinated it. Calenda, on the other hand, opened that fascination to a whole set of ontological instabilities that fundamentally shifted the centrality of that gaze, disrupting the distinctions of race and gender, human and nonhuman that subtend it. As a result, she argues, calenda produced a cultural practice that made possible new forms of identity, while simultaneously disturbing the way the trope of calenture functioned in the Romantic canon. Once viewed through the lens of its relation to calenda, calenture becomes a space that reimagines the status of personhood, and connects it to other histories and temporalities.

The following two essays broach the figure of Toussaint Louverture both as a writer and as someone *written into* the literary and historical record. In "Toussaint Louverture: Creating a Public Romantic Subject," Theresa M. Kelley explores a longstanding Romantic era trope as it bears on the public persona of the most visible leader of the Haitian Revolution.

Examining the ways Louverture presented himself in his own writings as well as the ways he was presented in other people's writing, Kelley analyzes the crucial difference between the classical conception of the Romantic subject as inwardly directed, and the thoroughly public Romantic subject of Louverture. Focusing on the way his public narrative is characterized by something other than the standard arc of "rise and fall," Kelley reads Louverture's status in the print culture of the era as a riposte to views of subjectivity predicated on Enlightenment liberalism and its Romantic inheritors. It does so by demonstrating the contradictions, created by slavery, between Enlightenment and Romantic concepts of subjectivity and the one Louverture exemplifies. Louverture, in Kelley's argument, is not a single, unified subject, but a set of shifting discourses and texts that reveals what is latent or unseen in existing European conceptions of subjectivity. Honing in on what she calls the "contingent" elements of this narrative, the ways in which the print record of Louverture was exposed not just to the contingency of history but to the contingency of interpretation itself, Kelley singles out several key tropes, including Louverture's insertion of himself into Abbé Raynal's seemingly prophetic claim about the eventual emergence of a "Black Spartacus." Kelley understands this insertion not as an assumption of mythic prophecy, but as a retrospective attempt by Louverture and others to negotiate the tenuous and contingent nature of the revolution itself. What emerges is the narrative of a Romantic "subject" riven by various contingencies it attempts to control, while opening itself to a futurity that it cannot.

In "Seeing into the Very Bones: C. L. R. James and William Wordsworth on Figure, Personhood, and Revolutionary Discourse," Brian McGrath examines the function of personification in James's *Black Jacobins* alongside Wordsworth's poem "To Toussaint L'Ouverture." Arguing that both texts claim that personhood, with its status as the source of rights, is a feature and function of language rather than a natural fact, McGrath examines how each text implies a potential revisioning of the category of personhood and who or what counts as a person. Arguing that the very category which Europeans used to justify the enslavement and brutalization of those deemed not to be persons is generated tropologically, McGrath's essay suggests that James and Wordsworth speak to each other across historical distances, as well as across the division between historiographic writing and poetry. Revisiting the question of whether Romanticism necessarily involves a retreat from history, McGrath begins by exploring how James's historical writing utilizes classic Romantic tropes—such as volcanos—to suggest the underground forces that make revolutionary outbursts possible. Contrasting James's invocation of Romantic tropes with Wordsworth's poem on Toussaint Louverture, McGrath demonstrates that the poem too is highly self-conscious about its use of rhetoric, connecting the role of personification in the poem to Wordsworth's equation of Louverture with

INTRODUCTION

"Man's unconquerable mind." The poem, McGrath contends, undercuts this apparently universalizing gesture by emphasizing the performative and tropological valence of "Man"—the very category used to enslave those who had fought alongside Louverture to liberate themselves from slavery. Thus, each author problematizes the trope of personification while also insisting on its necessity as an animating tool for rethinking the scope of personhood and its political applications.

Like McGrath's essay, with its discussion of Wordsworth, the following essays address the Haitian Revolution as it is figured in well-known works of European Romanticism. Kir Kuiken's essay "Unavowed Community in Kleist's *Betrothal in San Domingo*" reads Heinrich von Kleist's novella about a mixed-race pair of doomed lovers, situated in Haiti in 1804, as an exploration of forms of community that become possible in a revolutionary context only when they are conceived in ways that are not identified with the state. Focusing on the unavowed nature of the "betrothal" of the title, Kuiken argues that the novella proposes a form of social obligation that transcends existing legal or juridical contexts. This form of obligation animates the possibility—but not the reality—of the lovers' betrothal. Pitting the state—in this case the nascent Haitian state—against the lovers, Kuiken shows how something other than the friend/enemy distinction becomes operative in the unspoken vow that unites them. For a writer living in a divided Prussia that was itself occupied by the French, the setting of the Haitian Revolution provided Kleist not only with the shock of a fundamentally new form of revolution that had taken on the mantle of progress Kant had once identified with the French Revolution, but also with a means by which to explore how a community is formed without a state to support it. What Kleist articulates, Kuiken claims, is a "community of lovers" that destabilizes social contract theories of the state, along with biopolitical regimes (such as the French colonial slave regime) predicated on race or other identitarian structures. In the end, Kuiken argues, the novella figures two different conceptions of history, one that proves incapable of recognizing the unavowed community, and another that maintains a fidelity to its promise.

In "'Despair Begins with Stupefaction' : Unthinkable Agencies in Hugo's *Bug-Jargal*," Deborah Elise White explores blind spots structuring the main narrative of Hugo's novel. The narrator, Leopold d'Auverney, onetime heir to a Saint-Domingue plantation, repeatedly reveals his younger self's inability to conceive of an authentic Black political or erotic agency. As a result, his friendship with the slave Pierrot, who is secretly the revolutionary leader Bug-Jargal, is characterized by a quasi-pathological refusal to see what is in front of his eyes. Even when the narrative seems to imply a growing self-awareness, that awareness inevitably falls short. Focusing on Leopold's description of himself as stupefied by events, White traces the echoes and implications of that word (*stupeur*) across the text, showing the extent to which the narrative evokes (white, European) psychic collapse in the face of Black agency and self-sovereignty. However, although the novel invites one to critique Leopold's limitations, White argues that one must attend to the potential complacency of any reading that positions the reader altogether outside of Leopold's errors. She shows that the novel figures such a complacent critical reader in the Jacobin official sent to arrest Leopold as a counter-revolutionary: insisting on the universal character of the Jacobin project, the official subsumes events in Saint-Domingue to events in Paris, and is as blind to the specific character of the slave uprising as Leopold. In her conclusion, White suggests that a similarly unearned claim to universalism helped set to work Obama-era fantasies of a post-racial United States. In Hugo's novel, she argues, Leopold's stupefied language serves—if only inadvertently—to draw out the radicalism of the Haitian Revolution and its continuing challenge to both conservative and progressive narratives.

The volume's turn to the North American context starts with Brigitte Fielder's essay, "Revolutionary Resonances in Frances Watkins Harper's 'Triumph of Freedom.'" Fielder shows how the Haitian Revolution was a constant reference in the Black press of the nineteenth century, specifically as an example of a successful slave revolt that might act as a precursor for a future American abolitionist revolution. While Watkins Harper's story has usually been read in terms of its references to the insurrection at Harper's Ferry, Fielder shows that the Haitian Revolution's historical resonance forms a key part of Harper's attempt to construct a narrative arc of Black emancipation that both predates and follows out of that event. As such, the Haitian Revolution became a way of interpreting the conditions of possibility for American abolition not only as predictive but also as historically possible. Since the Haitian Revolution was consistently written about in the Black press, its ubiquity, Fielder argues, became a genre unto itself. Comprised of a variety of narratives, including histories of the revolution and biographies of its leaders, these tales were told and retold from the advent of the Black press in America into the next century. Fielder shows that the constant references to the Haitian Revolution were part of an attempt to deploy these stories in the service of the possibility of imagining a *global* Black emancipation. More than simply another retelling of the Haitian Revolution, Watkins Harper's story constitutes an attempt to contextualize the Revolution in terms of a broader history of Black emancipation and decolonization. Moreover, as Fielder shows, Watkins Harper's vision of this broader history underlines the importance of collective action. Emancipation and decolonization will not be the product of a single savior, even of a Toussaint Louverture, but the product of ordinary people working collectively and continually toward the future.

The volume concludes with Branka Arsić's "Revolutionary Shattering: Emerson on the Haitian Revolution," which charts how one of the key figures of American Transcendentalism—Ralph Waldo Emerson—connected his understanding of the relationship between natural, cultural, and mental phenomena to his praise for the Haitian Revolution. Far from

INTRODUCTION   17

simply a general commitment to abolitionism that remains distinct from the main body of his work, Arsić demonstrates that Emerson's core writing and philosophy is fundamentally connected to his understanding of the Revolution's significance. Examining some of the main texts in Emerson's *oeuvre*, Arsić argues that Emerson targets the conception of the independent self formulated by traditional liberal theory. Locke's conception of "property in one's own person," which forms the basis for his conception of property more generally, allows for a confusion between self and property that generates the conceptual basis for the slave system. Emerson, Arsić argues, develops a different conception of the self that challenges the confusion of property with the self, leading to an "I" that is in a state of constant becoming. The constantly revolutionized self forms the basic ontology for Emerson's conception of political revolution: if the mind is always being generated by its encounter with things and senses external to it, then it is in a state of constant alteration that gives no priority to the self or to its purported stability. Without a basis for identifying the self as belonging to itself, Emerson's approach shatters the notion of "property in one's own person," and reveals how democracy's grounding in a Lockean conception of personhood produces an inbuilt dogmatism that authorizes, and depends on, slavery. Seeing the Haitian Revolution as concomitant with Emerson's alternative conception of the self and as a concretization of his thinking, Arsić analyzes Emerson's comparison of the reforms instituted in British Antigua with the radical overthrow of the slave system in Haiti. Suggesting that revolution, not reform, is the only thing capable of the kind of transformation required to defeat slavery and prepare for the possibility of a "new and coming civilization," Arsić argues that Emerson turns Toussaint Louverture into a key figure for his conception of the self. He is the figure of a revolutionary becoming that transforms a slave into a non-slave and ultimately into an anti-slave, by transforming the notion of personhood itself, thereby radically altering the world. Throughout this volume, block quotations where the translation has a source are not enclosed within square brackets; translations enclosed in brackets are the author's.

In taking up Haiti's literary legacies the contributions gathered in this volume reflect a range of theoretical and methodological approaches as well as differing national and linguistic traditions. What they share is a commitment not only to think the unthinkable, but to reconceptualize and reimagine what has come to seem all too familiar in the discourses of Romanticism and literary studies. Read individually and as a collection, they also intervene in contemporary discussions about the legacy of the Haitian Revolution in ways that offer alternative genealogies of the *present* at a time when that present has been experienced, more than usual perhaps, as a moving target. Though the volume was conceived and underway by late 2019, most of the contributions were written in 2020 and we are deeply grateful to our contributors. Under the peculiar conditions of research and

Notes

1 Michel-Rolph Trouillot, *Silencing the Past: Power and the Production of History*, 20th-anniversary Edition (New York: Beacon Press, 2015), 73.

2 Ada Ferrer, "Talk about Haiti: The Archive and the Atlantic's Haitian Revolution," in *Tree of Liberty: Cultural Legacies of the Haitian Revolution in the Atlantic World*, ed. Doris Garraway (Charlottesville: University of Virginia Press, 2008), 21–40, 22.

3 Marlene Daut, "Haiti and the Black Romantics: Enlightenment and Color Prejudice after the Haitian Revolution in Alexandre Dumas's *Georges* (1843)," *Studies in Romanticism* 56 (Spring 2017): 73. Christopher Miller discusses later French literary responses to Saint-Domingue/Haiti in *The French Atlantic Triangle: Literature and Culture of the Slave Trade* (Durham, NC: Duke University Press, 2009) and argues that "France attempted to come to terms with the Haitian Revolution, long after it was over, through a calculated plan for forgetting" (246). Planned forgetfulness, like Ferrer's "thunderous" silence, points not only to the hypocrisies but to the genuine impasses involved in tracing Haiti's revolution across the historical-textual record. "Forget Haiti," the title of Miller's chapter on Jacques-François Roger, is an imperative that seems to pull the rug out from under its own demand. But as psychoanalysis insists and Miller understands, one can only genuinely forget something that has been properly remembered. For a psychoanalytically informed reading of the "disavowal" of the Haitian Revolution, see Sibylle Fischer, *Modernity Disavowed: Haiti and the Cultures of Slavery in the Age of Revolution*" (Durham, NC: Duke University Press, 2004). On the term disavowal, see pages 37–8.

4 Ferrer, "Talk about Haiti," 34. For a review of the reception and impact of Trouillot, cf. Alyssa Sepinwall, "Still Unthinkable? The Haitian Revolution and the Reception of Michel-Rolph Trouillot's *Silencing the Past*," *Journal of Haitian Studies* 19, no. 2 (2013): 75–103. Sepinwall argues that "although the essay has helped to make the Haitian Revolution more widely known, when non-Haitian scholars write about the Revolution, they often still do so in ways that Trouillot would denounce as 'banalizing'" (76).

5 C. L. R. James, *The Black Jacobins: Toussaint Louverture and the San Domingo Revolution*, 2nd ed., revised (New York: Vintage Books, 1963), ix. Cf. the more recent history of the revolution by Laurent Du Bois, *Avengers of the New World: The Story of the Haitian Revolution* (Cambridge: The Belknap Press of Harvard University Press, 2004), 6–7: "The impact of the Haitian Revolution was enormous. As a unique example of successful Black revolution, it became a crucial part of the political, philosophical, and cultural currents of the eighteenth and nineteenth centuries. By creating a society in which all people, of all colors, were granted freedom and citizenship, the

INTRODUCTION

Haitian Revolution forever transformed the world. It was a central part of the destruction of slavery in the Americas, and therefore a crucial moment in the history of democracy, one that laid the foundation for the continuing struggles for human rights everywhere. In this sense we are all descendants of the Haitian Revolution, and responsible to these ancestors."

6 Carolyn Fick, *The Making of Haiti* (Knoxville: University of Tennessee Press, 1990), 49.

7 Eugene Genovese, *From Rebellion to Revolution: Afro-American Slave Revolts in the Modern World* (Baton Rouge: Louisiana State University Press, 1979).

8 Fick, *Making of Haiti*, 55. She argues that one consequence of the military success of maroon fighters in Jamaica, Dutch Guyana, and elsewhere, were treaties that effectively neutralized them from impacting the ongoing political and social dispensation of the plantations.

9 Fick, *The Making of Haiti*, 56.

10 Eduardo Grüner, *The Haitian Revolution: Capitalism, Slavery and Counter-Modernity*, trans. Ramsey McGlazer (Cambridge, UK: Polity Press, 2020), 92.

11 Fick, *The Making of Haiti*, 59. Cf. 104f. and 240f on some of the difficulties of interpreting the weave of beliefs that shaped the leadership of the 1791 insurrection.

12 Grüner, *Haitian Revolution*, 94.

13 Nick Nesbitt, *Universal Emancipation: The Haitian Revolution and the Radical Enlightenment* (Charlottesville: University of Virginia Press, 2008), 2 (emphasis in original). On some of the complications and contradictions involved in the discourse of Universalism in the context of the Haitian revolutionary struggle with France, see Doris Garraway, "'*Légitime Défense*:' Universalism and Nationalism in the Discourse of the Haitian Revolution," in *Tree of Liberty: Cultural Legacies of the Haitian Revolution in the Atlantic World*, ed. Doris Garraway (Charlottesville: University of Virginia Press, 2008), 63–90. See, too, note 15.

14 Grüner, *Haitian Revolution*, 65 (emphasis in original).

15 Grüner, *Haitian Revolution*, 186 (emphasis in original). For a "narrative" reading of the constitution that addresses the complex interplay of universalism and particularism across different articles of the 1805 constitution, see Sibylle Fischer, *Modernity Disavowed*, 232–6.

16 Cf. Alain Badiou, *Polemics*, trans. Steve Corcoran (London: Verso Press, 2006), 388. We use "event" here in a sense primarily drawn from Badiou's analysis of other historical "events" such as the Paris Commune and the Cultural Revolution. For an extended political-theoretical account of the Haitian Revolution that draws suggestively on Badiou's "*politique d'émancipation*," see Nick Nesbitt, *Universal Emancipation*. Nesbitt cites Badiou's French phrase on page 27.

17 Laurent Dubois, *Haiti: the Aftershocks of History* (New York: Picador Press, 2012), 370. For an analysis that emphasizes continuities of *economic* exploitation between colonial Saint-Domingue and postindependence Haiti

20 HAITI'S LITERARY LEGACIES

see, for example, Jean Casimir, *The Haitians: A Decolonial History*, trans. Laurent DuBois (Chapel Hill: University of North Carolina Press, 2020).

18 The recent explosion of anglophone scholarly and cultural interest in Haiti can be exemplified by the recent publication of a *Haiti Reader* by Duke University Press and edited by Laurent Dubois, Kaiama L. Glover, Nadève Ménard, Millery Polyné and Chantalle F. Verna (Durham, NC: Duke University Press, 2020) and by the 2018 publication of Julius S. Scott's dissertation over three decades after it was written—three decades during which it had, nonetheless, circulated among scholars: *The Common Wind: Afro-American Currents in the Age of the Haitian Revolution* (London: Verso, 2018). Duke's publication in 2017 of *The Black Jacobins Reader*, edited by Charles Forsdick and Christian Høgsbjerg honors the importance to Haitian Studies of C. L. R. James's classic account of the Revolution first published in 1938 and republished with revisions in 1963. A (not exhaustive) sampling of recent twenty-first-century anglophone historical scholarship on the Haitian Revolution includes, in addition to works by Dubois, Ferrer, Grüner, and Nesbitt already cited in earlier notes: Julia Gaffield, *Haitian Connections in the Atlantic World: Recognition after Revolution* (Chapel Hill: University of North Carolina Press, 2015), Chelsea Stieber, *Haiti's Paper War: Post-Independence Writing, Civil War, and the Making of the Republic, 1804–1954* (New York: New York University Press, 2020); Karen Salt, *The Unfinished Revolution: Haiti, Black Sovereignty and Power in the 19th-century Atlantic World* (Liverpool: Liverpool University Press, 2019); and James Forde *The Early Haitian State and the Question of Political Legitimacy* (London: Palgrave, 2020); influential edited collections on the revolution published in this century include *The Impact of the Haitian Revolution in the Atlantic World*, ed. David Geggus (Columbia: University of South Carolina Press, 2001), *The World of the Haitian Revolution*, ed. David Patrick Geggus and Norman Fiering (Bloomington: Indiana University Press, 2009), as well as Alyssa Goldstein Sepinwall, *Haitian History: New Perspectives* (London: Routledge, 2013). The record in Francophone historical scholarship despite essential work by Yves Benot and others is not comparable. On the continued pertinence of Trouillot's critique and also taking up francophone historiography, see Sepinwall, "Still Unthinkable?" 75–103.

19 Miller, *The French Atlantic Triangle*, 246–50.

20 See note 18. For an example of how archival practice and historiographic lacunae can be mutually reinforcing, cf. Nesbitt writing a little over a decade ago in *Universal Emancipation*, 41: "A search of the Cornell library database on the historiography of the French Revolution reveals over 350 Library of Congress subject headings alone, and well over 7,000 individual volumes. A similar search for Haiti reveals twelve subject headings and a grand total of 235 volumes (many of them duplicates) on the events of 1791–1804."

21 Lauren Collins, "The Haitian Revolution and the Hole in French High School History," *New Yorker Magazine* (December 3, 2020). Her article goes on to discuss both previous and current attempts to reform the national curriculum.

INTRODUCTION

22 Up to a point, the disjunction of revolutionary event and discursive formation is a characteristic of modern revolution in general. The latter, as Hannah Arendt has written, "is inextricably bound up with the notion that the course of history suddenly begins anew, that an entirely new story, a story never known or told before is about to unfold." See Arendt, *On Revolution* (London: Penguin Books, 1963), 28. On Arendt and the Haitian Revolution cf. Nesbitt, *Universal Emancipation* 124–8. Despite her own lack of attention to the Haitian Revolution, Arendt figures in other discussions of Haiti (and of Trouillot) including Greg Beckett, "The Ontology of Freedom: The Unthinkable Miracle of Haiti," *Journal of Haitian Studies* 19, no. 2 (Fall 2013): 54–74.

23 On the planetary (as opposed to the "global" of a hegemonic and homogenizing globalization) see Gayatri Chakraborty Spivak, *Death of a Discipline* (New York: Columbia University Press, 2003), 72–102.

24 Trouillot, *Silencing*, 82 (emphasis in original).

25 Deborah Jenson, *Beyond the Slave Narrative: Politics, Sex, and Manuscripts in the Haitian Revolution* (Liverpool: Liverpool University Press, 2011), 9–10.

26 Cf. Jenson, *Beyond*, 47: "Without [Louverture's] communicative diplomacy in literary form, it is not clear that the Haitian Revolution would have 'translated' from paradigms of class and race upheaval to a paradigm of Black historical/national genesis, as it did in literary commemorations of Toussaint's legacies by writers throughout the nineteenth century." For Jenson on Louverture's proto-romanticism, see 70. For recent discussions of Louverture and Dessalines as *writers* see, too, Grégory Pierrot, *The Black Avenger in Atlantic Culture* (Athens: University of Georgia Press, 2019), 100–28; Daniel Desormeaux, "The First of the (Black) Memorialists: Toussaint Louverture," *Yale French Studies* 107 (2005): 131–45, and Garraway, "*Légitime Défense.*" In this volume Theresa Kelley offers further consideration of Louverture as both a revisionary Romantic "public" hero *and* writer.

27 A more developed reading of Article 14 would have to consider the role of the patriarch-magistrate in its metaphorical system and the potentially re-naturalizing implications of that figure for gendered power relations.

28 Grüner, *Haitian Revolution*, 185.

29 Michel-Rolph Trouillot, "The Odd and the Ordinary: Haiti, the Caribbean, and the World" was the keynote address for "Haiti in Comparative Perspective," sponsored by the Columbia/The New York University Consortium on Latin American and Caribbean Studies, New York University, New York, February 9, 1990; reprinted on the Sciello website: https://www.scielo.br/scielo. php?pid=S1809-43412020000100553&script=sci_arttext&tlng=en . Concern around just this issue—Haitian exceptionalism—seems to account for a great deal of the resistance provoked by Trouillot's use of the term "unthinkable."

30 Fischer, *Modernity Disavowed*, 10–11.

31 Marlene Daut, *Tropics of Haiti: Race and the Literary History of the Haitian Revolution in the Atlantic World 1789–1865* (Liverpool: Liverpool University Press, 2015), 44.

32 Daut's work mentioned above currently stands alone as a comprehensive literary history of the Revolution's impact in the first two-thirds of the nineteenth century. Important English-language collections on the cultural and literary impacts of the Haitian Revolution that extend beyond the nineteenth century include the 2005 "Haiti Issue" of *Yale French Studies* edited by Deborah Jenson and Doris Garraway's *Tree of Life* already cited. Christopher Miller's *Black Atlantic Triangle* offers a major overview of the francophone Black Atlantic that addresses several Romantic texts, though the peculiar nexus of Romantic literature and the Haitian Revolution is not central to his argument. Other important recent scholarship in this area includes scholarly editions and translations such as Deborah Jenson and Doris Y. Kadish's bilingual edition of Haitian nineteenth-century poetry translated by Norman Shapiro, *Poetry of Haitian Independence* (New Haven: Yale University Press, 2015) and Paul Youngquist and Grégory Pierrot's edition of Marcus Rainsford's 1805 *An Historical Account of the Black Empire of Hayti* (Durham, NC: Duke University Press, 2013). Online venues have also contributed to the recovery and dissemination of Haitian texts of the period: for example, the digital edition of *La Gazette Royal D'Hayti* and other journals of the Northern Kingdom of Hayti during Henry Christophe's reign (lagazetteroyale.com). For obvious reasons, most critical and interpretive work on the Caribbean by scholars of British Romanticism focuses on British colonies. This work—by scholars such as Alan Bewell, Elizabeth Bohls, Debbie Lee, Emily Senior, and Paul Youngquist—is, of course, highly pertinent to any discussion of the Haitian Revolution. Youngquist recalls Haiti's importance across the Caribbean in his introduction to the special issue of *Studies in Romanticism* on Black Romanticism mentioned above (For a selection of works that have engaged more directly with Romanticism's relationship to the Haitian Revolution see note 44.)

33 Emily Apter, *Against World Literature: On the Politics of Untranslatability* (London: Verso, 2013), 61 and 57. Apter opens her discussion by recalling how comparatist "literary history" "has been beset by what Christopher Prendergast, following Arjun Appadurai, calls the 'Euro-chronology' problem" (57).

34 In their introduction to a special issue of *Symbiosis* on "New Directions in Transatlantic Romanticism," Deanna Koretsky and Joel Pace have asked "if adding 'Black' to 'Romanticism' enables us to trouble its racist roots, is it still Romanticism?" but ultimately argue on behalf of "rethinking what we mean by romanticism itself" rather than dropping the term altogether. See their introduction to *Symbiosis: Transatlantic Literary and Cultural Relations*, 23.1 (Spring 2019), 6-7. In "Black Romanticism: A Manifesto" (to which Koretsky and Pace allude), Paul Youngquist refers to the Haitian Revolution's impact across the Caribbean and remarks that "In colonial terms, not the flowering of culture, not the triumph of right, but the recurrence of racial violence defines the Romantic era" *Studies in Romanticism* 56 (Spring 2017), 6.

35 Lovejoy's famous essay "On the Discrimination of Romanticisms" treats "Romanticism" as a test case of the crudeness of all such literary-historical terms, only to smuggle in the suggestion that "Romanticism" is, after all, the *most* problematic of them: "The categories which it has become customary to use in distinguishing and classifying 'movements' in literature or philosophy ... are far too rough, crude, undiscriminating—and none of them so hopelessly so as the category 'Romantic.'" Arthur Lovejoy, "On the Discrimination of Romanticisms," reprinted in *English Romantic Poets*, ed. M. H. Abrams (Oxford: Oxford University Press, 1960), 7.

36 On the emergence of "literature" as a "right to say everything" and its relation to a democracy and freedom "to come," see the interview with Jacques Derrida that opens *Acts of Literature*, ed. Derek Attridge (New York and London: Routlege, 1992), 37.

37 Percy Bysshe Shelley, *Shelley's Poetry and Prose*, ed. Donald H. Reiman and Neil Fraistat (New York: W. W. Norton, 2002), 535. Cf. from the same passage: "the most unfailing herald, companion, and follower of the awakening of a great people to work a beneficial change in opinion or institution is Poetry" (535).

38 Shelley, *Shelley's Poetry and Prose*, 535.

39 Shelley thus anticipates Derrida's account of literature in the interview cited above from *Acts of Literature*, ed. Derek Attridge, 37: "'What is literature?'; literature as historical institution with its conventions, rules, etc., but also this institution of fiction which gives *in principle* the power to say everything, to break free of the rules, to displace them, and thereby to institute, to invent, and even to suspect the traditional difference between nature and institution, nature and conventional law, nature and history. Here we should ask juridical and political questions. The institution of literature in the West, in its relatively modern form, is linked to an authorization to say everything, and doubtless too to the coming about of the modern idea of democracy. Not that it depends on a democracy in place, but it seems inseparable to me from what calls forth a democracy, in the most open (and doubtless itself to come) sense of democracy."

40 Nesbitt, *Universal Emancipation*, 2 (emphasis in original).

41 Orrin Wang, *Fantastic Modernity: Dialectical Readings in Romanticism and Theory* (Baltimore: Johns Hopkins University Press, 1996), 187.

42 Lovejoy, "On the Discrimination of Romanticisms," 7.

43 Susan Buck-Morss, *Hegel, Haiti, and Universal History* (Pittsburgh: University of Pittsburgh Press, 2009), 40. The chapter from which we are quoting, "Hegel and Haiti" first appeared in *Critical Inquiry* 26 (Summer 2000). Buck-Morss rightly describes the publication of her "Hegel and Haiti" in 2000 as "something of an intellectual event" (ix). In the context of the North American academy, it was an event not least for the way it made a certain kind of silence around Haiti audible—the silence that Trouillot had already analyzed and that Buck-Morss finds pervasive in contemporary Hegel scholarship. It was also an event touching a philosopher who, though a critic of early German Romanticism, looms large for later generations in the constellation of nineteenth-century Romantic writing.

44 Daut's *Tropics of Haiti* is a field transforming work that includes extended discussion of several authors revisited in this volume. Other important

recent anglophone scholarship not already mentioned in our references (and that contains at least some attention to Haiti and Romantic texts) includes Srinivas Aravamudan's *Tropicopolitans: Colonialism and Agency 1688–1804* (Durham: Duke University Press, 1999), Chris Bongie, *Islands and Exiles: The Creole Identities of Post/Colonial Literature* (Standford: Stanford University Press, 1998); Joan Dayan, *Haiti, History, and the Gods* (Berkeley: University of California Press) 1998; Dorish Kadish, *Fathers, Daughters, and Slaves: Women Writers and French Colonial Slavery* (Liverpool: Liverpool University Press, 2012) and Jared Hickman, *Black Prometheus: Race & Radicalism in the Age of Atlantic Slavery* (Oxford: Oxford University Press, 2017).

45 Joel Pace, "Afterthoughts: Romanticism, the Black Atlantic, and Self-Mapping," *Studies in Romanticism* 56 (Spring 2017), 115.

1

The Shadow of Voltaire: Early Haitian Literature and the Claims of Intertextuality

Chris Bongie

Un spectre épouvantable en tous lieux me poursuit ....
Que veut cet habitant des ténébreux abîmes?
Que vient-il m'annoncer?

—Voltaire[1]

At a meeting of the Port-au-Prince town council on December 10, 1791, there appeared before the municipal officers a certain Sieur Clemanson *fils*, owner of a plantation in the hills to the south of the town. Capital of the West Province of the French colony of Saint-Domingue, Port-au-Prince was in a state of chaos, a good part of it having burned to the ground three weeks before, after the collapse of a peace treaty signed on October 23 that had brought a momentary end to the armed insurrection launched by free people of color (*gens de couleur libres*) in late August, at precisely the same time as the slave revolt in the North. The plantation owner's deposition testifies, in miniature, to the renewal of hostilities in the West between white and free colored citizenry, but also to the complexity of a struggle in which some white settlers had, for a variety of reasons, allied themselves with the *gens de couleur* and in which both the warring parties were committed to preserving the institution of slavery. On the 8th of the month, Clemanson *fils* declared, citizens of colour, numbering from ten to twelve, arrived at the Clemanson plantation, headed by two white men, one of whom calls himself "little Voltaire" [*dont l'un s'appelle le petit Voltaire*]. Upon their arrival, they took hold of the negress Theresa, and wanted to force her to reveal the whereabouts of the white men and women whom they knew to be on the said plantation. They tied her down and put a rope around her neck, and it was only upon the urging of the other slaves that they let her go.[2]

The planter's deposition then goes on to describe the violence perpetrated by "the mulattoes" (*les mulâtres*) as they took control of the plantation, and the desperate flight of his family as they sought refuge in the bushes.

This archival anecdote serves as a telling reminder of why the free colored insurrection of 1791 has proved so difficult to incorporate into "the story of the only successful slave revolt in history," to cite the subtitle of C. L. R. James's 1930s play about the Haitian Revolution, *Toussaint Louverture*. Fought in the name of equal rights for all *free* citizens in Saint-Domingue, and expressly committed to the preservation of a colonial system grounded in the rule of slavery, this was an uprising in which the colony's slaves were viewed as mere pawns, subject to disciplinary violence as here, or strategically deployed against the whites as, most famously, in the case of the so-called Swiss—several hundred armed slaves integrated into the free colored army but then deported from the colony in the immediate aftermath of the October peace treaty, an act of appeasement on the part of leaders of the insurrection that would quickly become "a symbol of free colored perfidy ... in the propaganda war of the revolution."[3] The encounter at the Clemanson plantation testifies amply to these fraught relations between insurgent "citizens of color" and the slave population, while the story's momentary focus on the *négresse Thérèse* also serves to remind us of the violently gendered dynamics of what was a highly masculinized struggle for human rights. But for our purposes, what is of primary interest here is the figure of the "little Voltaire," positioned by the plantation owner (whether in reality or for rhetorical effect) at the head of this band of free colored citizens. The presence of this white collaborator serves as a veritable allegory for the problematic explored in this chapter: namely, the role played by Voltaire in helping shape what Kevin Olson has referred to as the "political imaginary" of the 1791 free colored insurrection, with its contradictory commitment to human rights and the rule of slavery.[4]

In what follows, I retell in some detail the story of this insurrection and its aftermath, focusing in particular on two archival documents in which intertextual references to Voltaire's tragedies play a key role in the performative displays of literacy whereby leaders of the free colored movement laid claim to the recognition of their equal rights as citizens. If the primary goal of my chapter is simply to flesh out an episode of the Haitian Revolution that is often reduced to a footnote (and a discomfiting

THE SHADOW OF VOLTAIRE

one at that, given its evident limitations when it comes to the project of universal emancipation), this historical narrative also opens out onto two cautionary arguments about the legacy of what I will be calling "(the other) 1791." First, in relation to the ongoing reconsideration (and valorization) of early Haitian literature that has become integral to our understanding of nineteenth-century Haiti, the archival material considered in this chapter establishes genealogical links between (the other) 1791 and the emergence of the Haitian literary field following upon independence in 1804, and in so doing suggests that we attend to the ways in which this literature does not simply break with but remains haunted by the particular "set of sociopolitical processes of differentiation and hierarchization" that shaped the free colored imaginary.[5] Second, in relation to figurations of identity that are both central to and questioned by (a particular articulation of) Black Studies, I suggest that looking back at the political demand for recognition that was a characteristic feature of the free colored imaginary is a useful exercise when it comes to thinking about the structural challenge of any rights-based politics of recognition in the present, namely, that "the entry fee for legal recognition," as Alexander Weheliye notes, "is the acceptance of categories based on white supremacy and colonialism, as well as normative genders and sexualities."[6] While this second cautionary argument is one that will be touched upon only at the end of the present chapter, the following section prepares the ground for the first, introducing a particularly well-known Haitian text from 1804 that will serve throughout as the touchstone for our investigation of the literary legacies of (the other) 1791.

* * *

Nowhere are the genealogical links between (the other) 1791 and the founding documents of postindependence Haitian literature, as mediated through the figure of Voltaire, more evident than in the Proclamation of April 28, 1804, signed by Jean-Jacques Dessalines, which justified the elimination of most of the "white Frenchmen" who had remained in Haiti after the declaration of independence on January 1. "The hour of vengeance has arrived," Dessalines proclaimed to his fellow Haitians, "and the implacable enemies of the rights of man have suffered the punishment due to their crimes." Any unregenerated Haitian who "thinks he has not fulfilled the decrees of the Eternal, by exterminating these blood-thirsty tigers [*tigres altérés de sang*]" is called upon to leave the country:

> Indignant nature discards him from our bosom; let him hide his infamy far from hence; the air we breathe, is not suited to his gross organs; it is the air of liberty, pure, august, and triumphant.
>
> Yes, we have rendered to these true cannibals [*vrais cannibales*], war for war, crime for crime, outrage for outrage; yes, I have saved my country; I have avenged America [*j'ai vengé l'Amérique*].[7]

This act of vengeance, which should cause the "tyrants, usurpers, scourges of the new world [*fléaux du nouveau monde*]" to tremble, has also, Dessalines stressed, had the salutary effect of drawing together "two classes of men, born to cherish, assist, and succour one another" but "whom the refined duplicity of Europe for a long time endeavoured to divide." These two classes, conceived of here in the hyper-racialized terms of "Blacks and Yellows" (*Noirs et Jaunes*), have been rendered "for ever one, indivisible, and inseparable," made "but one family" through this sacrificial rite of passage, their "perfect reconciliation sealed by the blood of our butchers." Bloody vengeance enacted by all members of the Haitian "family" lays to rest the long history of social divisions evident in the civil war of 1799–1800 between the forces of Toussaint Louverture and André Rigaud, or in the differing trajectories of slave revolt and free colored insurrection in 1791. Indeed, the Proclamation itself performatively enacts this unification of the "two classes of men" at its conclusion, where Governor General Dessalines's name as signatory is followed by that of his newly minted secretary general, Juste Chanlatte, responsible for the certified copy ("Le Gouverneur général, / Signé, DESSALINES. / *Pour copie conforme*, / Le Sécrétaire général, / JUSTE CHANLATTE."). A figure of some prominence during the free colored insurrection of 1791, Chanlatte had only just returned to Haiti from years of exile in the United States,[8] and his presence as under-signatory confirms the union of two classes that is being proclaimed in the body of the text.

As has only recently been recognized, the rhetorical force of the Proclamation was enhanced by the intertextual deployment of lines from Voltaire, most particularly from his New World tragedy *Alzire* (1736), a searing indictment of Spanish colonialism in the Americas, which contemplates the legitimacy of armed indigenous resistance to settler colonial rule while opting in the end for a "civilizing discourse" of acculturation, in a predictable recourse to "colonial paternalism" that serves to regulate "the impassioned rhetoric of political liberty and cultural autonomy that dominates the rest of the play."[9] Dessalines's claim to have "avenged America," for instance, echoes that of the Inca warrior Zamore, who, three years after being left for dead by his Spanish torturers, returns to Lima with a band of comrades who share his hatred of the colonizers and his desire to avenge America or die trying (*Ils sont dans nos forêts, et leur foule héroique / Vient périr sous ces murs, ou venger l'Amérique*; 2.4.177–78); while the characterization of Haiti's annihilated enemy, the French, as "scourges of the New World" repeats the indictment of the Spanish made by the noble-hearted former governor of Peru, Don Alvares, to his son Gusman, Zamore's former torturer and present rival for the affections of the Inca princess Alzire (1.1.85).

The use of Voltaire in Dessalines's Proclamation provides a fascinating example of postcolonial literacy through which "the theatrical words of Enlightenment [were appropriated] in the service of a very real act of vengeance against colonial tyranny,"[10] but it also raises the empirical

THE SHADOW OF VOLTAIRE

question of how this source found its way there: how, in the words of historian Laurent Dubois, who was the first to point toward this intertextual connection, the by-all-accounts "illiterate" Dessalines might have "capture[d] and reformulate[d] Voltaire's channeling of the history of European colonialism in his own writings and words," mobilizing it "within a political project of liberation, resistance, and vengeance against Europe itself."[11] It would be possible, of course, to produce hypothetical scenarios about how Dessalines might have become familiar with these lines from Voltaire, although it is perhaps telling that Dubois supplies none. Equally telling in this respect is the fact that literary critic Deborah Jenson, in an influential series of interventions between 2007 and 2016 that constitute the most concerted attempt at locating Desssalines's "conceptual fingerprints" in documents from 1804 bearing his signature, simply avoided any mention of the shadowy presence of Voltaire in the Proclamation, thereby obviating the need for any such scenarios in her engagement with "Dessalines's textual corpus—his *oeuvre*."[12] Intertextual connections of this sort evidently complicate arguments based on the claim that there is "a fluid, sustained, and critical structure of metaphor in the major Dessalinian texts, regardless of secretarial signature," and that this characteristic "structure of metaphor" allows us to identify Dessalines as the "primary authorial voice directing an admittedly complex redactive process."[13] From Jenson's perspective, these texts demand to be read as an expression of what she calls "Dessalines's 'life by metaphor,'" exemplified in the Proclamation, for instance, by "his metaphoric framing of death and death's agents, notably the colonist as 'bloodthirsty tiger.'"[14] Dessalines's reference to *tigres altérés de sang*, his "metaphor of the Haitians' ethical imperative to exterminate the bloodthirsty tiger," becomes, in this reading, a distinctive manifestation of "embodied cognition,"[15] rather than the mere reiteration of a stock phrase that crops up with great frequency in any number of revolutionary pamphlets from the 1790s and/or (more interestingly, from our perspective) the knowing redeployment of a line from Voltaire's tragedy *Zaïre* (which can itself be traced back to Corneille's *Horace*).

Although Jenson does acknowledge in places that the Proclamation was "composed with the assistance of secretary Juste Chanlatte,"[16] her argumentative focus on Dessalines's authority prevents her from recognizing, much less interrogating, intertextual connections of this sort. There is thus a significant foreclosure when it comes to the role of its under-signatory, Juste Chanlatte, one that is all the more glaring given the intense engagement with Voltaire that would characterize Chanlatte's *oeuvre* in subsequent decades, and especially in relation to *Alzire* as I have demonstrated elsewhere.[17] This foreclosure, I hasten to add, is *equally* characteristic of straightforward attributions of authorship to Chanlatte, based on "common-sensical" assumptions that, of course, the Paris-educated, light-skinned, well-to-do Chanlatte must have produced this eloquent text! How could it be otherwise?[18] This *banalizing* form of attribution, even were it true, plays into the condescending assumptions about the limits of Dessalines's conceptual vision that Jenson's argument has the great merit of questioning. If Chanlatte played a role, be it minor or major, in "writing" rather than simply "transcribing" the words of the Proclamation, then we need to *think* about his role rather than simply assume it, and there is no better place to start than with the shadowy presence of Voltaire in this text, which cannot be readily incorporated into a Dessalines-centric reading of it such as Jenson's.

Within the terms of conventional literary history, reading this intertextual evidence as a sure sign (as I believe it to be) of Chanlatte's compositional "assistance" would allow us to connect the Proclamation to other texts Chanlatte later signed in his own name, where the theatrical and philosophical works of Voltaire, and more broadly the classical literary tradition and its neoclassical avatars, play such a central role. A move such as this, neatly compatible with "Romanticism's sacralization of the author,"[19] would help promote the ongoing recuperation of Chanlatte as a writer of *individual* importance, perhaps even "the most important writer in Haiti's early postcolonial existence."[20] The argument pursued in this chapter, by contrast, leads us not forward but back, to Chanlatte's first emergence on the historical scene in 1791: it stakes out a sociological claim about Chanlatte as a *representative* figure, someone whose individual talent cannot be disentangled from his *collective* identity as a (in 1804, erstwhile) free colored citizen. The presence of Voltaire in the Proclamation is best *thought*, I argue, in genealogical terms: as the unsettling trace of a "political imaginary" that shaped the free colored insurrection of 1791 and its lingering aftermath; as the ambivalent recollection of a way of seeing the world and acting in it that Chanlatte had shared with other elite members of his social class, for whom the tragedies of Voltaire served as a source of inspiration and legitimization in their struggle for equal rights, for integration into the national family of "Frenchmen," and for the preservation of a colonial system founded upon the rule of slavery; as, in short, the shadow of colonial divisions that haunt the Proclamation's bewitching vision of anticolonial liberation and national unification in the postcolonial present.

* * *

In the first volume of his influential *Études sur l'histoire d'Haïti* (1853), nineteenth-century Haitian historian Beaubrun Ardouin mentions Juste Chanlatte as one of the free colored leaders from the parish of Arcahaye who took up arms on August 26, 1791, as part of a coordinated uprising of "men of color" across the West and South Provinces of Saint-Domingue. Chanlatte, Jacques Cameau (his soon to be father-in-law), and Jean-Baptiste Lapointe, like others of their class across the two provinces, "on 26 August 1791 ... simultaneously took up arms and organized themselves militarily, initiating that glorious struggle of which the final denouement, after numerous twists and turns, and cruel political calamities, would be the act of January 1, 1804."[21] Ardouin's emphasis on the "initiatory" role of the *hommes de couleur* in the struggle that led to Haitian independence offers a teleological reading that is strikingly off-kilter in relation to familiar narratives such as James's *The Black Jacobins*, which take as their epic point of departure the August 22 slave revolt in the North Province and the Bois Caïman vodun ceremony that preceded it. As an explanation of the origins of "the miraculous freedom of 1804,"[22] Ardouin's story makes little sense to us today. However, giving serious thought to his claim, inasmuch as it is possible (for us), requires some such unlikely reckoning with (the other) 1791, a willingness to forego the ready-made answers that constitute our own historiographical points of departure for understanding the Haitian Revolution by attending carefully to "the *twin* uprisings of August 1791."[23]

Longstanding tensions between Saint-Domingue's two free classes, white and colored, had been exacerbated by the outbreak of the revolution in France, and were further enflamed by the brutal execution in February 1791 of Vincent Ogé and Jean-Baptiste Chavannes, along with dozens of other *gens de couleur libres* who had participated in an armed uprising in October of the previous year launched with the intention of securing political rights arguably granted them in a "deliberately ambiguous" decree issued by the Constituent Assembly that March.[24] The martyrdom of Ogé, "ignominiously sacrificed to the ferocity of the European colonists, those bloodthirsty men," would become a rallying call for the movement.[25] However, the immediate stimulus for the insurrection in August was the colonial government's failure to enact the Constituent Assembly's law of May 15, 1791, which granted full political rights to a segment of the free colored population, those born of free fathers and mothers. Although news of this law arrived in the colony at the end of June, it was never officially promulgated there, and was strenuously resisted by white authorities, who argued that this "fatal decree" would destroy the necessary "line of demarcation" between "Whites and Blacks" that was embodied by the intermediary class of "freed men and mulattoes" (*les affranchis et les mulâtres*), and would thus have disastrous consequences that should "strike terror in the hearts of anyone who is not an *enraged* Philanthropist."[26]

In his rousing account of the significance of August 26, Ardouin makes a point of noting that the *hommes de couleur* of Léogâne, directly to the south of Port-au-Prince, were among those who did not join the common struggle that day, because they "followed the prompting of [Pierre] Labuissonnière, a timid soul," best known to us today as one of the main correspondents of Julien Raimond, whose tireless efforts in Paris on behalf of free colored rights and in conjunction with the Abbé Grégoire had helped pave the way for the May 15 legislation.[27] The "timidity" of Labuissonnière, or at least his desire to avoid retributive violence, is evident in a "journal kept by the citizens of color from the parish of Léogâne," dated June 5, 1791 (with an August 24 postscript), and addressed to the French National Assembly by its lead signatory Labuissonnière and almost fifty other "planters and property owners."[28] The journal describes the "deplorable situation" faced by the parish's free colored citizens since November 1789 when attempts had been made to seek representation in the newly constituted primary assemblies, resulting in the persecution and eventual imprisonment of their leaders, including Labuissonnière. The narrative tracks in detail the outrages to which they were subject by the whites in charge of Léogâne, culminating in a gripping scene of public humiliation when they were forced to their knees at a public assembly and ordered, "in this posture so humiliating for humanity but glorious for our persecutors ... to beg the whites' pardon and swear fidelity and unlimited submission to them," expressions of contrition that "the mouth uttered and the heart disavowed."[29] Armed resistance, it is pointed out, would have been possible, a collective retreat to the hills (*nos montagnes*) and the launching of a prolonged defensive war, but "the natural repugnance felt by humane men" at the act of shedding blood had ruled out such a response.[30] It is "our sentiments of humanity" that the signatories of the Journal wish to convey to the "legislators and restorers of French liberty" in the National Assembly: the fact that they are committed to "resisting oppression" in their quest for justice,[31] but will do so not in a "spirit of sedition or divisiveness" but "of union and concord," the very opposite of "the spirit of cruelty" that has always characterized the actions of their adversaries.[32]

The journal is prefaced by a series of apologetic statements about "our feeble pens, our feeble means" (*nos faibles plumes, nos faibles organes*), anticipating the "publicly performed self-consciousness" that rhetorically shapes early works of Haitian literature by the likes of Boisrond-Tonnerre and Baron de Vastey.[33] The collective subject that is given voice in the Journal asks its interlocutors to overlook "our lack of a talent for writing," "to excuse the baldness of our style, the incorrectly spelled words, their lack of order," and focus on the content itself, well aware that these signs of a "limited education" would be seized upon by their "enlightened" enemies (*des contradicteurs très éclairés et très animés*)[34]—the sort of men who, in the coming weeks, responding to news of the May 15 decree, would scoff that of the many thousand *hommes de couleur* in the colony "there wasn't a single one who had received the sort of education required for governing such a considerable island, *Chia, bichi, moi, pas, vellé, ca* being the sum total of what one can drag out of them."[35]

And yet this self-conscious opening is itself prefaced, and ironized, by an emphatic display of literacy at the very outset, in the form of an epigraph from Voltaire:

La vérité terrible avec des yeux vengeurs
Vient sur l'aile du tems et lit au fond des cœurs

Son flambeau redoutable éclaire enfin l'abîme
Où dans l'impunité s'était caché le crime.
Voltaire.[36]

[On the wings of time comes the dreadful truth of old,
With its avenging eyes scanning the depths of the soul,
Its mighty flame illuminating the dark abyss,
Revealing the crime that has gone unpunished.]

As the affirmation of a shared literary culture, the name of "Voltaire" here clearly suffices to promote the desired bonds of recognition between the oppressed and their transatlantic benefactors, serving, like the very act of writing in works of early Haitian literature, as "the evidence of a humanity that must claim its part of logos as a consequence of common understanding."[37] However, it also prompts more specific questions about what exactly we are being asked to recognize. These lines, it turns out, are from one of the lesser known of Voltaire's plays, *Eriphile*.[38] Pronounced in the opening act and scene of the play by the high priest of Jupiter, they are part of his augury that the crimes of Eriphile, the Queen of Argos, who was complicit in the murder of her husband Amphiarus at the hands of her devious suitor Hermogide fifteen years before, will come back to haunt her, as indeed they do in the form of an oedipal hankering for her unrecognized son Alcméon, whom she had abandoned as a baby because of a prophecy that he would kill her. Believing himself to be the son of a slave, raised by another slave, but now a military leader, fresh from resounding victories over Argos's enemies, Alcméon aspires to wed his Queen, only to learn the truth about his father's identity and his mother's role in Amphiarus's death. In the final act, taking vengeance against Hermogide, and urged on by the furies, Alcméon will accidentally stab his repentant mother, fulfilling the prophecy that Eriphile would die at her son's hand, this tragic ending balanced, however, by his ascent to the throne and the restoration of patriarchal order.

The tragedy's themes of (mis)recognition and (il)legitimacy thus allow for a self-identification on the part of the *gens de couleur* with the role of Alcméon (one that will be even more evident in our next archival document). The appropriation of Voltaire, moreover, in its emphasis on a vengeful unveiling of the terrible truth of racial oppression, and the associated use of light/dark imagery to understand the abyssal past's relation to the revolutionary present, arguably anticipates what Raphael Hoermann has termed a "radical Gothic" mode of understanding the Haitian Revolution, one that deploys but inverts the "demonizing" recourse to Gothic rhetoric in "hegemonic" representations of "the horrors of Saint-Domingue," and that finds expression in fiercely anticolonial documents like the Proclamation.[39] If the free colored imaginary provides a genealogical point of departure for such documents, of course, the colonial limits of that imaginary are equally clear when we consider the restorative trajectory of Alcméon's story, which carries him beyond tragedy to a place in which he can be recognized as the legitimate successor to his father.

On August 24, Labuissonnière's colleague Joseph Alvarez appended a note to the Journal confirming its account of his arbitrary incarceration in April; two days later, the coalition of free colored forces took up arms in the West Province, achieving rapid success over the next several weeks in a series of minor skirmishes. White plantation owners in the parishes surrounding Port-au-Prince were from the start inclined to negotiate with the free colored insurgents, being themselves at odds with the increasingly radical direction taken by the whites in control of Port-au-Prince, the so-called *patriotes*, whose anti-royalist and autonomist inclinations were being fuelled by a growing underclass of *petits blancs* in the city intent on consolidating their own position. If it meant the preservation of property rights and putting the "radical" whites of Port-au-Prince in their place, then *grands blancs* such as Hanus de Jumécourt were willing to legitimize the formal erasure of a "line of demarcation" between the two classes, signing a treaty on September 7 that would provide the basis for a subsequent *concordat* agreed to shortly thereafter by the suddenly beleaguered whites of Port-au-Prince. Sanctioning the "beneficent decree" of May 15, this September 11 *concordat* looked forward to a "reunion of the citizens of all classes" based on the understanding that "equality, precious and sacred, shall be the basis and the result of all future actions, and that there shall be no difference between them [the citizens of color] & the white citizens other than those that are necessarily due to merit and virtue."[40]

Contested by white "patriots" whose grip on Port-au-Prince waxed and waned over the following six weeks, the September *concordat* eventually became the basis of a province-wide treaty, which, among other things, officially abolished the racialized distinction between white and colored citizens. Authored, like the preceding one, by free colored leader Pierre Pinchinat, a lawyer who had practiced in France during the 1780s, it was signed at the Damiens plantation on October 23 (including by Juste Chanlatte as a representative of the parish of Arcahaye), and was greeted by its supporters as "a treaty that should serve as the basis for bringing about the regeneration of the Colony, the destruction of abuses & the execution of laws; a treaty that should put an end to systems which lead to dissension, anarchy & discontent," and thereby effect the "reunion of brothers" who might otherwise have destroyed themselves in civil war.[41]

Only weeks after the signing of the treaty and the free colored army's triumphant entry into Port-au-Prince, a fragile equilibrium was shattered by the arrival of news from France that the Constituent Assembly had, on September 24, overturned the May 15 decree, returning the power of determining local laws (and thus the policing of voting rights) to the existing white-elected assemblies. In Saint-Marc to the north of Port-au-Prince, free colored leaders

THE SHADOW OF VOLTAIRE

35

headed by Jean Savary (in his capacity as "President of the Army of Saint-Marc") reflected on the potentially dramatic consequences of this reversal in a November 16 letter to the newly constituted French Legislative Assembly. The letter begins by explaining how (what its authors perceived as) the recognition of their rights in the March 1790 decree had exacerbated existing tensions between themselves and the white population, who gave vent to "a hatred of us a thousand times more implacable than what they had expressed before, and like lions roaring with anger their glaring eyes became the signs of our proscription" (*semblables à des lions rugissants de colère leurs regards devenaient pour nous des signes de proscription*).[42] News of the September 24 decree had emboldened these angry lions, who were ready to "bind us with new chains," but their prospective victims were resolved to fight back: "Fortified by our courage, our unity, and the principles that you have established for us [in the Declaration of the Rights of Man], we will resist oppression [*nous résisterons à l'oppression*] to our last breath."[43] Proclaiming their readiness "to *live free or die*," Savary and his colleagues conclude the letter with an expression of hope that "the voice of nature" can still make itself heard in the National Assembly, that virtue will triumph, and that the oppressed (*les opprimés*) will be granted their desire for recognition: "Look upon us in an equitable way [*Jetez un regard d'équité sur nous*], and you will see Frenchmen inviolably attached to the Nation, the Law, & the King!"[44]

The appeal to "un regard d'équité" at the end of the Saint-Marc letter follows through on an earlier admonition that should men such as their white adversaries, who are "governed by their passions, find it impossible to be equitable," they would do well

> to call upon the supreme Being, to go and consult nature in all its variety, to examine their conscience, and then will they say as the author of *Zaïre* says,

> Les mortels sont égaux, ce n'est point la naissance
> La seule vertu fait leur différence.[45]

> [Mortals are equal, it is not their birth, hence,
> But virtue alone that makes the difference.]

This tidy couplet from Voltaire was a familiar one in the context of the revolutionary struggle for equal rights, and is most commonly linked to his play *Le fanatisme, ou Mahomet le prophète* (1741), where these lines are uttered by the prophet's second-in-command Omar when justifying why he has sworn allegiance to the low-born Mahomet—a nice-sounding philosophical justification that is, however, when taken in context, riddled with irony, given the play's overall representation of the fanatical prophet as an anything but virtuous, hypocritical imposter. However, Voltaire had originally deployed these same lines in a much more straightforward manner a decade before in *Eriphile*, and given the reference to that play in the Léogâne Journal there is every reason to believe that their use here should be traced back to this source, where they are not subject to the sort of contextual irony at play in *Mahomet*. In *Eriphile* this egalitarian credo is uttered by the worthy Alcméon, the adopted son of a slave, as we have seen, who has risen to the top of the military ranks precisely on the basis of his talents. At this early point in the tragedy (the first scene of Act Two), Alcméon has ambitions of marrying the Queen of Argos, whom he does not yet know to be his mother, and is arguing against the "wretched prejudice" (*préjugé malheureux*) that would condemn him to the lowly condition of his birth regardless of his accomplishments, which are those, he proudly declares, of a self-made man, someone who has taken the "shameful chains" (*ces fers si honteux*) in which he was born and used them to shackle the hands of his enemies, someone who sees who he is and not who he was, and believes himself to be at least as worthy as the kings whom he has vanquished.[46] The ultimate irony of Alcméon's dismissal of *la naissance* as a criterion for social recognition, of course, is that his ancestors *do* matter, for, it turns out, he never was the son of a slave whom he believed himself to be but the legitimate offspring of the king of Argos.

It is not hard to understand the appeal of this particular play by "the author of *Zaïre*" to free colored readers. As a self-made figure of civic virtue and military prowess, Alcméon, "this proud Citizen," provides a ready source of identification for those intent on gaining their fair share of power in a colony imperilled by "the barbarism, injustice, and arrogance of the European colonists."[47] But no less than the Enlightenment vision of Voltaire, whose "fixist, polygenetic view of humankind" stands as "one of the first pseudo-scientific views of the African's fundamental dissimilarity from Europeans,"[48] the free colored imaginary had decided limits when it came to the matter of equality. The Saint-Marc letter begins, for instance, with fulsome praise of the National Assembly's "declaration of the rights of man in society, which is a masterpiece of the human spirit," while pointing out that the "general" terms in which it was couched at first appeared to include even "non-free persons"—an alarming appearance, it is added, that was happily put to rest by subsequent decrees.[49] Here we have a classic example of how, to recall Kevin Olson's analysis, the free colored imaginary invests deeply in the "normative aura" of the idea of the rights of man, while at the same time restricting its revolutionary commitment to "the equality of all property owners."[50] This initial stress on the "inalienable and imprescriptible rights" guaranteed to all *free* persons by the 1789 Declaration is then buttressed by a practical commitment to preserving those rights and their limits when the letter proceeds to emphasize the ongoing role of this class of twenty-five thousand oppressed Frenchmen (*hommes français*) not only in helping preserve Saint-Domingue from disloyal whites eager to declare

THE SHADOW OF VOLTAIRE

the colony's independence but in taking up arms "to defend the properties of all citizens and, on their own volition, to drive back the blacks in revolt [*les noirs révoltés*] in the North Province"—an effort at restoring calm that, should it be crowned with success, would result in "their being recognized by Equity and Justice as the saviours of Saint-Domingue."[51] This active response to the slave revolt follows through on the Léogâne Journal's earlier commitment to the National Assembly that, notwithstanding any dissension between the two classes of free citizens, should a "slave insurrection" arise from the general anarchy that reigns in the colony "you would see us rally round the Whites to defend them to the last drop of our blood."[52]

The letter from Saint-Marc would arrive at its transatlantic destination in late January 1792, by which time the situation on the ground in the West Province had been utterly transformed by the cataclysmic events of November 21–22, when enraged mobs of whites in Port-au-Prince, emboldened by news of the Assembly's reversal of the May 15 decree and seizing on an isolated incident of interracial violence, went on a rampage, murdering free colored citizens, pillaging their homes, and burning (whether inadvertently or not) a good portion of the capital to the ground. After their mass exodus from the city, the free colored army (along with their mostly royalist white allies) reassembled in neighboring Croix-des-Bouquets and prepared to lay siege to Port-au-Prince, exhorting their brethren in other regions of the province "to plunge our blood-stained arms, avengers of perfidy and betrayal, into the breasts of these monsters from Europe," to quote from what is no doubt the best known document associated with the 1791 free colored insurrection, an intercepted letter presumably dating from late November that was published by Port-au-Prince *patriotes* as evidence of the "monstrosity" of the *hommes de couleur* and identified at the time as the work of its lead signatory Pierre Pinchinat, although it is now more commonly attributed to Juste Chanlatte, one of its many cosignatories.[53] On December 10, when Clemanson *fils* made his deposition to the municipal authorities in Port-au-Prince, the fate of the province, and hence of the entire colony, seemingly lay in the balance. Was a reconciliation between the two warring parties still possible, despite the perfidious backtracking of the whites and the desire for vengeance it had provoked? Would "reason and sound policy" prevail, Pinchinat and his colleagues at Croix-des-Bouquets asked their adversaries, the unhinged colonists (*les insensés colons*), in a letter dated December 31 in which they pointedly identified themselves as "French citizens formerly of color"? Would their eyes finally be opened to "the imperious necessity of there being a single class of citizens if the domestic enemy who menaces you from every side [i.e., the slaves in revolt] is to be successfully resisted"?[54] Or would those "true cannibals [*vrais cannibales*] who arrogate to yourselves the right to slake your thirst for human blood" continue in their destructive ways, leaving the *citoyens français ci-devant de couleur* in despair and with no other option than to become "new Samsons, bring down the columns of the temple, and bury themselves with the Philistines under the ruins of the edifice, making but a vast tomb of the entire colony"?[55]

It is at this point of uncertainty, as the soon-to-be-jettisoned Gregorian calendar moves from 1791 to 1792, that my detailed account of the free colored insurrection must break off, given limitations of space, even though the insurrection's extended aftermath is vital for the sort of genealogical arguments being mounted here. The briefest mention of subsequent events must suffice by way of returning us to the 1804 Proclamation and its vengeful denunciation of the "true cannibals" who colonized America. Chief among these would be passage of the law of April 4, 1792, through which the French Legislative Assembly unequivocally granted all "hommes de couleur & nègres libres" in the colony the political rights for which they had fought. Charged with enforcing this decree, Civil Commissioners Léger-Félicité Sonthonax and Étienne Polverel would, after their arrival in the colony in September, help usher in a new epoch for free colored citizens, many of whom took on prominent roles in the colony: Labuissonnière and Savary would become, respectively, the mayors of Léogâne and Saint-Marc; Pinchinat would be named to the twelve-person (six white, six colored) *Commission intermédiaire* in charge of governing the colony in the lead-up to promised new elections. On December 10, 1792, one year to the day after the deposition of Clemanson *fils*, Juste Chanlatte (Chanlatte *fils*) conveyed the mood of optimistic reconciliation, addressing the municipality of Port-au-Prince as part of a ceremony in which the free colored army led by Louis-Jacques Beauvais handed over its flag to municipal officers, including Chanlatte's father, as part of their integration into the town's national guard: "We abjure every form of hatred; we swear for all time to bear arms in defense of the *patrie* and in the interests of this commune. We will perish rather than ever separate ourselves from the new flags under which the law now joins us together."[56]

In the months to come, while still working in tandem with free colored forces to eliminate white resistance to the law of April 4 and put an end to the slave revolt, the Civil Commissioners, through both force of circumstance and philosophical inclination, would be drawn in increasingly radical directions, which culminated in the abolition of slavery throughout the colony, starting with Sonthonax's declaration of *liberté générale* in the North Province on August 29, 1793. The elimination of the distinction between citizens and non-free persons, a distinction so integral to the free colored imaginary of 1791, would prove a step too far for the many *gens de couleur* who saw it not as the logical culmination but the very antithesis of the egalitarianism they espoused. While some prominent leaders such as Rigaud and Pinchinat remained loyal to the Commissioners, firm in the belief that the "cause of liberty will triumph here," in the words of Juste Chanlatte's uncle Antoine, one of Sonthonax and Polverel's most indefatigable officers,[57] many others

THE SHADOW OF VOLTAIRE

broke ranks in the closing months of 1793, some still professing their loyalty to France and holding out hope that it would not sanction the abolition of slavery, and others going so far as to align themselves with France's enemies, the British and/or the Spanish.

In Saint-Marc, notably, the imprescriptible right of "resistance to oppression" became the rallying call of Savary's *Conseil de paix et d'union*, which in November urged parishes across the colony to join their coalition and strike back against "the perfidious policy" of the Civil Commissioners, a call that would be answered in the affirmative by, among others, Labuissonnière and his colleagues in the parish of Léogâne.[58] In a circular letter addressed to his "brothers and friends" in the West and South Provinces, the Conseil's deputy from the parish of Arcahaye warned them to step back from the abyss into which they were being led by the Commissioners, those "bloodthirsty despots, those unfaithful emissaries of a nation that is as humane as it is generous." These *despotes sanguinaires* were plotting and had in part executed "the destruction of free men" (*la destruction des hommes libres*), having already reduced the North Province to "a second Nigritia" (*une nouvelle nigritie*). Citing the ongoing disarmament of "the free population" and the "expedited use of the guillotine on our imprisoned brothers" in Port-au-Prince, this deputy urged those who were still sitting on the fence that they cease being the "passive spectators" of these and other such "scenes of horror" orchestrated by the Commissioners. Rather than "await, in culpable inaction, the moment when their *tigricity* (for there are so many new words for unheard of crimes!) sates itself on our unfortunate fellow citizens," he exhorted, "let us take up arms! Unite our efforts against a common enemy! .... Resistance to oppression! It is the primary right of man."[59]

As the deputy conjures up the various manifestations of this *tigricité*—bands of *nègres* in Port-Républicain (Port-au-Prince), for instance, armed by the Commissioners and "rendered cruel by the example of crime, ... roaming the streets and sowing terror"—one cannot help but wonder about the individual trajectory that led Juste Chanlatte, the signatory of this "revolutionary" call to arms,[60] from the understanding of resistance (and of tigers) that caused him to bemoan the abolition of slavery in the North Province and its consequent transformation into a *nouvelle nigritie* to the very different sentiments voiced in Dessalines's Proclamation of April 28, 1804. There is a redemptive story to be told here about Chanlatte, one that can stand as emblematic of the overcoming of past divisions between "two classes of men" now "blended together" through a nation-building act of sacrificial vengeance against the "blood-thirsty tigers" who once bent them "under an iron yoke." This is a story all the more compelling in light of Chanlatte's subsequent refusal to join his (erstwhile) free colored brethren in the October 1806 coup mounted against Dessalines, "that tiger thirsting for the blood of his fellow men"—as leaders of the revolt put it in their manifesto "Résistance à l'oppression,"[61] (re)claiming their imprescriptible right to lead the former colony of Saint-Domingue on the grounds that, unlike the assassinated Emperor/former (Black) slave, they were "the men likely to think, those ultimately capable of ensuring the sublime principles of true liberty" (*les hommes susceptibles de penser, ceux capables enfin de faire triompher les sublimes principes de la vraie liberté*).[62] Chanlatte's refashioning of himself in 1804 in the service of Dessalines's "anticolonial, antislavery empire," and subsequently, after 1806, as an exemplary Christophean writer, "displacing and destabilizing the (heretofore universal) authority of French colonial discourse,"[63] is a story well worth telling, one that nicely lends itself (to anticipate a point made in the concluding section of this chapter) to "the lexicons of resistance and agency ... [which] assume full, self-present, and coherent subjects working against something or someone."[64]

Compelling as that story of *individual* guilt and redemption might be, however, the genealogical connections that I have been establishing here between 1804 and (the other) 1791 take us in a different, sociological direction, toward an encounter with a collective imaginary and habitus—grounded in the distinction between race-less citizens and abjected non-free persons—that is not simply worked against and overcome, but that continues to work upon its subjects in social fields as seemingly distinct as those of politics and literature, long after the need for its disavowal has become apparent.[65] Approached from this direction, what makes itself heard in the 1804 Proclamation is the ghostly "presence" of the free colored voice, the remainder and reminder of a "thoughtful" disposition that thwarts our understandable desire to read this and other such texts as a straightforward reworking of the language of a famous European writer by an individual, be it Dessalines or Chanlatte, who could be understood as simply wresting it away from its colonial moorings (or, alternately, activating their latent potential). Instead of this decisive, "cannibalistic" relation between colonial (French) and postcolonial (Haitian) texts, between old endings and new beginnings, what we have come to recognize here is a mediated form of intertextuality troubling the clear lines of demarcation that would allow us, for instance, to make forceful literary-historical claims on behalf of "a Haitian Romanticism that *began* in 1804" and that was "instantiated" by texts such as the January Act of Independence and the April Proclamation with their seemingly original "fusion of enlightenment poetics into revolutionary politics."[66] The shadow of Voltaire in the Proclamation tells of something over and beyond the new historical epoch that is being proclaimed (and the new literary aesthetic with which one might wish to identify it): what that *spectre épouvantable* announces is that this fusion of poetics into politics has a history, and a "guilty" one at that, and in revealing this "dreadful truth of old" what it foretells to us is the tragic possibility, soon to be actualized in the "thoughtful" resistance of Pétion and his republican allies to Dessalines's "oppressive" empire, that (the other) 1791 will always have a future in 1804.

* * *

The preceding analysis of the uses to which the author of *Zaïre*'s tragedies were put during the free colored insurrection provides a cautionary genealogy for thinking about the emergence of a specific national literary tradition, but it also opens out onto more general considerations bearing on the logics of *recognition* that are integral both to any instance of intertextual understanding and, in a different but related manner, to the political imaginary of (the other) 1791. For *gens de couleur* such as Labuissonnière, Savary, Pinchinat, and Chanlatte, as we have seen, intertextual references to French literature served as evidence of a common language through which recognition of the oppressed could be mediated, conveying both the promise of reconciliation between the colony's two slave-owning classes and a warning of the tragic consequences that would ensue from a failure of recognition. This poetics was of a piece with their politics, the politics of a rights-based struggle for the legal recognition of citizens of color. The ideological limits of this particular struggle—its disappointing failure to recognize the full scope of the rights discourses that inspired it, its commitment to preserving rather than abolishing the colonial system—make the free colored insurrection difficult to incorporate into a progressive understanding of the Haitian Revolution, of the sort required, say, by "a certain Romantic historicism."[67] This very failure, however, in all its specificity, speaks eloquently to general problems with the politics of recognition that drove this insurrection: it draws valuable attention to the high cost of the "entry fee" for legal recognition, something that can be more easily forgotten in relation to less evidently "guilty" rights-based movements, as Alexander Weheliye points out in *Habeas Viscus*, his seminal contribution to what he characterizes (in the wake of Sylvia Wynter) as Black Studies' pursuit of "a politics of global liberation beyond the genocidal shackles of Man."[68] The "successes" of certain contemporary movements Weheliye argues (citing as examples "mainstream feminist, civil rights, and lesbian-gay rights movements"), facilitate "the incorporation of a privileged minority into the ethnoclass of Man at the cost of the still and/or newly criminalized and disposable populations (women of color, the black poor, trans people, the incarcerated, etc.)."[69] The "sociopolitical processes of differentiation and hierarchization" so painfully evident in the struggle of the *gens de couleur* for recognition of their rights as citizens, to the exclusion of enslaved persons, continue on into the present, part of a revolutionary legacy that will, Weheliye argues, continue to haunt us as long as we have not merely identified but acted upon the "dire need of alternatives to the legal conception of personhood that dominates our world."[70]

A return here, at the end, to our point of departure in this chapter, the scene at the Clemanson plantation, can help draw out the (unending) end-game of the hierarchical (and always-already racialized) politics of recognition critiqued by Weheliye (and, by extension, a Black Studies committed to the project of "imagining worlds after and alongside Man"[71]). Like so much of what we "know" about the Haitian Revolution, the events at the Clemanson plantation come to us filtered through a white voice that is all too recognizable, an authoritative (one might even say "authorial") voice supplying a hegemonic framework within which recognizable figures of difference are contained. Clearly, these figures demand to be read otherwise, in terms of another story, about the resistance to oppression, that Clemanson cannot tell. The prominence given the free colored citizens in this white narrative makes them the most obvious subjects for recuperation in any such counter-hegemonic story. But there are other potentially recognizable subjects present at the margins of this scene, who also lend themselves to being "understood within the lexicons of resistance and agency," and in terms of their imprescriptible rights as "full, self-present, and coherent subjects working against something or someone": the figure of Theresa, for instance, who demands to be rescued from the "inattentions to the complications of gender" characteristic of the "Franco-Haitian revolutionary lexicon";[72] and the other slaves whose fraught relations to the central actors in the scene can be read as anticipating the unequal "power relations between elites and those who fought for a 'counter plantation' existence" in postindependence Haiti.[73] Necessary as such recuperation might be from a rights-based perspective, the translation of these shadowy, abjected figures into distinct, recognizable subjects would risk, for Weheliye, losing sight of other possible "modes of analyzing and imagining the practices of the oppressed in the face of extreme violence": modes that could envision and sound "the manifold occurrences of freedom in zones of indistinction," and that could recognize, as it were, that "putatively abject modes of being need not be redeployed within hegemonic frameworks but can be operationalized as variable liminal territories or articulated assemblages in movements to abolish the grounds upon which all forms of subjugation are administered."[74]

An abolitionist perspective of the sort envisioned here by Weheliye would allow one to register and operationalize the indistinct movements arising from the "demonic grounds" of the Clemanson plantation, reorienting our relation to Theresa, the other slaves, and perhaps even, in the final instance, unlikely as it might seem given our analysis in this chapter, those intrusive "citizens of color" and their doomed (in a white supremacist world) struggle for recognition. Locating such figures in, and as, "liminal territories" and "articulated assemblages," not simply alongside but, prospectively, after the world of Man, is part of the imaginative labor that Black Studies can perform, Weheliye argues (and augurs), once one has ceased to credit the belief that legal and other such demarcating forms of recognition and inclusion are in any way fundamental to "the radical reconstruction and decolonization of what it means to be human."[75]

In returning to the scene at the Clemanson plantation, and reorienting oneself in such a way as to sense its potentiality, however, the question remains as to what, if anything, can be done along these lines (of flight) with the shadowy figure of Voltaire, be it the little one whose fugitive life of "collaboration" with the *gens de couleur* escapes our archival grasp, or the great one whose name we cannot fail to recognize, and whose literary legacies include, as I hope to have shown in this chapter, a formative role in shaping the free colored insurrection of 1791 and its spectral resurgences in postindependence Haiti. How can we track the intertextual deployment of this great man's words without, in every sense of the word, recognizing them? This, it strikes me, is the very question, writ small, that a collection of essays such as the present one largely poses, devoted as it is, and as it cannot help being, to the recuperative task of identifying Haiti's literary legacies and the ways in which (representations of) the Haitian Revolution can contribute to a renewed understanding of something called "Romanticism." In the light of this difficult, and perhaps unanswerable, question, a return to the "guilty" history of (the other) 1791 is, I would venture, less of a digression from the task at hand than it might at first appear, and altogether more central than literary critics and historians invested in shedding new light on the Haitian Revolution and its legacies might wish to any reckoning of the part we continue to play in silencing the very voices we are so rightly intent upon hearing.

Notes

1 *Eriphile. Tragédie de M. de Voltaire, Représentée par les Comédiens ordinaires du Roi, le Vendredi 7 Mars 1732* (Paris: n.p., 1779), 12–13. ("A frightful spectre pursues my every step. ... Arisen from the shadowy depths, what does he want? What is it he foretells to me?" Unless otherwise noted, all translations from the French in this chapter are my own.)

2 "Extrait des minutes de la municipalité du Port-au-Prince," Archives Nationales (henceforth AN), Pierrefitte-sur-Seine, DXXV 67 675.

3 David Patrick Geggus, "The 'Swiss' and the Problem of Slave/Free Colored Cooperation," in *Haitian Revolutionary Studies*, ed. D. Geggus (Bloomington: Indiana University Press, 2002), 116–17.

4 See Kevin Olson, *Imagined Sovereignties: The Power of the People and Other Myths of the Modern Age* (Cambridge: Cambridge University Press, 2016), 119–24. Throughout this chapter I will be referring to the "free colored insurrection," with a self-conscious awareness of the many problems associated with such wording (and which are rendered starkly visible by comparing it with C. L. R. James's use in *The Black Jacobins* of "Mulatto

revolution" to describe these same events). Placing the emphasis on "free people of color"—that is to say, *all* non-enslaved non-whites irrespective of phenotype—at the very least attenuates the historiographical tendency toward conflating legal and quasi-biological categories (a conflation that was, of course, ubiquitous in white discourse, as we see in Clemanson's oscillation between "citoyens de couleur" and "mulâtres").

5   I am drawing here on Alexander G. Weheliye's analysis of race/racialization in *Habeas Viscus: Racializing Assemblages, Biopolitics, and Black Feminist Theories of the Human* (Durham, NC: Duke University Press, 2014), 5.

6   Weheliye, *Habeas Viscus*, 5.

7   *Proclamation. Jean-Jacques Dessalines, Gouverneur Général, aux habitans d'Haiti* (Au Cap: Pierre Roux, 1804), available at https://haitidoi. com/2015/10/30/dessalines-reader-28-april-1804 (henceforth referred to as the Proclamation). I am using Marcus Rainsford's nearly contemporaneous translation of this text, included as an appendix to his *An Historical Account of the Black Empire of Hayti* (1805); see Paul Youngquist and Grégory Pierrot's critical edition of Rainsford's book (Durham: Duke University Press, 2013), 264–7.

8   For a summary of what little is known about Chanlatte's life during the revolutionary period, see Grégory Pierrot, "Juste Chanlatte: A Haitian Life," *Journal of Haitian Studies* 25, no. 1 (2019): 44–50.

9   Madeleine Dobie, *Trading Places: Colonization and Slavery in Eighteenth-Century French Culture* (Ithaca: Cornell University Press, 2010), 163.

10 Chris Bongie, "The Cry of History: Juste Chanlatte and the (Unsettling) Presence of Race in Early Haitian Literature," *MLN* 130, no. 4 (2015): 819.

11 Bernard Camier and Laurent Dubois, "Voltaire and Dessalines in the Theater of the Atlantic" (unpublished manuscript, December 2011). This translated version of an article that originally came out in French in 2007 includes concluding reflections on Dessalines and *Alzire* that were left out by the editors of the published article (Dubois, pers. comm., June 10, 2020).

12 Deborah Jenson, *Beyond the Slave Narrative: Politics, Sex, and Manuscripts in the Haitian Revolution* (Liverpool: Liverpool University Press, 2011), 89.

13 Jenson, *Beyond*, 90.

14 Deborah Jenson, "Living by Metaphor in the Haitian Declaration of Independence: Tigers and Cognitive Theory," in *The Haitian Declaration of Independence: Creation, Context, and Legacy*, ed. Julia Gaffield (Charlottesville: University of Virginia Press, 2016), 73.

15 Jenson, "Living," 74, 79.

16 Jenson, *Beyond*, 46. In an early article from 2007, Jenson refers to Dessalines and Chanlatte as "co-authors," and speaks of "hybrid authorial productivity between an illiterate ex-slave leader and more privileged blacks," language that is edited out of the later book version of this article, which enforces a stricter line of demarcation between Dessalines's "dictation" and Chanlatte's "transcription"; see Jenson, "Before Malcolm X, Dessalines: A 'French'

THE SHADOW OF VOLTAIRE   45

Tradition of Black Atlantic Radicalism," *International Journal of Francophone Studies* 10, no. 3 (2007): 333.

17   Bongie, "Cry," 816–19. On Chanlatte's "affinity" for Voltaire, see also Marlene Daut, "'Nothing in Nature is Mute': Reading Revolutionary Romanticism in *L'Haïtiade* and Hérard Dumesle's *Voyage dans le nord d'Hayti* (1824)," *New Literary History* 49, no. 4 (2018): 505–7.

18   See, for instance, David Geggus, ed., *The Haitian Revolution: A Documentary History* (Indianapolis: Hackett, 2014), 180–1.

19   Lucy Newlyn, *Reading, Writing, and Romanticism: The Anxiety of Reception* (Oxford: Oxford University Press, 2000), 15.

20   Chelsea Stieber, *Haiti's Paper War: Post-Independence Writing, Civil War, and the Making of the Republic, 1804–1954* (New York: New York University Press, 2020), 273.

21   Beaubrun Ardouin, *Études sur l'histoire d'Haïti, suivies de la vie du Général J.-M. Borgella*, vol. 1 (Paris: Dezobry et E. Magdeleine, 1853), 201.

22   Nick Nesbitt, *Universal Emancipation: The Haitian Revolution and the Radical Enlightenment* (Charlottesville: University of Virginia Press, 2008), 127. ("The miraculous freedom of 1804 lay in the spontaneous creation of utterly new sequences in human history such as decolonization and universal abolition.")

23   Geggus, "Swiss," 104 (my italics).

24   David Geggus, "Racial Equality, Slavery, and Colonial Secession during the Constituent Assembly," in *Haitian Revolutionary* Studies, ed. D. Geggus, 165. For an overview of white/free-colored relations between 1789 and 1791, see John D. Garrigus, *Before Haiti: Race and Citizenship in French Saint-Domingue* (New York: Palgrave Macmillan, 2006), 227–63.

25   Jean Savary and 23 other signatories, "À Messieurs les membres de l'Assemblée Nationale à Paris," Saint-Marc, November 16, 1791, fol. 2. AN DXXV 110 867.

26   *Extrait d'une Adresse à la Paroisse de Torbeck, province du Sud de Saint-Domingue. Sur le Décret du 15 Mai. Assemblée du 24 Juillet 1791* (n.p.: Les Cayes, 1792), 2, 10 (consulted at AN DXXV 113 895). Emphasis in original.

27   Ardouin, *Études*, 1.201. On Labuissonnière's correspondence with Raimond, see Florence Gauthier, *L'aristocratie de l'épiderme: Le combat de la Société des Citoyens de Couleur, 1789–1791* (Paris: CNRS Éditions, 2007), 203–8.

28   Pierre Labuissonnière and 49 other signatories, "Journal tenu par les citoyens de couleur de la paroisse de Léogâne pour être présenté à vous Messieurs de l'Assemblée Nationale séante à Paris," fol. 10. AN DXXV 110 867.

29   Labuissonnière et al., "Journal," fols. 8–9.

30   Labuissonnière et al., "Journal," fol. 5.

31   Labuissonnière et al., "Journal," fol. 1: ("Vous avez permis de résister à l'oppression, nous sommes opprimés, nous réclamons votre justice"). As we will see, the phrase *résistance à l'oppression*, from the Declaration of the

Rights of Man and the Citizen (Article 2), would become a formative point of reference for the free colored imaginary.

32 Labuissonnière et al., "Journal," fols. 1–2.

33 Labuissonnière et al., "Journal," fol. 1. On the "publicly performed self-consciousness" of early Haitian literature, see Marlene Daut, *Baron de Vastey and the Origins of Black Atlantic Humanism* (New York: Palgrave Macmillan, 2017), 15.

34 Labuissonnière et al., "Journal," fol. 1.

35 J. H. Paulian, *Pétition adressée à l'Asssemblée Nationale, Relative au Décret du 15 Mai, concernant les Hommes de Couleurs [sic]; Par un Habitant de Saint-Domingue, député pour cet effet* (Paris: Imprimerie de Calixte Volland, n.d. [1791]), 3 (consulted at AN XXV 114 899).

36 Labuissonniére et al., "Journal," fol. 1.

37 Doris Garraway, "Print, Publics, and the Scene of Universal Equality in the Kingdom of Henry Christophe," *L'Esprit Créateur* 56, no. 1 (2016): 89.

38 Voltaire, *Eriphile*. 9. This play was first performed in 1732, immediately before the far more successful *Zaïre*, but would only be published posthumously, and against the author's express wishes, in 1779.

39 See Raphael Hoermann, "'A Very Hell of Horrors'?: The Haitian Revolution and the Early Transatlantic Haitian Gothic," *Slavery & Abolition* 37, no. 1 (2015): 195–7 for an analysis of the Proclamation as a text that "harness[es] the power of the Gothic in [its] rhetorical warfare."

40 *Concordat passé entre les citoyens du Port-au-Prince & les citoyens de couleur de la même partie de Saint-Domingue* (Port-au-Prince: J. Barthelemy, 1791), 4, 10, 3.

41 "Nouvelles coloniales," *Journal du Port-au-Prince*, October 27, 1791 (137), and November 17, 1791 (191).

42 Savary et al., "À Messieurs," fol. 1.

43 Savary et al., "À Messieurs," fol. 2.

44 Savary et al., "À Messieurs," fols. 3–4.

45 Savary et al., "À Messieurs," fol. 2. The second line should read, "C'est la seule vertu qui fait leur différence."

46 Voltaire, *Eriphile*, 19–20 (*Mes grandeurs sont à moi: mon sort est mon ouvrage; / Et ces fers si honteux, ces fers où je naquis, / Je les ai faits porter aux mains des ennemis. … Je vois ce que je suis, & non ce que je fus; / Et crois valoir au moins des Rois que j'ai vaincus*).

47 Savary et al., "À Messieurs," fol. 3.

48 Andrew S. Curran, *The Anatomy of Blackness: Science and Slavery in an Age of Enlightenment* (Baltimore: Johns Hopkins University Press, 2011), 141, 138.

49 Savary et al., "À Messieurs," fol. 1 (*un chef d'oeuvre de l'esprit humain, quoiqu'elle paraissait comprendre ici dans sa généralité des personnes non libres*).

THE SHADOW OF VOLTAIRE

47

50 Olson, *Imagined Sovereignties*, 121.

51 Savary et al., "À Messieurs," fol. 3 (*que l'Equité et la Justice feront reconnaître pour les sauveurs de St. Domingue*).

52 Labuissonnière et al., "Journal," fols. 5–6.

53 *Copie d'une lettre des chefs des gens de couleur de la Croix-des-Bouquets, à ceux du quartier de l'Artibonite* (Port-au-Prince: Imprimerie Nationale, n.d. [1791]), 1, as translated in Geggus, ed., *Haitian Revolution*, 70–1.

54 Pierre Pinchinat and 36 other signatories (including Juste Chanlatte), "Réponse à Monsieur Thomas Millet membre de l'assemblée ci-devant séante à St. Marc, par les citoyens français ci-devant de couleur," Croix-des-Bouquets, December 31, 1791, fol. 20. AN DXXV 110 872.

55 Pinchinat et al., "Réponse," fol. 15 and fol. 19.

56 "Discours prononcé par le citoyen Chanlatte, au nom des citoyens armés de la ville du Port-au-Prince, lors du dépot de leur drapeau, à la municipalité de la ville du Port-au-Prince," in *Extrait des registres des délibérations de la municipalité du Port-au-Prince: Séance du 10 Décembre 1792* (Port-au-Prince: n.p., n.d. [1792]), 2–3 (consulted at AN, Paris, F3 198).

57 Antoine Chanlatte (Chanlatte *jeune*) to Étienne Polverel, Plaisance, September 15, 1793, fol. 2. AN DXXV 21 216.

58 For a detailed account of Savary's actions and the November 13 "Résistance à l'oppression" manifesto for which he was lead signatory, see Ardouin, *Études*, 2.300–16.

59 "Copie d'une lettre écrite par Chanlatte, deputé de la paroisse de l'Arcahaye, au conseil de paix et d'union séant à St-Marc, aux paroisses de l'Ouest et du Sud, non encore coalisées," *Courrier politique de la France et des ses colonies*, no. 55 (January 23, 1794): 222–3.

60 For verification that this letter was written by Juste Chanlatte (Chanlatte *fils*), and not by his uncle Antoine (Chanlatte *jeune*), as was assumed by Louis Gatereau, editor of the Philadelphia paper in which it was published months after it was first circulated, see the fourth volume of Jean-Philippe Garran's *Rapport sur les troubles de Saint-Domingue* (Paris: Imprimerie Nationale, 1799), 173, 185.

61 Étienne Gérin, Alexandre Pétion, and 47 other signatories, "Résistance à l'oppression," October 16, 1806, in *Copies des Lettres et Pièces écrites au Général en Chef de l'Armée d'Haïti* (Au Cap: Pierre Roux, n.d. [1806]), 16. For an extended commentary on this manifesto and the "1806 Republican Revolution," as well as Chanlatte's refusal to participate in it, see Stieber, *Haiti's Paper War*, 48–57.

62 Gérin, Pétion, et al., "Résistance," as translated in Stieber, *Haiti's Paper War*, 53.

63 Stieber, *Haiti's Paper War*, 32, 79.

64 Weheliye, *Habeas Viscus*, 2.

65 Given limitations of space, I cannot elaborate upon, much less critique, here the ways in which this genealogical argument builds upon Hénock Trouillot's

seminal if contentious efforts in the 1960s at uncovering the social origins of early Haitian literature, which he traced back to the "school" of "Pinchinat, Beauvais, Raimond, Ogé, Chavannes, in a word the freed men [*affranchis*] of Saint-Domingue," claiming that "the mindset [*esprit*] of these men has predominated in Haitian politics, and it is this same mindset that has produced our literary works." Trouillot, *Les origines sociales de la littérature haïtienne* (Port-au-Prince: Imprimerie N. A. Théodore, 1962), 87, 98.

66   Daut, "'Nothing,'" 495, 498, 497 (my italics).

67   David Scott, "The Theory of Haiti: *The Black Jacobins* and the Poetics of Universal History," in *The Black Jacobins Reader*, ed. Charles Forsdick and Christian Høgsbjerg (Durham, NC: Duke University Press, 2017), 121–2.

68   Weheliye, *Habeas Viscus*, 4.

69   Weheliye, *Habeas Viscus*, 81.

70   Weheliye, *Habeas Viscus*, 81.

71   Alexander G. Weheliye, "Conversations in Black: Alexander G. Weheliye," interview by Monica Miller and Christopher Driscoll, *Marginalia Review of Books*, September 1, 2015, https://marginalia.lareviewofbooks.org/conversations-in-black-alexander-g-weheliye/

72   Marlene Daut, *Tropics of Haiti: Race and the Literary History of the Haitian Revolution in the Atlantic World, 1789–1865* (Liverpool: Liverpool University Press, 2015), 293.

73   Karen Salt, *The Unfinished Revolution: Haiti, Black Sovereignty and Power in the Nineteenth-Century Atlantic World* (Liverpool: Liverpool University Press, 2019), 44.

74   Weheliye, *Habeas Viscus*, 2, 82.

75   Weheliye, *Habeas Viscus*, 4.

2

Romantic Fevers: Calenture and Calenda in the Americas

Mary Grace Albanese

This essay traces a developmental trajectory between two distinct but intimately linked Atlantic phenomena: the first is *calenda* (also known as *kalinda* or *calinda*), a Caribbean and Latin American dance often associated with Afro-diasporic belief systems, particularly Haitian Vodou. The second is *calenture*, a febrile hallucination, which was frequently reported by white mariners and which became a recurring trope in US and European Romantic literature. Both etymologically (their names derive from the Spanish *calentura*, meaning fever) and politically (both phenomena are born of oceanic mobility, exploitation, and bondage) these twinned concepts adumbrate an Atlantic world of unstable ontologies. In British and US Romanticism, this unruliness of human, animal, and environmental materials often manifests through the lurid horrors of what Colin Dayan has called "Gothic convertibility."[1] Yet if we turn to Afro-Caribbean spiritual traditions, other forms of relation emerge. Haitian Vodou, I argue, embodies a porousness of personhood that establishes a revolutionary Kreyòl voice at the heart of modernity, offering alternative paradigms to global northern histories of calenture and of Romanticism, more broadly.[2]

In British Romanticism, in particular, calenture has occupied a privileged position in literary criticism. A favored trope in the writings of Wordsworth, Coleridge, and Byron, calenture was both a literary device and a commonplace medical pathology.[3] Most contemporary readers would have understood calenture as a fairly widespread illness, denoting a very specific nautical phenomenon: a hallucination of fields onto a seascape, into which a sailor would sometimes throw himself, often fatally. Invocations of the phenomenon were strikingly recurrent not only in contexts relating specifically to nautical and medical conditions, but also in literary, political, and religious writings from the seventeenth century until the early twentieth century. Although "calenture" is hardly common parlance today, anecdotal evidence suggests that the phenomenon still occurs: a good friend who grew up on a boat in the South Pacific nodded with immediate recognition when I described the phenomenon. For her, it was merely a banal occurrence for those who live at sea. Another acquaintance, raised in Manhattan, claimed that he once glimpsed Central Park's Sheep Meadow projected upon the waves while sailing.

In the Romantic tradition, however, calenture was more than a bothersome trick of the eye: it was an ontological problem that staged the indeterminacy of sea and land, the foreign and the domestic, in an age of rapid global expansion. Yet despite the conceptual mobility of calenture, it is nearly always, in the Romantic tradition, limited to the perspective of white European men: with very few exceptions, representations of calenture are both written by white men and suffered by white men. If this is the case, one might wonder, what can the white colonist's calenture possibly have to tell us about the Black dance calenda, besides its shared etymology? I will venture to say quite a lot. To begin, the first references to both calenda and calenture emerge in the Atlantic world. The *Oxford English Dictionary* places the first use of calenture as 1593, but the term doesn't begin to gain rhetorical traction until the early eighteenth century: that is to say, concurrent to the use of calenda.[4] Second, and perhaps more importantly, the conceptual instability of calenture—at once a deadly threat, a siren song, an oceanic pathology, and a flickering illusion—mirrors colonial misreadings and misappropriations of Black social, political, and spiritual life. Far from a hermetically sealed Romantic trope, calenture instead absorbs the contours of Atlantic, and specifically Haitian, cultural influences.

What, then, does calenture tell us about the calenda? Or, to invert the question, what can the calenda tell us about calenture? Here, I would like to offer some limitations and qualifications to my approach. If Black dance can help critics understand US and European Romanticism, I do not believe US and European Romanticism can help critics understand Black political and spiritual life. Nor do I believe that the calenda should be absorbed into a Romantic tradition and indeed, I would argue that global northern romanticizations—in the colloquial sense—of Vodou have done as much harm to Haiti as have more explicit denigrations by the likes of foreign evangelicals, newscasters, and journalists (denigrations I will not reprint here but which are likely exhaustingly familiar to anyone who follows US or French news outlets). In this respect, I follow Brenda Marie Osbey, who

ROMANTIC FEVERS

has criticized the violence of romanticization, albeit within the context of Louisiana voodoo:

> What I see as the larger problem than our not talking with you about our religion is the fascination it holds for so many of you. And this, I think, stems from the many and peculiar prejudices of the colonial mind ... Combine such inbred white superstition and fear with the inability to distinguish among folklore, popular myth and religion—or simply between folk and formal religion—and you have the makings for a popular narrative in which anything can be believed or stated with impunity.[5]

While respecting the independence and autonomy of Black cultural practices, however, I do believe the calenda can say something about the development of a specifically *Haitian* Romanticism. Critical studies of Haitian Romanticism have tended to focus on elite francophone cultural production, from the Hugo and Lamartine inflected writings of the 1830s group *Le Cénacle* to the early stirrings of twentieth-century *indigènisme*.[6] As Caryn Cossé Bell has argued, Haitian Romanticism took its cues from European Romanticism, beginning with the appellation Le Cénacle, the Port-au-Prince version of the Parisian cénacle of Lamartine, Hugo, and Dumas.[7] Yet these accusations of colonial mimicry often overlook the fact that elite Haitian literary producers found inspiration in Black peasant traditions, including but not limited to Kreyòl proverbs, the reproduction of Vodou songs, and retellings of oral histories and folklore. As J. Michael Dash has convincingly argued, French Romanticism helped "liberate the Haitian creative imagination" and in doing so contributed to the creation of a uniquely Haitian literature.[8] Following Dash, I would like to push beyond the paradigm of mimicry, which retains the logics of a directionality of cultural output that flows from Europe to the Caribbean. In contrast, when we understand calenture/calenda as constitutive of European and US Romanticism, we reverse these cultural channels, which often imply that colonial literature is dependent on, or passively influenced by, European artistic and political ideologies. Instead the indeterminacy of calenda/calenture stems from the Caribbean to Europe.

Moreover, we can attain a fine-grained and more nuanced framework for comparative Romanticisms if we take seriously the indeterminacy of these phenomena. Calenture/calenda not only reverses white supremacist hierarchies, but effectively destabilizes the boundary between colonial margin/canonical center, Caribbean fringe/European metropole by blurring the contours—quite literally—of visual and epistemological orientation that have allowed for the construction of these binaries. As Katherine McKittrick has argued of the production of Black geographic space "margin-politics are, in fact, underacknowledged geographies bound up in embodiment, metaphor, knowledge and ownership" an empty metaphor which, she claims, "simultaneously marks place and takes place."[9] Following McKittrick, I would like to propose the relationship between calenture/calenda as a fragile coupling, which dislodges the global northern logic of the "margin" and instead allows us to imagine spaces that reject settler colonial assumptions regarding personhood, property, and ontological stability. Instead, the flickering contours of these two phenomena reveal how Haiti seeps into and, in doing so, not only influences but *displaces* what we have come to historicize as the canonical Romantic center.

Fever, Nostalgia, and the Revolutionary Atlantic

Calenture was born of slavery. One of the term's earliest uses in English language occurs in *Robinson Crusoe* (1719), when Crusoe recounts "being thrown into a violent Calenture by the excessive Heat of the Climate"[10] while slave trading on the Guinea Coast. Jonathan Swift underscores the collusion between the pathology and the Atlantic slave trade in the first chapter of *Gulliver's Travels* (1726) in which Gulliver claims "I had several Men died in my Ship of Calentures, so that I was forced to get Recruits out of Barbadoes, and the Leeward Islands."[11] Given the context of both usages, we are given to understand that both Swift and Defoe are using calenture in its simplest sense: as *calentura*, or fever. Underlying this fever, however, is a more complex pathology. Five years earlier, Swift writes of calenture in "Upon the South-Sea Project":

> So, by a calenture misled,
> The mariner with rapture sees,
> On the smooth ocean's azure bed,
> Enamell'd fields and verdant trees:
>
> With eager haste he longs to rove
> In that fantastic scene, and thinks
> It must be some enchanted grove;
> And in he leaps, and down he sinks.[12]

By collating nautical fever with enchantment, Swift's calenture of *Gulliver* and "The South-Seas" makes explicit the contiguities between migration, both compulsory and volitional, and fantastical hallucination. These contiguities were formalized in Johnson's *Dictionary*, where, quoting the medical writer

John Quincy, the Doctor describes the pathology as "a distemper in hot climates wherein [sailors] imagine the sea to be green fields."[13]

The term gains further texture when, in 1794, Erasmus Darwin merges the Swiftian notion of calenture as enchanted hallucination with another contemporary pathology: nostalgia. In his two-volume medical treatise, *Zoonomia; or the Laws of Organic Life*, Darwin sutures conceptual (physical, mental, aesthetic) to national (French, English, Swiss, and Spanish) categories in the following definition:

> *Nostalgia*. Maladie du Pais. Calenture. An unconquerable desire of returning to one's native country, frequent in long voyages, in which the patients become so insane as to throw themselves into the sea, mistaking it for green fields or meadows. The Swiss are said to be particularly liable to the disease, and when taken into foreign service frequently desert from this cause, and especially after hearing or singing a particular tune, which was used in their villages dances, in their native country, on which account the playing or singing this tune was forbid by punishment of death. Zwingerus.
>
> Dear is that shed, to which his soul conforms,
And dear that hill, which lifts him from the storms.
—Goldsmith[14]

It is important to note that the introduction of nostalgia into Darwin's definition does not offer a sentimentalizing (as its modern invocation might) or even a psychologizing of the illness.[15] Furthermore, in contrast to twentieth- and twenty-first-century understandings of nostalgia, *Zoonomia* locates the illness's particularity not in longing for a stable *temporal* point, but in the *spatial*: calenture is therefore caused and cured by the very act of mobility.[16]

This mobile quality has allowed many critics to read literary representations of calenture as symptomatic of colonial expansion and its attendant anxieties. Alan Bewell, for example, argues that the medical phenomenon constitutes "a mistaken superimposition of a 'native' landscape onto a 'foreign' one."[17] I hesitate to adhere too closely to Bewell's rather allegorical reading of calenture; after all, the flickering nature of the hallucination would preclude a stable "superimposition" of any sort, the pastoral is not necessarily synonymous with the colonizer's home, and the ocean should not, perhaps, be so quickly analogized to colonized territories. However, Bewell astutely reveals how the confusions provoked by calenture are contiguous with a period of violent movements, social as well as spatial. I am inclined to agree with Kevis Goodman's reading of the disease, which proposes that the pathology's tropological power derives from its very instability and, moreover, from the way that instability manifests in individual bodies. Goodman writes that calenture's victims are "ex-static in a precise sense: they have been 'put out of place' ... and seem to occupy another place."[18] Rather than propose a one-to-one correspondence between the pathology and colonial ideologies, Goodman is concerned with the novelty of movement that was constitutive of exploitative Atlantic economies. Such a reading effectively highlights the fantasy of calenture: in an age when men can be turned into objects, the poor into the wealthy, the locally bound into the itinerant, why, after all, couldn't one imagine water becoming land?

Goodman's and Bewell's work is situated in a British context which is unsurprising for calenture was especially popular in late-eighteenth- and early-nineteenth-century British literature, most notably in Romantic poetry. Wordsworth in his "The Brothers, a Pastoral Poem," Byron in the verse play "The Two Foscari," and Coleridge in "The Rime of the Ancient Mariner" all evoke, to varying extents, the phenomenon. Wordsworth, writing of calenture in "The Brothers" describes how

> the broad green wave and sparkling foam
> Flash'd round him images and hues, that wrought
> In union with the employment of his heart,
> He, thus by feverish passion overcome,
> Even with the organs of his bodily eye,
> Below him, in the bosom of the deep
> Saw mountains, saw the forms of sheep that graz'd
> On verdant hills, with dwellings among trees,
> And Shepherds clad in the same country grey
> Which he himself had worn.[19]

This description of Leonard's illness concludes with a footnote: "This description of the Calenture is sketched from an imperfect recollection of an admirable one in prose by Mr. Gilbert, Author of the *Hurricane*."[20] Wordsworth's note gives the reader an important insight into the origins of calenture: best known for his poem "The Hurricane: A Theosophical and Western Eclogue" (1796), William Gilbert was a white lawyer in Antigua, who upon returning to Britain in 1796, moved to Bristol and established a friendship with Coleridge. The latter would eventually publish Gilbert's *Fragment by a West Indian*, in the final issue of *The Watchman* (May 13, 1796). Wordsworth's reference to Gilbert not only places "The Brothers" within a lineage of British Romantic calenturist poetics, but adumbrates a revolutionary Atlantic specter which is quite literally buried—that is to say, footnoted—but unspoken in the poem. Although Gilbert's reasons for returning to Britain are unknown, we can speculate that 1796 was an uncomfortable year for white colonists. The Haitian Revolution was already well underway, and fear of revolutionary contagion had spread throughout the circum-Caribbean. Enslaved people in British, Spanish, and Dutch colonies took the events in Haiti as their inspiration, launching their own freedom struggles in Guyana, Grenada, Curaçao, Saint Lucia, Venezuela, Dominica, and the British Virgin Islands. Gilbert's abandonment of Antigua, compounded by his apocalyptic evocation of calenture in "The Hurricane" that same year, reveals the intimate conceptual contiguities between Caribbean revolution, Romantic illusion, and perceived colonial threat. Or, as Gilbert writes:

> The European subjugation of AMERICA, the AMERICAN MIND OF LIFE only suffered a powerful affusion of the European; and, that as the solution proceeds it acquires a stronger and stronger tincture of the Subject, till at length that, which was first subdued, assumes an absolute, inexpungable predominancey and a FINAL.[21]

As Alan Bewell, Paul Cheshire, and Frank Mabee have argued, Gilbert stages the destruction of European culture through its invocation of these apocalyptic Americas, where natural disasters and diseases—rather than political revolution—usurp Europe's global standing.[22] While Gilbert's pastoral invokes revolutionary freedom struggles in the American hemisphere, Wordsworth's georgic cannot confront the violence which necessitated these struggles. Conceived as "the concluding poem of a series of pastorals," "The Brothers" overlays the trauma of the Atlantic passage with an elegy for English rural labor, mourning the fate of the shepherd James, who falls off a cliff while his brother Leonard is at sea.[23] Critics have frequently noted Wordsworth's juxtaposition of rural and maritime labor— James's landlocked somnambulism structurally paralleling Leonard's calenture—thus thwarting the promise of ancestral restoration. As Mabee has argued of the poem "Wordsworth depicts the Ewbanks' insolvency via James's somnambulism and Leonard's failure to use the profit from his colonial labor to repurchase the familial land."[24] Yet Mabee overlooks the crucial fact that Leonard's "colonial labor" is sustained by *stolen* labor from Black subjects ("with some small wealth / Acquir'd by traffic in the Indian Isles / To his paternal home he is return'd" (64–6)). Wordsworth's failed georgic is not merely symptomatic of pastoral loss but violently displaces the trauma of Atlantic economies within a white familial tale bound to "the mountains of Cumberland and Westmoreland," thus reproducing the logics of white settler colonialism (135n). In this respect, even James's unmarked grave erases and occupies the space of the Atlantic passage, displacing the imperative to perform what Christina Sharpe might call "wake work" within a pastoral poetics of white British loss.[25]

Despite calenture's clearly transnational and specifically Atlantic revolutionary, conceptual structure, little to no critical work has considered the pathology outside of a British framework. Calenture, a disease of oceanic mobility, remains ironically married to one nation. But we see calenture manifest in hispanophone (Lope de Vega, Calderón de la Barca, and Cervantes) francophone (Charles Baudelaire and Eugène Sue), and US literary traditions (the letters of Thomas Jefferson, the poetry of Philip Freneau, and the prose of Cotton Mather, James Russell Lowell, William Henry Channing, and especially in the US American Romantic movement, including the writings of Poe, Thoreau, and Melville). One of the earliest US literary references to the illness can be found in Philip Freneau, who from late autumn 1775 to June 1779 was based in Saint-Croix, and made extensive trips to Jamaica and Saint-Domingue. Freneau's colonial experience perhaps inflected his description of fever in his long poem "The House of Night" (1779; revised 1786).

> There wakes my fears, the guileful *Calenture*
> Tempting the wanderer on the deep-sea main
> That paints gay groves upon the ocean floor,
> Beckoning her victim to the faithless scene![26]

Note that Freneau genders calenture as a siren, adding a sexualized, feminine current to what is otherwise a stridently masculine poem. Indeed, we might read this lyric invocation of calenture as the underside of the virile narratives of Defoe and Swift; if calenture was traditionally figured as a masculine disease of the sea, it manifested through other kinds of bodies. In 1786, Freneau felt obliged to define calenture in a footnote, yet a survey of nineteenth-century US literature reveals that calenture was used freely—its meanings fraying to encompass a number of conditions, from simple fever to the specific hallucination as defined by Freneau and Johnson. Although less common a figure in US nautical accounts than it was in Britain, calenture's stature in European literature clearly translated to a US audience: calenture appears in manifold forms and genres including historical chronicles, religious tracts, medical literature, and popular gothic and sensational fiction.

Calenture continued to flourish in US Romantic and Transcendentalist movements. Thoreau alludes to the pathology in his journal on July 14, 1855 in *Cape Cod Notes*: "The sea has the same streaked look that our meadows have in a gale."[27] Similarly, Edgar Allan Poe's *The Narrative of the Life of Arthur Gordon Pym of Nantucket* (1838) dramatizes calenture when Pym finds himself aboard a leaking vessel without sufficient food or water:

> Shortly after this period I fell into a state of partial insensibility, during which the most pleasing images floated in my imagination; such as green trees, waving meadows of ripe grain, processions of dancing girls, troops of cavalry, and other phantasies. I now remember that, in all which passed before my mind's eye, *motion*, was a predominant idea ... When

ROMANTIC FEVERS 57

I recovered from this state ... I was firmly convinced that I was still in the hold of the brig, near the box, and that the body of Parker was that of Tiger.[28]

But it is (perhaps unsurprisingly) in Herman Melville that the phenomenon of calenture achieves a complexity equal to its treatments in British Romanticism, appearing in "The Piazza," the *Confidence-Man* and multiple times in *Moby Dick*. In the chapter "The Gilder," for example, the malady is described in the following poetic terms:

There are the times, when in his whale-boat the rover softly feels a certain filial, confident, land-like feeling towards the sea; that he regards it as so much flowery earth; and the distant ship revealing only the tops of her masts, seems struggling forward, not through high rolling waves, but through the tall grass of a rolling prairie.[29]

Much like in Freneau, calenture is explicitly gendered: however while, in Freneau, calenture manifested as erotic temptress, Melville's "filial" sentiment, compounded by the invocation of "flowery earth," offers a maternal, if patently illusory, security not dissimilar to Wordworth's georgic. Moreover, this hallucination indexes the material conditions of the whaling economy, alluded to in an earlier chapter of the novel entitled "The Street:" describing the landscape of New Bedford, Ishmael notes "all these brave houses and flowery gardens came from the Atlantic, Pacific, and Indian oceans. One and all, they were harpooned and dragged up hither from the bottom of the sea."[30] If the maternal fantasy of "The Gilder" provides a calenturist respite from the industrial relations of the whaling voyage, "The Street" invokes calenture only to reveal the violent modes of extraction at the heart of gendered and domesticated labor.

Freedom Flights

Although calenture flourished in the predominantly white, male literary circles of the United States and Europe, it also held a powerful—albeit frequently medicalized—place in Caribbean discourses. Colonial medical accounts, particularly those from the West Indies, adumbrate our understanding of the role of nostalgia and calenture in Romantic literature, frequently evoking Darwin's "mal du pays" or homesickness as a cognate for "calenture." For example, Pierre Victor, the Baron de Malouet, a commissary in Saint-Domingue from 1767 to 1774, and owner of several sugar plantations, reflects on Saint-Domingue in the 1770s from the standpoint of his return to France in 1804. Describing military mortality in Saint-Domingue, he writes: "Sur un envoi de troupes d'Europe, les 2/5ème

58   HAITI'S LITERARY LEGACIES

éprouvent la maladie du pays dans la première quinzaine, et de sept il en périra deux dans les chaleurs; s'ils fatiguent et qu'ils ne soient pas nourris très sainement il en périra trois." (In an envoy of European troops, 2/5th of them experienced nostalgia [*maladie du pays*] in the first fortnight, and two out of every seven died in the heat; three out of every seven died if exhausted and malnourished.).[31] In his 1805 defense of Rochambeau's regime of terror, Philippe-Albert de Lattre, "Propriétaire, ex-Liquidateur des dépenses de la guerre à Saint-Domingue" notes the exacerbating effects of nostalgia on epidemics suffered by French soldiers in Saint-Domingue through a comparison between colonial conquest and the Italian campaign of the French Revolution:

> Durant les dix années de la révolution française, nos troupes ont continuellement été garnies de gale et de vérole, prises en Italie, où ces maladies ne sont pas bénignes. Est-il étonnant … que la complication de ces maux réunis à la maladie du pays, ait produit autant de mortalités?[32]

> [During the ten years of the French Revolution, our troops consistently suffered from scabies and pox [meaning, likely, syphilis] caught in Italy, where such maladies are not benign. Is it surprising then, … that the complication of these illnesses, united with the "maladie du pays," was the cause of so many deaths?]

Like the Baron de Malouet, Lattre's account of colonial illness suggests that both the "maladie du pays" and the physical afflictions of scabies and pox operate on physical levels. Perhaps of greater interest, however, is the positioning of the Italian campaign of the French Revolutionary Wars against the French colonization of Saint-Domingue, as though to suggest that French colonization of Saint-Domingue was in some way consonant with republican expansion in Europe (an expansion, moreover, that impinges on the sexual decadence of the eroticized locales Italy and Saint-Domingue).

The medicalized understanding of calenture as contagion—one which evokes now familiar histories of revolution, republicanism, and the yellow fever endemic to the end of the eighteenth and early-nineteenth centuries— extends back to the seventeenth century with the emergence of a purportedly feverish and infectious dance, known as the calenda. The etymology of this dance has been disputed: some ethnographers trace the word to the Congo; others to Guinea; some believe it is a remnant of the Roman New Year winter festival ("calends" from which we get the word calendar); a nineteenth-century theory that has been dismissed as particularly silly contends it simply means "que linda" ("how pretty" or "how nice"); many ethnographers now believe the word is a creolization of the Spanish "la calentura"—meaning, simply "fever."[33]

Writing in 1694 of his voyages to Guadeloupe and Martinique, the French priest Père Labat offers one of the earliest observations of the calenda:

Les danseurs sont disposez sur deux lignes, les uns devant les autres, les hommes d'un côté, et les femmes de l'autre. Ceux qui sont las de danser, et les spectateurs font un cercle autour des danseurs et des tambours. Le plus habile chante une chanson qu'il compose sur le champ, sur tel sujet qu'il juge à propos, dont le refrain qui est chanté par tous les spectateurs, est accompagné de grands battemens de mains. A l'égard des danseurs, ils tiennent les bras à peu près comme ceux qui dansent en joüant des castagnettes. Ils sautent, font des virevoltes, s'approchent à deux ou trois pieds les uns des autres, se reculent en cadence jusqu'à ce que le son du tambour les avertisse de se joindre en se frappant les cuisses les uns contre les autres, c'est-à-dire, les hommes contre les femmes. A les voir, il semble que ce soient des coups de ventre qu'ils se donnent, quoiqu'il n'y ait cependant que les cuisses qui supportent ces coups. Ils se retirent dans le moment en pirouettant, pour recommencer le même mouvement avec des gestes tout-à-fait lascifs ... De tems en tems ils s'entrelassent les bras, et font deux ou trois tours en se frappant toujours les cuisses, et se baisant. On voit assez par cette description abregée combien cette danse est opposée à la pudeur.[34]

[The dancers are drawn up in two lines, one before the other, the men on the one side and the women on the other. Those who are tired of dancing, and the spectators, form a circle around the dancers and the drums. The most adept sing a song which they make up on the spot, on whatever subject they judge to be timely, whose refrain is sung by all the spectators and which is accompanied by a great clapping of hands. As for the dancers, they hold their arms, a bit like those who dance while playing the castanets. They leap, pirouette, come within two or three feet of each other, and then retreat to the rhythm of the music until the sound of the drum directs them to come back together, hitting their thighs against each other, that is to say the man against the women. To all appearances it seems that they are hitting each other with their stomachs, although it is actually the thighs which deliver the blows. They then retreat, pirouetting, only to begin the same movements again, with altogether lascivious gestures ... From time to time they interlock arms and turn about two or three times, always striking the thighs and kissing. One easily sees from this abridged description the extent to which this dance is opposed to decency.]

Beneath Labat's voyeuristic prose is a cultural performance which, if not entirely independent from his regulatory gaze, does an unexpected kind of work. This display of a collective identity offers a social arena and a

60   HAITI'S LITERARY LEGACIES

historical practice that connects dancers not only to one another (through modes of kinship otherwise denied to them) but enjoins their practice to both past and future. Past, in its repetition of dances from severed African nations and future through the forms of kinship it produces. Through the eyes of Labat, this future can only be reproductive: his evident discomfort with the dance's sexuality (he at one point frets that it even contaminates slave children) is dismissed as "postures indécentes, et tout-à-fait lascives" (indecent and utterly lascivious postures).

But I would like to suggest that something escapes Labat: though men and women may begin in two cleanly demarcated lines (*les hommes d'un côté, et les femmes de l'autre*) note how *undifferentiated* men and women are in its actual practice. The dancers leap and skip and make "virevoltes"—a kind of pirouette, but more specifically, an about turn, a reversal. The notable body parts in this hypersexualized dance are not in fact sexed: they are stomachs, arms, and thighs; moreover, these bodies are *entrelacés* in such a way that suggests confusion rather than copulation. Outside the reproductive logics of slavery (i.e., the notion of the female body as mere storehouse for future labor) the dance allows for a cultural practice of Black futurity untethered from the exploitative demands of propagation. As scholars such as M. Jacqui Alexander, Omise'eke Natasha Tinsley, and Roberto Strongman have argued, Vodou's cosmologies allow for an expanded sense of gender and sexuality that does not necessarily correspond to global northern forms of identification.[35] In Strongman's words, Afro-Caribbean spiritual beliefs produce "transcendental moments in which the commingling of the human and the divine produces subjectivities whose gender is not dictated by biological sex."[36] Despite Labat's attempted rhetorical disciplining of the calenda, the dance's interlaced, ever-turning celebrants dislodge the global northern gender binary.

Moreover, this practice troubles not only gender divisions but also racial lines. Labat notes that: "Les Espagnols l'ont apprise des Nègres, et la dansent dans toute l'Amerique de la même maniere que les Nègres." (The Spanish learned it from the Nègres, and danced it throughout America in the same manner as the Nègres.)[37] It is unclear, from Labat's description, whether or not these dances are practiced separately, or if the Spanish dance alongside the people they enslave, however he discloses a clear anxiety around cultural miscegenation. This anxiety is perhaps most striking in Labat's account of that pinnacle of white cleanliness: the nun. He observes that: "les religieuses ne manquent guère de la danser la Nuit de Noël, sur un théâtre élévé dans leur Choeur, vis-à-vis de leur grille, qui est ouverte, afin que le Peuple ait sa part dans la joye que ces bonnes âmes témoignent pour la naissance du Sauveur" (Even nuns do not stop dancing it, on Christmas night, on an elevated theatre in their Choir, facing their railings, which are open so that the People can share in the joy that these good souls have in celebrating their Savior's birth).[38] What troubles here is *not only* that calenda embodies a form of slave sociality, but that it reveals the porousness of categories around which the colonial project organized itself. Virginal avatars of whiteness become sexualized creatures, quite happy to rub their thighs and bellies together, without the help of any man. Similarly, Spaniards mimic the people they have enslaved; and gender distinctions dissolve from two straight lines into the interlaced contours of dance. Upending distinctions of race, gender, and sexuality, the calenda cannot quite be contained by Labat's regulatory prose. Even the spectacular dimensions of Labat's account serve less, I would argue, as a function of Labat's censorious and titillated gaze, but instead allow for a performative structure of identity, in which an independent community emerges through the very act of its articulation.

French colonists swiftly legislated against this independent community: the Code Noir, first established by Louis XIV in 1685, outlawed assembly, drumming, and dancing. Article III states:

> Interdisons tout exercice public d'autre Religion que celle de la catholique apostolique et Romaine; voulons que les contrevenans soient punis comme rebelles et désobéissans à nos commandemens; défendons toutes assemblées pour cet effet, les quelles nous déclarons conventicules, illicites et séditieuses, sujettes à la même peine qui aura lieu même contre les maitres qui les permettront, ou souffriront à l'égard de leurs esclaves.[39]

> [We forbid any religion other than the Roman, Catholic, and Apostolic Faith from being practiced in public. We desire that offenders be punished as rebels disobedient of our orders. We forbid any gathering to that end, which we declare to be conventicle, illegal, and seditious, and subject to the same punishment as would be applicable to the masters who permit it or accept it from their slaves.]

Yet, as Alfred Métraux and Carolyn Fick have argued, the Code was likely ineffective as the following century saw a series of further mandates attempting to control Black dance. Such mandates are particularly significant given that, as Fick suggests, the calenda was likely used as a catch-all term for all Vodou practices.[40] A 1704 ordinance prohibited enslaved people from "gathering at night under the pretext of holding collective dances;" another law prohibited the calenda after nine o'clock in the evening, and only permitted the dance to be practiced with a judge's license; and the manager of a plantation in Bois de l'Anse was fined 300 livres for having "allowed a gathering of Negroes and a calenda" on his property.[41] In 1765, a militia by the name of the *Première Légion de Saint-Domingue* was formed with the express purpose of "breaking up Negro gatherings and calendas."[42]

Moreau de Saint-Méry was one of the white colonists who found himself both fascinated with and terrified by this dance. A white Creole lawyer so preoccupied with the fiction of purity that he took the trouble of creating a taxonomy of 128 different racial mixtures, Saint-Méry published the authoritative *Description topographique, physique, civile, politique et historique de la partie française de l'isle Saint-Domingue* from Philadelphia in 1789. The treatise includes some of the earliest descriptions of Vodou practices, and specifically of Afro-Caribbean dances associated with Vodou traditions. The invocation of spiritual Black collectivity which we see a century earlier in Labat, gains further weight in Saint-Méry's description of the calenda, which explicitly yokes the dance to rebellion. Saint-Méry forms a genealogy of insurrection structured around the intersection of the Makandal legend and the emancipatory potential of the calenda.

François Makandal's story has occupied a unique place in Haitian Revolutionary historiography.[43] As Monique Allewaert has argued, Makandal represents a fundamental division between traditional global northern historians and the diasporic vernacular tradition "drawing on two different archives, two different theories of the archive, and at least two different methods of interpreting the archive."[44] Of these two different traditions, we can reconstruct the contours of Makandal's life: possibly born in Islamic West Africa, Makandal was kidnapped as a child, and sold to the Saint-Dominguan planter Lenormand de Mézy in the district of Limbé (incidentally, Bwa Kayiman—the Vodou ceremony which launched the Haitian Revolution—would be held on the outskirts of Lenormand's property fifty years later).[45] After purportedly losing a hand in a sugar mill accident in the 1740s, Makandal fled his enslavers, escaping to Cap Français. From there, he built a network of resistance, which included both enslaved and self-emancipated people. It was the former category which appeared to most terrify colonists, as they blurred the boundary between domestic safety and foreign threat. And it was precisely this erosion of boundaries that Makandal profited from, encouraging his followers to concoct and distribute poisons (also called *makandals*) to the whites of the island. According to Saint-Méry:

> Pendant sa désertion il se rendit célèbre par des empoisonnements qui répandirent la terreur parmi les nègres, et qui les soumit tous. Il tenait école ouverte de cet art exécrable, il avait des agents dans tous les points de la colonie, et la mort volait au moindre signal qu'il faisit. Enfin dans son vaste plan il avait conçu l'infernal projet de faire disparaître de la surface de Saint-Domingue tous les hommes qui ne seraient pas noirs.[46]

> [Over the period of his desertion, he achieved fame through poisonings which spread terror among the Negroes, and to which they all submitted. He held an open school in this execrable art, he had agents in every corner of the colony, and, at his slightest signal, death would

ROMANTIC FEVERS   63

fly. Eventually, in his vast plan, he conceived of the infernal project of making disappear from the surface of Saint-Domingue all men who were not black.]

What for Saint Méry reads as an autocratic reign of terror became in diasporic folklore a form of collective freedom. Indeed, Saint Méry's gothic language of "flying death" might even be read as the lurid distortion of emancipatory diasporic traditions that have celebrated Makandal's flight from death: according to legend, Makandal escaped his execution by transforming into a fly.

Saint-Méry's misreading of Black political and spiritual life anticipates the question Alejo Carpentier would ask of Makandal, nearly 200 years later: "What did the whites know of Negro matters?"[47] Saint-Méry's distortion of Makandal's fugitive poetics extends into his description of the *calenda*, the dance at which Makandal purportedly was arrested in January 1758 in the Limbé parish. Saint Méry reports the following: "Un jour les nègres de l'habitation Dufresne, du Limbé y avaient formé un calenda nombreaux. Macandal qui était accoutumé à une longue impunité, vint se mêler à la danse" (One day, the *nègres* of the plantation Dufresne, in Limbé, formed a numerous calenda. Macandal who was accustomed to a long period of impunity, came to mix himself in the dance.) While Saint-Méry misinterprets this dance in the same dismissive tone with which he would dismiss Vodou ring dances elsewhere in his treatise, he also reveals the political potency of calenda. It is precisely—much like in Labat—its emphasis on porous borders which threatens Saint-Méry's white colonial ideologies. His invocation of the verb—to mix or "se mêler"—evokes at once the poisons Makandal composed and distributed to planters, the miscegenation Saint-Méry so clearly feared, and the messy contours of rebellious dance. Calenda emerges here as not just a vehicle for slave sociality but a very metonym for Haitian rebellion.

The spiritual and political dimensions of the *calenda*, and Vodou dance more broadly, in Haitian historiography establish a form of personhood that cannot be contained within a single body. Colonial accounts of the *calenda* reveal the ways in which enslaved people resisted not only white supremacist systems which sought to dehumanize them, but the very ontological premises of European ideologies of selfhood, based in property, self-same consistency, and the policing of personal borders.[48] In Labat's and Saint-Méry's accounts, biased as they may be, we see how Black diasporic traditions muddled global northern definitions that attempted to regulate distinctions between the male and female, the human and non-human, the natural and unnatural world. Instead, Vodou transcorporeality, the belief in the constitutive porosity of personhood, dislodges European Cartesian fantasies with what Strongman has identified as "the Afro-diasporic self [as] removal, external and multiple."[49]

To understand the self as an externalized collective means to understand one's relation to history, time, and the natural world as radically different from Cartesian understandings of the hermetically sealed self. Turning back to calenture, what would it mean to think of the pathology as, not merely symptomatic of white colonial anxieties, but an outgrowth of these transcorporeal Vodou belief systems? Rather than reading the metamorphosis of the sea into land within an allegorical framework of settler colonialism, might a shift toward a Vodou perspective enable other forms of relation? Can we not also read the indeterminacy of *calenture* as the joyous movements of resistance practiced by dancers of the *calenda*? Or as the fugitivity of Makandal? Or perhaps as the offerings of plants, food, and fruits of the earth which are floated on small rafts to sea, honoring Agwe Tawoyo, the powerful Vodou water *lwa* and spirit of the Middle Passage? Viewed through the philosophy of Haitian Vodou, calenture's shifting borders between sea and land, its spatial and temporal flux, establish a very different register from the white colonist's nostalgia. Rather than understanding calenture as a longing for a European pastoral homeland, might we instead think of it as a spiritual bridge, a spatial and temporal unloosening of natural and human borders, which connects individual history to that of the intergenerational and diasporic collective? Far from Wordworth's settler colonialist fantasy of not only stolen Black labor but also stolen Black affect—that is to say, the erasure of Black trauma by the pastoral elegy of white domestic grief— calenture, when approached through the genealogy of the calenda, instead manifests as a transcorporeal poetics of mourning and communal healing. Or, as the Vodou song "Sou lanmè," translated by Erol Josué and Laurent Dubois, claims: "In the bottom of the ship/we are all one."[50]

Calenda, much like calenture, troubles racist colonial hierarchies that sustained themselves on the fiction of personal property, Romantic individualism, and ontological differences between male/female, domestic/ foreign, white/Black. Just as the pathology of calenture collapses the distinction between the sea and the land, the calenda dance erodes global northern modes of binary thinking. This convertibility of the sea and the land, the pastoral fantasies of the plantation and the violence of the Atlantic passage, reconstructs the romantic oceans which enchanted the likes of Wordsworth. By reading these two phenomena together, we can understand Romantic accounts of calenture and calenda as a space that stages the fantasy of the self-identical person, even as they reveal other ways to imagine, practice, and sustain personhood across space and time.

Notes

1 Colin [Joan] Dayan, *Haiti, History, and the Gods* (Berkeley: University of California Press, 1998), especially 63–4. See also Jonathan Bate,

ROMANTIC FEVERS 65

Romantic Ecology: Wordsworth and the Environmental Tradition
(London: Routledge, 1991); Scott Hess, *William Wordsworth and the Ecology of Authorship: The Roots of Environmentalism in Nineteenth-Century Culture* (Charlottesville: University of Virginia Press, 2012); Allan Bewell, *Romanticism and Colonial Disease* (Baltimore: Johns Hopkins University Press, 2003) and *Natures in Translation: Romanticism and Colonial Natural History* (Baltimore: Johns Hopkins University Press, 2017); Kevis Goodman, *Georgic Modernity and British Romanticism Poetry and the Mediation of History* (Cambridge: Cambridge University Press, 2004); Richard Grove, *Green Imperialism: Colonial Expansion, Tropical Island Edens, and the Origins of Environmentalism, 1600–1860* (Cambridge: Cambridge University Press, 1995); Anahid Neressian, *Utopia, Limited: Romanticism and Adjustment* (Cambridge, MA: Harvard University Press, 2015).

2 On Black diasporic ecology as a counterpoise to Enlightenment anthropocentrism, see Kamau Brathwaite. *The Arrivants: A New World Trilogy: Rights of Passage, Islands, Masks* (Oxford: Oxford University Press, 1973); *Barabajan Poems 1492–1992* (Kingston and New York: Savacou North, 1994); *Ancestors: A Re-invention of Mother Poem, Sun Poem, and X/Self* (New York: New Directions, 2001); Édouard Glissant *Poétique de la relation*, Paris: Seuil, 1990); *Soleil de conscience* (Paris: Gallimard, 1997); *Le Discours antillais* (Paris: Gallimard, 1997); Sylvia Wynter, "Unsettling the Coloniality of Being/Power/Truth/Freedom: Towards the Human, After Man, Its Overrepresentation—an Argument," *CR: The New Centennial Review* 3.3 (2003); "1492: A New World View" in *Race, Discourse, and the Origin of the Americas: A New World View*, ed. Vera Lawrence Hyatt and Rex Nettleford (Washington, DC: Smithsonian Institution Press), 5–57. More recently, see *Caribbean Literature and the Environment Between Nature and Culture*, ed. Elizabeth M. DeLoughrey, George B. Handley, Renée K. Gosson (Charlottesville: University of Virginia Press, 2005); Monique Allewaert, *Ariel's Ecology: Plantations, Personhood, and Colonialism in the American Tropics* (Minneapolis: University of Minnesota Press, 2013); Jana Evans Braziel, *Riding with Death: Vodou Art and Urban Ecology in the Streets of Port-au-Prince* (Oxford, MI: University of Mississippi Press, 2017); Karen McCarthy Brown, "Staying Grounded in a High-Rise Building: Ecological Dissonance and Ritual Accommodation in Haitian Vodou," in *Gods of the City: Religion and the American Urban Landscape*, ed. Robert A Orsi (Bloomington: Indiana University Press, 1999), 79–102; Valérie Loichot, *Water Graves: The Art of the Unritual in the Greater Caribbean* (Charlottesville: University of Virginia Press, 2020); Sonya Posmentier, *Cultivation and Catastrophe: The Lyric Ecology of Modern Black Literature* (Baltimore: Johns Hopkins University Press, 2017).

3 See Alan Bewell, *Romanticism and Colonial Disease* (Baltimore: Johns Hopkins University Press, 2003); Kevis Goodman, "'Uncertain Disease': Nostalgia, Pathologies of Motion, Practices of Reading," *Studies in Romanticism* 49, no. 2 (2010); Helmut Illbruck, *Nostalgia: Origins and Ends of an Unenlightened Disease* (Chicago: Northwestern University Press, 2012); Jonathan Lamb, *Scurvy: The Disease of Discovery* (Princeton: Princeton University Press,

2016); Celeste Langan, *Romantic Vagrancy: Wordsworth and the Simulation of Freedom* (Cambridge: Cambridge University Press, 1995). According to Goodman, British medical accounts of calenture appeared in works by Thomas Trotter (*Observations on the Scurvy*, 1792), William Falconer (*A Dissertation on the Influence of the Passions upon Disorders of the Body*, 1792), Joseph Banks (*Journal of the Right Hon. Sir Joseph Banks*, 1768–71), Robert Hamilton (*History of a Remarkable Case of Nostalgia, affecting a native of Wales, and occurring in Britain*, 1786–87), Thomas Arnold *(Observations on the Nature, Kinds, Causes, and Prevention of Insanity, Lunacy, or Madness*, 1782), George Seymour (*Dissertado Medica Inauguralis de Nostalgia*, 1818). Cited in Goodman "Uncertain Disease," 205.

4 "calenture, n.1." OED Online, Oxford University Press, September 2020, www.oed.com/viewdictionaryentry/Entry/11125. Accessed August 1, 2020.

5 Brenda Marie Osbey, "Why we can't talk to you about voodoo," *Southern Literary Journal* 43, no. 2 (Spring 2011): 5–6. On global northern misrepresentations of Haiti, see also Dayan, *Haiti, History, and the Gods* and Gina Athena Ulysse, *Why Haiti Needs New Narratives: A Post-Quake Chronicle* (Middletown: Wesleyan University Press, 2015).

6 See Caryn Cossé Bell, *Revolution, Romanticism, and the Afro-Creole Protest Tradition in Louisiana, 1718–1868* (Baton Rouge: LSU Press, 1997), especially pp. 99–105; J. Michael Dash, *Literature and Ideology in Haiti, 1915–1961* (London: Macmillan Press, 1981); Joseph Délide, "Genèse du Nationalisme Culturel Haïtien," *Cahiers d'études africaines* 1, no. 237 (2020): 63–88; Jacquelin Dolcé, Gérald Dorval, and Jean Miotel Casthely, *Le romantisme en Haïti: la vie intellectuelle, 1804–1915* (Pétionville: Éditions Fardin, 1983); Jean Prince-Mars, *Ainsi Parla L'oncle Suivi De Revisiter L'oncle* (Montreal: Memoire d'encrier, 2009); Chelsea Stieber, *Haiti's Paper War Post-Independence Writing, Civil War, and the Making of the Republic, 1804–1954* (New York: New York University Press, 2020).

7 Bell, *Revolution*, 104.

8 Dash, *Literature and Ideology*, 7.

9 Katherine McKittrick, *Demonic Grounds: Black Women and Cartographies of Struggle* (Minneapolis: University of Minnesota Press, 2006), 55.

10 Daniel Defoe, *Robinson Crusoe* (New York: Modern Library, 2001), 16.

11 Jonathan Swift, *Gulliver's Travels* in *The Prose Works of Jonathan Swift*, ed. Herbert Davis (Oxford: Oxford University Press, 1939–68), 11:221.

12 Jonathan Swift, "Upon The South Sea Project," in *Jonathan Swift: The Complete Poems*, ed. Pat Rogers (New Haven: Yale University Press, 1983), 209–10.

13 Samuel Johnson, *A Dictionary of the English Language*. 4 vols.

14 Erasmus Darwin, *Zoonomia; or the Laws of Organic Life*, 3rd ed., correct (1801), in *The Collected Writings of Erasmus Darwin*, intro., Martin Priestman, 9 vols. (Bristol: Thoemmes Continuum, 2004), 8: 82–3.

ROMANTIC FEVERS   67

15 Much like Darwin's linguistic triad, the original definition of nostalgia is itself a hybrid. Coined in 1688, by the Swiss physician Johannes Hofer, the neologism combines the Greek word *nostos*—"return to native land"—with *algos*, or pain. The symptomology included "continued sadness, meditation only of the Fatherland, disturbed sleep ... attending to nothing hardly, other than an idea of the Fatherland"—and the etiology, simply a return to home. Though in crafting his definition, Hofer borrows from the pre-existing German *heimweh* and the French *maladie du pays*, many seventeenth-century scholars believed that nostalgia was unique to landlocked Switzerland. Tellingly, nostalgia, unlike calenture, does not appear in Johnson's *Dictionary*. It was not until the mid-eighteenth century that diagnoses of the illness appear in Britain.

16 Nicholas Dames, for example, ascribes the rise of nostalgia in the English novel—which he locates in Jane Austen's hermetically sealed novels—as a response to a set of late-eighteenth-century dislocations, such as colonial expansion, the French Revolution, and the mass emigration that ensued, the Napoleonic Wars, and the distant movements of increasingly conscription-based armies. Nicholas Dames, *Amnesiac Selves: Nostalgia, Forgetting, and British Fiction, 1810–1870* (Cambridge, MA: Harvard University Press, 2001), 32. It is not for nothing, then, that calenture, as imagined by Darwin, not only spans from the sciences to the arts, but traverses national borders. Darwin's cosmopolitan definition invokes the Swiss nostalgia, the French "maladie du Pais," and the Spanish-inflected calenture, thus stylistically enacting the spatial dislocation that purportedly generates the illness.

17 Bewell, *Romanticism and Colonial Disease,* 60.

18 Goodman, "'Uncertain Disease," 207.

19 William Wordsworth, "The Brothers," *Lyrical Ballads*, ed. R. L. Brett and A. R. Jones (London: Routledge, 1991), pp. 135–50; II. 51–60.

20 Wordsworth, "The Brothers," II. 51–60.

21 Paul Cheshire, *William Gilbert and Esoteric Romanticism: A Contextual Study and Annotated Edition of 'The Hurricane'* (Oxford: Oxford University Press, 2018), 105.

22 Bewell, *Romanticism and Colonial Disease*, 61–3; Paul Cheshire, *William Gilbert and Esoteric Romanticism: A Contextual Study and Annotated Edition of 'The Hurricane'* (Oxford: Oxford University Press, 2018); Frank Mabee, "'The Sea as Green Fields': Calenture and Wordsworth's Rural Ocean," in *The Sea and Nineteenth-Century Anglophone Literary Culture*, ed. Martha Elena Rojas and Steve Mentz (Surrey: Ashgate Press, 2016).

23 Wordsworth, "The Brothers," p135n.

24 Mabee, "'The Sea as Green Fields': Calenture and Wordsworth's Rural Ocean," 137.

25 Christina Sharpe, *In the Wake: On Blackness and Being* (Durham: Duke University Press, 2016).

26 Philip Freneau, "The House of Night," in *Early American Poetry: Selections from Bradstreet, Taylor, Dwight, Freneau, and Bryant,* ed. Jane Donahue Eberwein (Madison: University of Wisconsin Press, 1978), 219.

27 Henry David Thoreau, *Journal of Henry D. Thoreau* vol 7 (Boston: Houghton Mifflin, 1949), 441.

28 Edgar Allan Poe, *The Narrative of the Life of Arthur Gordon Pym of Nantucket*, ed. J. Gerald Kennedy (New York: Oxford World's Classics, 2008), 89.

29 Herman Melville, *Moby Dick: or, the Whale*, 1851. Reprint (New York: Modern Library of America, 2000): CXIV: 703–4.

30 Melville, *Moby Dick*, 234.

31 P. V. Malouet, *Collection de mémoire et correspondances officielles sur l'administration des colonies*, Paris, 5 volumes, loc. cit., t. IV, chap. V, pp. 228–9. All translations, unless otherwise indicated, are my own.

32 A. P. de Lattre, *Campagnes des Français à Saint-Domingue et réfutation des reproches faits au capitaine-général Rochambeau* (Paris: Chez Locard, 1805), 77–8.

33 See, for example, Sebatián de Covarrubias's definition of calenda in *Tesoro de la lengva casrellana* (Madrid, 1611; Barcelona: S. A. Horta, 1943, p. 269). On the history of the calenda, see Maureen Warner-Lewis, *Central Africa in the Caribbean: Transcending Time, Transforming Cultures* (Kingston, Jamaica: University of West Indies Press, 2003); Yvonne Daniel, *Caribbean and Atlantic Diaspora Dance: Igniting Citizenship* (Urbana: University of Illinois Press, 2011); Julian Gerstin, "Tangled Roots: Kalenda and Other Neo-African Dances in the Circum-Caribbean," *New West Indian Guide/Nieuwe West-Indische Gids* 78, no. 1 (2004): 2.

34 Jean-Baptiste Labat, *Nouveau voyage aux isles de l'Amérique*, 6 vol (Paris: G. Cavelier and P.-F. Giffard, 1722), 4:154.

35 M. Jacqui Alexander, *Pedagogies of Crossing: Meditations on Feminism, Sexual Politics, Memory and the Sacred* (Durham: Duke University Press, 2005); Omise'eke Natasha Tinsley, *Ezili's Mirrors: Imagining Black Queer Genders* (Durham: Duke University Press, 2018); Tinsley, "Songs for Ezili: Vodou Epistemologies of (Trans) gender," Feminist Studies, 37, no. 2 (2011): 417–36; Tinsley, "Black Atlantic, Queer Atlantic: Queer imaginings of the Middle Passage," GLQ 14, nos. 2–3: 191–215; Roberto Strongman, *Queering Black Atlantic Religions: Transcorporeality in Candomblé, Santería, and Vodou* (Durham: Duke University Press, 2019); Strongman, "The Afro-Diasporic Body in Haitian Vodou and the Transcending of Gendered Cartesian Corporeality," *Kunapipi* 30, no. 2 (2008).

36 Strongman, *Queering Black Atlantic Religions*, 4.

37 Labat, *Nouveau Voyage*, 154.

38 Labat, *Nouveau Voyage*, 156.

39 Le *code noir ou Receuil des règlements rendus jusqu' à présent* (1685, reprint Basse -Terre: Société d'Histoire de la Guadeloupe, 1980) Archives de l'Outre-Mer, Aix-en-Provence, Col F/390. Translation by John Garrigus.

40 Carolyn Fick, *The Making of Haiti: The Saint-Domingue Revolution from Below* (Nashville: University of Tennessee Press, 1990), 40–53; Alfred Métraux, *Le Vaudou haïtien* (Paris: Gallimard, 1958).

41 See Métraux, *Le Vaudou haïtien*, 109; see also Kate Ramsey, *The Spirits and the Lwa: Vodou and Power in Haiti* (Chicago: University of Chicago Press, 2011), 36.

42 "Ordonnance du Gouverneur Général, portant creation d'un Corps de Troupes Légères, désignés sous le nom de Première Légion de Saint-Domingue, du 15 janvier 1765," in Moreau de Saint-Méry, *Loix et constitutions des colonies françoises de l'Amérique sous le vent* 6 vol. (Paris: chez l'auter n.d.) 4: 825–31. Cited in Ramsey *The Spirits and the Lwa,* 36.

43 The literature on Makandal is vast. See, in particular, Hérard Dumesle, *Voyage dans le nord d'Hayti, ou, Révélations des lieux et des monuments historiques* (Port au Prince: Imprimerie du Gouvernement, 1824); Thomas Madiou, *Histoire d'Haïti* 3 vols. (Port-au-Prince: Impr. de J. Courtois, 1847); David Patrick Geggus, *Haitian Revolutionary Studies* (Bloomington: Indiana University Press, 2002); Carolyn Fick, *The Making of Haiti*; Geggus, "Marronage, Voodoo, and the Saint-Domingue Slave Revolt of 1791," *Proceedings of the Meeting of the French Colonial Historical Society* 15: 22–35; Karol K. Weaver, *Medical Revolutionaries: The Enslaved Healers of Eighteenth-Century Saint-Domingue* (Urbana and Chicago: University of Illinois Press, 2006). On the popular afterlives of Makandal, see Alejo Carpentier, *El Reino de este mundo* (Barcelona: Seix Barral, 1949), Nalo Hopkinson, *The Salt Roads* (New York: Warner Books, 2003); or diasporic performing arts, including Edouard Duval-Carrié and Carl Hancock Rux's opera *Makandal* (premiered at the Guggenheim in 2013); Duval-Carrié's 2016–2017 series of portraits of Makandal, part of his exhibition "Metamorphosis" at the Museum of Contemporary Art in North Miami in October 2017; or the performance work of the Brooklyn-based dance company, named "La Troupe Makandal."

44 Monique Allewaert, "Super Fly: François Makandal's Colonial Semiotics," *American Literature* 91, no. 3 (2019): 460–1.

45 Fick, *Making of Haiti*, 60.

46 Moreau de Saint Méry, *Description topographique, physique, civile, politique et historique de la partie française de l'isle Saint-Domingue* (Philadelphie, 1797) tome 2: 629–30.

47 Alejo Carpentier, *The Kingdom of this World*, trans. Harriet de Onís (New York: Farrar, Straus, and Giroux, 2006), 44.

48 I am thinking specifically of a European genealogy of personal identity that foregrounds consciousness as the basis for the self (e.g., Descartes' *cogito*, or Locke's "sameness of rational Being"). See John Locke, *An Essay Concerning Human Understanding*, ed. Peter H. Nidditch (Oxford: Oxford University Press, 1975), 2.27.9; Descartes, *Meditations on First Philosophy* (Meditationes de prima philosophia), trans. George Heffernan (Notre Dame: University of Notre Dame Press, 1990). This genealogy has received lively criticism in recent years from critics such as Louis Sala-Molins, David Scott, and Sylvia Wynter, who have foregrounded the violent erasure of Black subjectivity from Enlightenment fictions of rationality. Wynter, for example, argues: "In the wake of the West's reinvention of its True Christian Self in the transumed terms of the Rational Self of Man, however, it was to be the peoples of the militarily expropriated New World territories (i.e., Indians), as well as the enslaved peoples of Black Africa (i.e., Negroes), that were made to reoccupy the matrix slot of Otherness—to be made into the physical referent of the idea of the irrational/subrational Human Other" Sylvia Wynter, "Unsettling the Coloniality of Being/Power/Truth/Freedom: Towards the Human, After Man, Its Overrepresentation—an Argument," *CR: The New Centennial Review* 3.3 (2003), 266. See also David Scott, *Conscripts of Modernity: The Tragedy of Colonial* Enlightenment (Durham: Duke University Press, 2005); Louis Sala-Molins, *Dark Side of the Light: Slavery and the French Enlightenment* (Minneapolis: University of Minnesota Press, 2006).

49 Strongman, *Queering Black Atlantic Religions*, 21.

50 "Sou lanmè," in *The Haiti Reader History, Culture, Politics*, ed. Chantalle F. Verna, Kaiama L. Glover, Laurent Dubois, Millery Polyné, Nadève Ménard (Durham, NC: Duke University Press 2020), 13–15.

3

Toussaint Louverture: Creating a Public Romantic Subject

Theresa M. Kelley

Introduction

This essay asks what it means to read Toussaint Louverture as a revolutionary subject in the time of Romanticism. As a Black Haitian leader of the only successful slave revolution in the Caribbean, he is an historical being who for a time fulfills the Romantic desire for a future time when freedom from bondage, human and political, would or might arrive. Unlike other Romantic writers and protagonists whose inner striving for freedom is what makes them subjects, Louverture is a public subject who becomes that subject as he acts and writes in a print culture as richly textured as a psyche. The difference I conjure with here is that between an inner, putatively Schillerian, Romantic subject and a public subject and revolutionary hero in the contingency laden world of revolutionary Haiti. Looking back in *An Historical Account of the Black Empire of Hayti*, published in 1805, Marcus Rainsford describes Louverture as a man of action, indefatigable and ever in command of the field. As Paul Youngquist and Grégory Pierrot remark, Rainsford's Louverture is "a man with no inner contradictions to compromise his devotion to liberty and his people ... gifted in understanding but unburdened by interiority."[1]

Louverture inverts the paradigm of the inner Romantic subject in ways and by means that are instructive for thinking about Romanticism as a public and contestatory space writ large across its print and visual cultures. He made good in historical time, and for a time, on the Romantic desire for a

72 HAITI'S LITERARY LEGACIES

hero-subject who makes freedom possible. So construed, he resolved (before Byron wrote it) the problem (and the pun) in the opening lines of *Don Juan*:

I want a hero: an uncommon want,
When every year and months sends forth a new one,
Till, after cloying the gazettes with cant,
The age discovers he is not the true one.[2]

As the Romantic hero who was wanted because he had for so long been wanting, Louverture filled a vacancy at the core of Romanticism that Romantic writers and their subject/protagonists struggled to fill. No more so, and no more complexly so, than in the enslaved Caribbean, where what it meant to be a subject exposed the internal contradictions in Romantic liberal thought about what it means to be a human and have rights. Born in slavery and, until he was manumitted, subject (more or less) to others, he became the heroic subject the age (or some) had wanted. In doing so, he also fulfills, or appears to fulfill, the Abbé Raynal's famous prediction that a Black leader would liberate his enslaved people somewhere in the Caribbean.

As remarkable as this story is, it is not sufficient. To begin with, what happened from 1791 to 1803, the years of Louverture's public life and death, is a more complicated revolutionary story. He was born a slave, but he had been freed, acquired property, including slaves, long before he joined other Haitian revolutionaries. He did so cautiously, after a series of slave revolts had become a revolutionary movement. He argued against Haitian slavery but only after the French official Léger-Félicité Sonthonax (whom Louverture later characterized as a traitor to France) had already issued the decree that abolished slavery. Later, as the general and de facto leader of Haiti, he ordered former slaves to return to their plantations to work, sometimes for their former masters, to keep Haiti's prosperous sugar economy going. He was unmoved by complaints that returning to those plantations often meant returning to working conditions that looked like enslaved labor, with a small pay increase. In the end, Napoleon removed Louverture from office. He was exiled in 1802, imprisoned in a fort in the Jura mountains of France. He died there in 1803, after sending Napoleon several versions of a detailed memoir defending his loyal service to France. Napoleon never answered.[3]

I argue in this essay that this more problematic narrative about Louverture opens a way to think about Romantic subjects—public and private—that is wary of a narrative arc of rise and fall, or prediction and fulfillment, which is to say the arc of Romantic prophecy.[4] Instead, his career as a political and military actor and a writer invites a different reading of Romantic narratives in which revolutionary desire cannot find a clear, inevitable path to fulfillment. Seeing how Louverture negotiates this version of a middle passage, with all the overtones this phrase contains, invites us to consider how other Romantic subjects make their way or do not toward a future they and their writers desire.

Celebrated or scorned, Louverture entered the political imaginary in the 1790s as a stunning military strategist and someone who wrote copiously and published his own versions of what happened. Commentators from the 1790s to the present have created many more versions in their effort to sort out who he really was and what his motives were for repeated shifts in his political loyalties to, then away from, one faction to another in Haiti; from France to Spain to England and back again, perhaps, to France. No wonder, Philippe Girard remarks, that it is difficult if not impossible to say who (or where) Louverture was as the public Haitian subject who is by turns hidden and exposed in the print record he helped to create, including but not limited to the gazettes Byron scorned.[5]

No one understood this point better than Louverture. My argument begins with this half-relation between Byron's wanting/wanted hero, whose absence is visible in the ebb and flow of print culture, and Louverture, whose emergence as a public and heroic subject required a proliferating print culture that included gazettes, printed speeches, proclamations, and published versions of diplomatic correspondence to justify his conduct and declare his motives. Behind all of these is an incomplete manuscript history that includes or identifies hundreds, perhaps thousands, of letters he wrote to enemies and allies to explain his actions. Written across this print and manuscript record, Louverture bridges but also exposes the fault line between enslaved and liberal subjects in the time of Romanticism.

Heard, overheard or in his own voice, Louverture is everywhere in the print history of Haiti. There, claims about what he said, wrote, or did—his own claims and those of many others—inhabit a thickly textured resonance machine that is by turns suppositional and declamatory. This record is topological: events and words touch, separate, and repass each other. He remained a highly visible yet elusive figure in the historiographic record long after he was no longer around to shape it or add to it. Accounts of what he said are versional rather than verbatim, among them his remarks as he boarded the ship that carried him to exile.[6] Across this print record, now running to over two hundred years and too many pages to count, its print medium (and the manuscript collections behind it) mixes tenses and claims. Who said what, where, when, and why is at issue whether Louverture speaks or someone reports what he said. In this print array, he is not a single unified poetic subject and hero. The same might be said about other public subjects who are both highly visible and yet not fully legible. Public subjects are hard to read.

Scholars have discovered more about Louverture's private life and early history than he chose to record.[7] Like the *lieu dit* (unnamed place) labels on maps of the island that Louverture's secretaries created, much is missing or misattributed. What he chose to say often served political ends. He spoke to rebellious ex-slaves in Fon, the African language he inherited, and used Kreyol, French or Kreyol-French, a mixed dialect spoken and written in Haiti in the 1790s. He reported that he and his wife spoke French at home. A fervent Catholic, he permitted a day of public African ritual to celebrate his appointment as the governor of Haiti.[8] Louverture operates off or on the page as though he were a curiously public, governmental version of Haitian maroon communities. Like them, he hides out, sometimes in plain sight as well as on the page, skirmishing, finding opportunities to take what he wants, then slipping back into hiding.[9] Louverture's motives, like his lines of march, were by turns transparent and opaque, making their appearance in print when Louverture was ready to go public, which was often. Contrived contingency may be an oxymoron, yet it is one that Louverture inhabited by modeling how to make contingency into opportunity.

His regard was public, both in the sense of what he regarded and how others regarded him. As a military commander and as a writer and rhetorician, he wrote as someone who spoke to that public, often to more than one addressee. He published diplomatic correspondence to Napoleon and other French officials and inserted proclamations he had published in Haiti into American and French newspapers.[10] At times he may have operated behind the curtain, like a puppeteer, to shape contemporary reports about what he read and did. He cuts a figure, as Keats said of Byron, that is dramatic, writ large across a global stage where many sought to dominate the wealthiest slave economy of the Caribbean in the last decades of the eighteenth century.[11]

He acted and wrote as if he knew that he inhabited a revolutionary plotline that could at any time come unhinged by a stitch or fold, a wayward event, encounter, or desire. He took a chance, actually many chances, to make contingencies into opportunities. His was more than a bet on the future. He backed it, call it insurance, like the insurance schemes that slavers and their backers devised to make a profit on those enslaved in the hulls of ships, with rhetorical and strategic military finesse that he mustered to shape circumstances and a print record that tracked every shift in Haiti's and his revolutionary enterprise.[12] He could do nothing about his place in the ever-expanding print history of the revolution after he died, although (I speculate) he would very much have liked to control his posthumous future.

Black and by turns visible and invisible in the print record, Louverture is the public subject who makes the Romantic and modern world uncomfortable. Writ large, he shifts the geographic and racialized ground of European accounts of being a subject. As a public subject who was once subject to others, he makes visible the seamy underside of the Romantic liberal subject, its contradiction between Enlightenment liberalism and imperial expansion and enslavement.[13] For these reasons and in all these ways, he returns us to the Romantic subject and its modern reincarnation by a different route, written across a print culture that was as versional as Wordsworth's *Prelude,* but via different means and purposes. Public facing though he was, Louverture was no more a single, unified subject than those Romantic subjects who negotiate inner psychic landscapes. This odd mix of affinity and estrangement, not the unified interiority that Charles Taylor claims as the Romantic origin for the emergence of a modern self, is what makes subjects, whether Romantic, modern, interior, or public.[14] Louverture's emergence as a public Romantic subject is backlit by unsettled oscillations between prophetic desire, anticipation, and doubt that haunt other Romantic subjects.[15]

Romantic Subjects

As a political and public subject, Louverture foregrounds what is at times hidden or suppressed in stories, philosophical or not, about what makes (or breaks) the subject. At the unsettled core of theories of the subject from German Romantic philosophy to the present, two terms—contingency and futurity—are entangled. Differences among these theories turn on how each construes the subject's relation to contingency as the way things are and behave in the world. Here the prospect or even the possibility of futurity is uncomfortably bound to contingency. As a public being whose actions and words responded to what happened as it happened, he kept the future, his own and that of revolutionary Haiti, on the near horizon. He presented himself as an autonomous public leader on a par with European adversaries and allies (who were, like himself, often both at once), but I surmise that in doing so he recognized the risk of becoming someone else's subject, even as free Haiti feared it would be re-enslaved. He makes this double image of what it means to be a Romantic subject vivid and unmistakable. That he does so by transforming himself and formerly enslaved Black Caribbeans from being subject to others into political subjects is critical to this story. C. L. R. James puts it this way:

> [Alphonse de] Beauchamp in the *Biographie Universelle* calls Toussaint L'Ouverture one of the most remarkable men of a period rich in remarkable men ... The history of the San Domingo revolution will therefore largely be a record of his achievements and his political personality ... Yet Toussaint did not make the revolution. It was the revolution that made Toussaint. And even that is not the whole truth. Great men make history, but only such history as it is possible for them to make.[16]

James's caveat, by way of Marx, specifies the zone of limitation and possibility where Louverture knew or soon learned how to make things happen, as best he could. For a decade he turned unexpected occasions, whether opportunities and emergencies, to his own account. He operated in a world marked by contingency, in the sense of the term that Christina Lupton distinguishes from chance, probability, and prediction: "a contingent event is one that has happened, but in a way that makes it apparent that it need not have been that way ... a tree falling in one's path is contingent."[17] Imagine that you are walking in a forest with different paths you might take. You choose one path over others, on a whim or perhaps, say, because you like what you see ahead. Somewhere on the path you have taken, you walk under a tree as it cracks and a big branch or the whole tree falls on your head. This event is unwelcome, but it is not inevitable. It happens without appeal to chance or bad luck or prophecy or an intended causal relation. Your path through the woods was not predetermined. There is no evil doer hiding in the woods who brilliantly works out, on the fly, how to fell this particular tree so that it falls on you.

Lupton's distinction challenges the terminological disarray in eighteenth-century and Romantic usage, where chance, contingency, fate, prediction, probability, and speculation were at times near synonyms, if not entirely synonymous.[18] Yet all these, with contingency their disturbed middle term, have everything to do with what can be said about how subjects, including Romantic subjects, act in the world. Be they eighteenth-century, Romantic, or modern, efforts to ally contingency with probability or prediction or even chance suppress what makes contingency very much of the world. In word and action Louverture was impressively alert to this point. So are theories of the subject from Schiller to Luhmann. Mapping differences among these theoretical accounts makes visible the degree to which Louverture and other Romantic subjects are, for all their differences, looking in the same direction: toward the future.

For Schiller, whose *Letters on Aesthetic Education* appeared in 1795, things (and subjects) are not so simple, nor is it clear that the subject in the process of becoming a Person, that is the Romantic subject, will triumph over things. Even if the becoming subject manages to "lift up" sensuous life into a higher level of being, Schiller argues, the tug of sensuous life and the material world can at any moment waylay the progress of the desiring subject whose inner striving and desire are one Romantic engine of revolutionary freedom.[19] Schiller's theory of how all this might happen begins with its two competing drives, the sensuous and the formal or rational. The becoming subject's task is to learn how to hold both drives in a productive relation, call it an energizing polarity.

What makes or breaks the subject's capacity to activate political freedom is a shadowy third drive, which comes into aesthetic and philosophical play when the perceiving, becoming subject can recognize the beauty of a sensuous work of art.[20] At that moment, and for Schiller it is only a moment, the becoming being glimpses the possibility that sensuous and formal or rational drives might collaborate. Only in this way can the sensuous being become a conduit to, rather than a drag on, the work of becoming a Person whose rational, formal being approximates an absolute subject. At such a moment, it becomes possible to imagine a rational and true subject.

What impedes this philosophical project is *Zustand* (state or condition), as in, one's state of affairs, or situation, a collective term for the world of material nature and time as an ever shifting temporality rather than eternal time—in other words, contingency. For Schiller, *Zustand* or Condition is arrayed, in all its parts, against Person or Personhood (*Persönlichkeit*). Like so many Romantic contraries, this one is hostage to itself: "Person and Condition—the self and its determining attributes—which is the Absolute Being we think of as one and the same, are in the finite being eternally two."[21] In the turnings of Schiller's syntax, plurals become singulars and what is in absolute terms "one and the same" turns out to be irreconcilably different. Schiller's philosophical project—and the difficulty at its core—require having it both ways. He would prefer that there be only the time of eternity, no material nature, and no contingency. Yet all these are where sensuous beings live.

Paul de Man argues that Schiller is unable to recognize the tension between what he and the Romantic subject desire and what they cannot have.[22] The charge is misplaced: the rhetoric and syntax Schiller uses to graft his argument to the epistolary format of *Aesthetic Education* insist on just this point. Some letters defend the possibility of striving for the absolute; others insist that condition frustrates this possibility. Neither claim, Schiller recognizes, can be pulled apart from the other. Together they specify the unremitting difficulty at the core of his theory of the subject.[23] The development of that subject depends, at first, on an inward impulse or longing, that (if all goes well, although it rarely does) leads the developing person to imagine or perhaps enact political freedom in the world. Yet a host of impediments make this outcome uncertain.

Novalis's 1798 essay "Pollen" reworks Schiller's earlier recognition that *Zustand*, state or condition and contingency, make trouble for the Romantic subject. For Novalis, "things" (*Dinge*) in the world are arrayed against what is "unconditioned" or "unconditional" (*Unbedingte*), that is, what is independent of and superior to things. The German word play—*Ding/Unbedingte*—suggests that what is "un"—not a thing, not conditioned—undoes things. The agent of this undoing is man, who "can get outside himself" to become a "supersensible being" and as such control the world of things: "all the accidents [*Zufälle*] of life are materials from which we can fashion whatever we want."[24] Novalis's *Zufälle* (accidents) replace Schiller's *Zufälligkeit* (contingency). If ever there was an example of how cognates can unravel a shared etymological origin, this is it.

Novalis's "accidents" are so many trees falling in the forest, knocking heads or other trees. Schiller's *Zufälligkeit* insists that what is at issue is not accident, singular or plural, but accident-ness as part of *Zustand* (condition) of living in the world and being of it. Singular, nominative, and substantive, *Zustand* and *Zufälligkeit* are arrayed against the project of aesthetic education—to become a Person or subject modeled on the Absolute subject that is reason, freedom, and eternity. Schiller understands, as will Badiou and Luhmann, *Zufälligkeit,* a German compound made from the adjective *zufällig* and the noun *Keit*, to mean the state or condition of being "accident prone" in the world and in time. Novalis asserts that the becoming subject can and will master the world as a political actor who seeks political as well as individual freedom. What Schiller offers instead is a space for thinking, in the time of Romanticism, about how becoming a subject is entrammeled in the conditions or restraints of the world. It is just here, and in ways that Badiou and Luhmann make explicit, that the possibilities of the Romantic subject open toward Louverture as a public subject for whom contingency is the field of play, the work at hand, the vehicle that he requires.

Alain Badiou's *Theory of the Subject*, which he recast in *Being and Event*, moves the theory of the subject into the direction Schiller had resisted, but could not put aside. In *Theory of the Subject*, he insists that the subject is inextricable from the world. Instead this relation, which he calls "torsion," is ever twisting, ever misaligned. Citing Friedrich Hölderlin, Badiou describes torsion as a topological operation which loops without a break between claims about subject and claims about world.[25] Working with accounts derived from Hegel's idealism, Lacan's successive formulations of the "Real" and Marxist accounts of subject and world, Badiou argues that the subject who exists in the world may seek comfort from an ego who imagines that the subject is recognizable, fully coherent with itself, and above all normative. Following a line of inquiry he takes up from Jacques Lacan, Badiou supposes that the unconscious subverts the ego by inviting or making an excess that eludes a strict partition between it and the Real. This excess points to how subjects might exceed the terms imposed by the world on acting and being.

To secure this bifold of subject and world, Badiou argues that the question to ask is not "what is a subject in politics," but "what makes a subject." His answer links the subject to what happens, in any given place or time: "a subject is such that, subservient to the rule that determines a place, it nevertheless punctuates the latter with the interruption of its effect."[26] The chiastic shape of this sentence captures the self-correcting (at times self-cancelling) relation between subject and forces or shifts that define the subject not as a being impervious to them but as one whose existence— fluctuating, never fixed—arises from them.

In *Being and Event*, Badiou argues that the ongoing but not fixed condition of the world and being is aleatory, a matter of chance.[27] It is not possible to protect the subject from the fluctuating character of time and place. To claim that a subject is stable over time is, he suggests, the fantasy logic of the future anterior, which understands the present as continuous with the past, as having already happened. So construed, the subject is a stable identity because he is what he was, and will be the same going forward. The arc of being such a subject is fueled, Badiou remarks, by desire. Its ground is, he says, wryly and perhaps hopefully too, "indiscernible." Its linguistic and syntactic anchor depends on producing "names whose referent is in the future anterior." The "entire being" that this idea of the subject seeks to defend must ever "encounter terms in a militant and aleatory trajectory." Badiou's subject is "the latent, errant being" that lives in and by chance.[28] As a name for what goes on and on, Badiou's chance puts extra pressure on Schiller's contingency. For although these terms are not strictly speaking synonymous, they both belong to an orbit of uncertainty and event that can make no appeal to an architectonic causality.

Badiou's argument has everything to do with the public subject that Louverture became in the time of Romanticism. However much Louverture and others wished to claim that he had already been predicted as the Black liberator who would free his people, the certainty of that temporal imaginary was put in doubt by the world historical moment that Louverture inhabited in print. There his claim to be a public and autonomous subject was always in the making, or unmaking.

Niklas Luhmann takes up the consequences of thinking about contingency and the subject in social systems that operate in a world of matter and event and being. Neither systems nor subjects can be contained within a theological or cosmological system that is ordered and stable. Instead, the world and its subjects turn and torque each other to create double contingencies that multiply on both sides and continue to turn in their relation to each other. Luhmann comments that some accounts of contingency in social relations posit a gradual reduction of contingency as unexpected encounters and outcomes settle into a stable pattern that reduces uncertainty. To the contrary, he contends, social systems look and probably act more like chance.[29] So understood, operations and persons netted together in a shifting arc of double contingencies live within each other, neither directed, nor caused, imperfectly aligned. In such a world you do what you can with contingencies as they arrive. Or you do not.

From Schiller on, contingency puts unrelenting pressure on the claim that the subject might not be subject to the world and other beings. You can say a subject exists across time, you can use the future anterior tense to make this claim, but for Schiller, Badiou, and Luhmann these claims are deceptions. Thinking about contingency as these philosophers do, however differently each does it, invites rethinking the claim that Romantic subjects necessarily predict revolutionary outcomes and make them happen. It also invites us to consider how an inner, striving Romantic subject is barely, if at all, prepared to take on a world of contingencies, let alone harness that world to a future that will have always been what one intended it would have always been. Consider these instances: Blake's prophetic characters who stumble toward but also away from imaginative and political freedom;

80 HAITI'S LITERARY LEGACIES

Percy Shelley's failed revolutionaries in the *Revolt of Islam*; Mary Shelley's fictional narratives of failure: from species creation to revolutionary mishap to a pandemic that wipes out all but one human being who knows that he is the last man on earth but imagines that someone will read his words later on. It is tempting to suppose that these failures or misfired arrivals are the whole story. I suggest that Louverture's unremitting attention to what happened as it happened invites us to look more carefully at narrative middles, where the work of becoming a Romantic subject happens. Here, his apparent difference from other Romantic subjects assists a surprising but important alignment. Living in the world, including the fictional worlds of Romantic narratives, is the work at hand. Revolutionary aspirations may fail, as they often do but that is not the end of reading. The work of reading, like the work of being a subject, requires paying attention to what happens along the way. In public and for a reading and listening public, Louverture is at every turn attuned to the work at hand.

A Crumpled Sheet of Paper

Sometime in the 1790s, a British general described the mountainous topography of Haiti to George III by "crumpling up a sheet of paper" and throwing it on the table: "Sire, Haiti looks like that." Or was it a British admiral, or perhaps a French admiral? Or was it Columbus describing Haiti to Queen Isabella of Spain four centuries earlier? Or perhaps it was a French general, no, several French generals who met Louverture, or did not, on a field of battle that was no field, but fold after fold of mountain ranges and deep valleys. Ralph Korngold repeats the British/George III version of the story to characterize Louverture's military brilliance. Whoever said it, it has become part of the landscape. US and Haiti government publications, including a geological survey, explain that the topography of Haiti is "crumpled."[30]

I read this crumpled sheet of paper as a figure for Louverture's manifold relation to the print culture of revolutionary Haiti. Anchored by its material substrates, mountains and paper, this figure aptly describes the double itinerary of Louverture's career in the field and on the page:

> Nobody knew what he intended doing, whether it was his intention to stay or go, whence he came, where he was going. Often he would announce that he was in Le Cap when he was at Port-au-Prince. When everybody imagined him to be at Port-au-Prince, he would be at Les Cayes, at Môle St. Nicholas, at St Marc. He would depart on a journey in a carriage, but a few miles from the starting point would mount his horse, order the vehicle and the guards to proceed, while he would appear where he was least expected accompanied only by a few officers.[31] He drafted letters at

all hours of the day and night ... answering 100, 200, 300 letters in a day are for him an ecstasy, a need ... [To ensure secrecy, his secretaries] wrote a portion of his most sensitive letters, which he then assembled in private like an alchemist synthesizing a dangerous chemical compound.[32]

As he emerges in these reports, Louverture is dazzling, secretive, and everywhere. Moving across a geography shaped by enslaved plantation labor, he masters a topography whose "rifts of broken earth," Kathryn Yusoff argues, constitute the historical geography of slavery and, not incidentally, the topography that made it possible for Maroon communities to survive, well hidden in Haiti's folded mountainous terrain.[33] Louverture never stopped writing and riding, to the chagrin of his adversaries in the field (remember the general or generals who crumpled that sheet of paper) and, likely, the horror of his secretaries, who had to keep at their desks as they translated his mix of Creole and Creole-inflected French into French.[34] In both reports he is the controlling syntactic subject, named and unnamed. No wonder Spanish authorities who were eager to keep him on their side gave him paper and pens as gifts. No wonder Napoleon had him sent to a remote prison in the Jura mountains, and then took away paper, pen, and Louverture's last secretary. And no wonder Louverture hid the last version of the memoir—an extended defense of his public actions—he had addressed to Napoleon, who refused to read it.[35]

Across thousands of pages in archives, on library shelves and digital platforms, Louverture is a highly public subject. He is also a fractal rather than single, unified subject. In some measure he is so because his life and times so required: he had to shift and turn to keep the field against many, and alongside some, players. The print record, which makes him and other public subjects who they are or become, stretches across a manifold of differences and echoes. So assembled and dispersed in the print record, public subjects like Louverture are strangely audible and discursive. What gets heard across the record that accrues to a public subject is a special version of what Michel Serres calls "noise" in the French sense, that is, a murmuring beneath the level of recognizable words or categories.[36] What public subjects say and what others say about them is highly audible but also so densely textured that claims about the character or even the actions and intentions of this subject are difficult to sort out. In the field and on the page, Louverture is such a subject. As such, he amplifies comparable uncertainties about other Romantic subjects. He is their inverted double: Black, public, and heroic.

In the print record of his life and times, Louverture inhabits an historical time whose contours and folds Serres imagines:

If you take a handkerchief and spread it out in order to iron, you can see in it certain fixed distances and proximities. If you sketch a circle in one area, you can mark out nearby points and measure far-off distances. Then take the same handkerchief and crumple it, by putting it in your pocket. Two distant points suddenly are close, even superimposed. If, further, you tear it in certain places, two points that were close can become very distant. This science of nearness and rifts is called topology, while the science of stable and well-defined distances is called metrical geometry.[37]

Finding one's way in the crumpled folds of historical time as Serres describes it is like finding one's way across the crumpled geology of Haiti: never a clear line of march. Like Louverture, readers live in the space-time manifolds of a print record that often supposes, but never captures, the future he or they desire. No wonder Louverture is hard to track across a print record that is scattered and at times in contradiction with itself and with manuscript sources. In what follows I present three episodes in which Louverture figures as a speaker or narrator, in his own voice or others' reports. In each the print record is thick and versional, its times and claims crumpled together. All the episodes are Blakean moments, which is to say that their time signature is layered but imperfectly aligned. Three topics or motifs recur in these reported episodes: prediction, Blackness, and futurity.

The first moment is the most widely reported. Louverture himself and many after him have suggested that Louverture fulfilled the Abbé Guillaume-François-Joseph Raynal's prediction that a Black leader would free his enslaved brothers. The second reports an exchange between Louverture and a white woman who offers to name him the godfather of her newborn son. The third is a reported dialogue between Louverture and the French official Sonthonax who had decreed the abolition of slavery in Haiti and thereafter became Louverture's ally, but in the end his enemy. Unlike the other two episodes, in the third Louverture reports what he said in print. Here too, though, the question of who said what remains at issue.

Reading Raynal

The Abbé Raynal's famous prediction of a Black Spartacus (not a quotation but a moniker invented and assigned to Raynal) appeared in the 1774 edition of his *Histoire philosophique et politique des établissemens et du commerce des européens dans les deux Indes*, translated and abbreviated as *History of the two Indies*. Like other eighteenth-century speculative histories, Raynal's posits a future based on a history whose speculative engine presents global commerce as a civilizing agent. It understates the matter to note that Caribbean slavery sits uncomfortably inside this narrative plot. From its first edition of 1770, the *History of the Two Indies* included an extended critique of New World slavery. Raynal added the famous prediction to the second edition of 1774. He removed it in the third and last edition of 1780.

Raynal's prediction replays (and plagiarizes) a scene in Louis-Sébastien Mercier's 1772 *The Year 2440*, a futurist novel that looks back on the past, which is to say the time when Mercier and Raynal were writing. In the not-as-yet-arrived future narrative time of the novel, Mercier's narrator sees a heroic statue that towers over a scattered group of statues whose abject postures and expressions convey their shame.

The Raynal-Mercier ping-pong of editions, reprints, and translations continued into the early nineteenth century. With each print iteration, their exchange set the stage for Louverture's emergence as the Black liberator of Raynal's prediction and Mercier's utopian backward glance. I am interested less in Raynal's plagiarism (hardly unusual in eighteenth-century print culture) than I am in the tense markers that distinguish his version from Mercier's future anterior, which he uses to imagine as having already happened what had not yet happened in the 1770s. The subtitle of Mercier's novel, "The future that never was," mocks its future anterior plot. Unlike the double move of Mercier's title and subtitle, Raynal's prediction is hedged and speculative:

il ne manque aux Nègres qu'un chef assez courageux, pour les conduire à la vengeance & au carnage.

Où est-il ce grand homme, que la nature doit peut-être à l'honneur de l'espèce humaine? Où est-il, ce Spartacus nouveau, qui ne trouvera point de Crassus? Alors disparoîtra le *code noir*; que le *code blanc* sera terrible, si le vainqueur ne consulte que le droit de représailles![38]

the negroes only want a chief, sufficiently courageous, to lead them to vengeance and to slaughter.

Where is this great man to be found, whom nature, perhaps, owes to the honour of the human species? Where is this new Spartacus, who will not find a Crassus? Then will the *black code* be no more; and the *white code* will be a dreadful one, if the conqueror only regards the right of reprisals.[39]

Raynal's syntax blends an anticipatory present and indicative future with notice of their counterfactual status in the present time of writing.[40] The hero is wanted or lacking, "'where is he,' where is this new Spartacus?" What Mercier imagined as having already happened, Raynal presents as at best not yet. Nonetheless, by the 1790s Louverture was identified with the Black liberator who, in the future anterior logic of Mercier's narrative time, had already been, done his job, and departed. Mercier's ironic subtitle and Raynal's decision not to present the Black liberator of slaves as someone who had already arrived entertain the rhetoric and syntax of contingency that would become Louverture's. As Mercier and Raynal stage it, prediction

84   HAITI'S LITERARY LEGACIES

is at best only a sometime thing. Even Mercier's future anterior claim that
a Black liberator had already freed slaves is circumstanced by Mercier's
subtitle and the timing of writing, when no liberator and no glorious
liberation had happened.

Marlene Daut and other scholars have tracked multiple versions of the
Raynal legend. In 1795, "it is said" that General Étienne Laveaux, who would
name Louverture lieutenant general of the Haitian army, proclaimed him
the hero Raynal had predicted.[41] Then and now it is not certain whether, as
C. L. R. James asserted, "Toussaint had read his Raynal."[42] Louis Dubroca,
among the most vitriolic of Louverture's critics, ridiculed this claim on the
grounds that he could scarcely speak, let alone read, French.[43] Among those
who said he could and did read Raynal, Cousin D'Avallon claimed that
Raynal was Louverture's "guidebook."[44] Pamphile de Lacroix reported
Louverture to have said, as the Haitian Revolution began, that he heard a
"secret [and inner] voice telling him, "now that blacks (*les noirs*) are free,
they need a leader (*chef*) and it is I who must be the leader predicted by the
Abbé Raynal."[45] As Louverture is said to have told it, Haiti wants a hero, a
terrible desire.

Perhaps the most widely circulated publication to convey Louverture's
inferred management of the Raynal story for his own purposes is an
anonymous 1799 article published in *Le Moniteur universel,* sometimes
identified as *La Gazette nationale* or *L'Ancien Moniteur*. Identified only
as "un citoyen nouvellement arrivé de Saint-Domingue," the unidentified
correspondent recalls at some length his visit to Louverture, at ease and
at home. This ease was at once domestic and political. By 1799, a fact
the correspondent notes, Louverture had become general-in-chief of the
French army in Haiti. During the visit, the *Moniteur* correspondent says,
Louverture reflected on events that had shaped his decision to take up a
military and political career. As the unidentified correspondent describes this
scene of self-instruction, Louverture asked himself about the strange logic of
slavery whereby the color of one's skin determines who is master and who
enslaved. This reflection led him to read the oft cited critique of slavery in
Raynal's *History,* and in particular the page where Raynal "paraît annoncer
le libérateur qui devrait arracher à ses fers un grande portion de l'espèce
humaine" (appeared to announce the liberator who would/must release
from its irons a great part of the human species). In the next sentence, the
Moniteur writer names this conditional to come "prediction." Returning
incessantly (*sans cesse*) to Raynal's "prediction," Louverture, the reader
is told, noted further that nevertheless (*cependant*) the French Revolution
had proclaimed the "éternels" (eternal) rights of man. From this train of
thought, the reader learns, Louverture arrived at the idea of the role he had
since taken.[46]

The French text of this account is more nuanced than its English
translation. "Cependant" signals a contrast between a prior assertion

and the declaration in which the adverb appears. In this case, the implied contrast is between the conditional future tense of Raynal's "appeared to announce" what would happen (or might happen) and the present moment of the French declaration of the "eternal rights of the human species." Louverture's phrasing, or the unidentified writer's report, introduces two key adjustments: "eternal" for "universal" and human species for "men" or "mankind." The first substitution makes those rights for all time as well as worldwide; the second, which he (or the writer) picks up from Raynal's text, makes the claim that Louverture insists on in his 1801 Haitian Constitution—that Haitians (men) are citizens of France, and as such they "are born, live and die free and French," not a subhuman species whose existence invited or required enslavement.[47]

All of this is reported. In later paragraphs, the writer quotes Louverture directly, but not here. Yet here, in reported speech, it seems likely that we hear what Deborah Jenson recognizes in Louverture's dictated and published speeches: he is a consummate "spin doctor" who knows how to represent himself to a wide audience within and beyond Haiti.[48] Here the writer of this *Moniteur* article does Louverture's publicity for him by presenting him as the philosophical and reflective Black Haitian general-in-chief whose career path took shape as he reflected on slavery, becoming a predicted liberator and, thanks to the French declaration of rights, the moment when that liberator had in a sense already arrived. The stage was already set when Louverture decided to step onto the historical scene.

The *Moniteur* sketch may be the only version of the Raynal story that hesitates, as Raynal had, between the arrival of a liberator whom he "appeared to announce" and a more emphatic "prediction" of that arrival, as the *Moniteur* writer also suggests. Perhaps Louverture read Raynal more closely than his commentators did. Perhaps not. Gathered together, versions of this moment in print and time amplify the figure of Louverture as a public subject who faced the future.

Black and White

The second moment, reported as a dialogue between Louverture and a white woman, appears in print less often than the Black Spartacus legend. It is virtually unchanged in all reports. After her husband had asked Louverture for work and been refused, the woman approached him to request that he become the godfather to her son. The unidentified narrator quotes Louverture's reply:

> Why, Madame, do you wish me to become your son's godparent? Your initiative has no goal but to make me give your husband a position; for your heart lies about the request you make to me.—How, general, can you believe this? My husband loves you; all the whites are attached to

you. Madame, I know the whites [*les blancs colons*]; if I had their skin, yes; but I am black [*noir*], and I know their aversion for us. Have you reflected carefully about the request you make to me? If I accept, what will your son say to you when he reaches the age of reason, seeing that a black is his godparent, would he not reproach you?—Madame, (pointing to heaven), he who governs all is the only god, I am general, it is true, but I am black [*noir*]. After my death, who knows whether my brothers will not be returned to slavery, and perish again under the whips of whites [*les blancs*]? The work of men is not enduring. The white colonists are enemies of the blacks [*les noirs*].[49]

The clause that follows Louverture's open-ended "who knows?" suggests he does know: "who knows *whether my brothers will not be returned to slavery, and perish again under the whips of whites?*" The reason for this unwilling admission is in plain sight. Black skins, white lies. He could have called himself *nègre* (*neg* in Haitian Creole). Sometimes he did, at others he did not. Replying to Sonthonax's declaration of his abolitionary fervor, "I am white but have the soul of a black man," Louverture snapped, "And I am black but I have the soul of a white man."[50]

These stories do not easily align with Louverture's public policy on race. Recognizing that Haiti's economic survival required that former slaves, whites and *hommes du couleur* work together, he resented the charge that he hated *hommes du couleur*; he told former slaves when he urged them to go back to work on plantations that he was Black and African, like them; and he argued that Haitians were neither Black nor white nor colored. If you mix red and white wines, he said, demonstrating his point by doing just that, the result is neither white nor red.[51] And yet, in the exchanges I have quoted, he was sharply attuned to the color line others drew between degrees of Haitian and African blackness and French whiteness.[52]

Louverture Addresses His Public(s)

In 1797, Louverture published what he claimed was an extensive series of exchanges with Sonthonax, the sometime ally become enemy whom Louverture exiled to France. Staged as a dialogue and running to thirty-nine pages in print, the document is addressed to the executive branch of the French Directory. As he frequently did when he wished to speak for himself in public, he also published the dialogue for all to read.[53] Purportedly a verbatim record of his exchanges with Sonthonax, the dialogue is highly dramatic and likely invented, a history play whose hero is Louverture, the Black "chief," as he names himself within the dialogue, who is a loyal citizen of free France, as he signs himself in diplomatic correspondence.

Louverture insists that he remembered exchanges between the two men that occurred over several months and that he kept notes after every exchange to be certain of his accuracy. How, scholars have asked, could he recall and then record long conversations that purportedly took place in many separate conversations over several months? In an attempt to defend himself against Louverture's charge of treason against France, Sonthonax objected that Louverture could not have spoken so eloquently in French, nor could he have transcribed Sonthonax's elegant French.[54] The charge is amusing, inasmuch as Louverture had done precisely what he is not supposed to be able to do. Yet it also speaks to a persistent doubt about whether he can be described as the author of what others transcribed and what he then signed and often published. Deborah Jenson argues persuasively for a complex practice that he sets in motion by dictating to several secretaries, who transcribed what he had said into a more or less accurate French. Louverture completes the authorial cycle, or recycling of his words, by comparing different transcriptions to determine whether his meaning had been accurately reported.[55]

Complete with intervals, scene changes, and stage directions, the dialogue claims to document Sonthonax's repeated attempts to persuade Louverture to declare Haiti, still a French colony, independent of France. Scene by scene, the dialogue stages a series of rhetorical skirmishes that create an unsteady rhythm of suspicion, doubt, and conniving, a wary verbal fencing match that Louverture dominates in part because he is telling the story. From scene to scene, the dialogue keeps restaging possible outcomes. As he presents Sonthonax, he is a shifty character who keeps coming up with new scenarios, new rationales. As Louverture parries again and again, he invites a return to Lupton's forest of contingent and forking paths. Louverture masters them all, meeting each unexpected (as he presents them) temptation or stratagem that Sonthonax puts in play easily, turning it aside, choosing to take another path, insisting again and again on his unwavering loyalty to France.

It is not possible, in any format, to give the full measure of Louverture's strategic self-representation as the "chef noir," who acts in Haiti on behalf of France.[56] When Sonthonax insists that the French are poised to capture Haiti and re-enslave its people, Louverture reports that he replied: "Hasn't France decreed general liberty? Can it take back its decrees? Does not the constitution guarantee us our rights?" The rhetorical form of these questions insists that the answers must be clear. Yet as Louverture created this dramatic account of the backstory that led to his dismissal of Sonthonax, the answers to all these questions might have been yes, of course, and it could happen any time. By 1797 the guarantee of Haitian freedom was neither general nor universal. Many in France, above all Napoleon, believed that the French declaration of rights did not extend to Black Haitians. Above all, members of the French Directory and Napoleon, along with some white colonists in

Haiti, hoped to re-enslave Haiti, as they attempted to do after Louverture was captured, exiled to France, and died.

As a narrative of what happened and what was said, as Louverture reported it, the dialogue claims to master the time of history. When Sonthonax says on his own behalf that he has only made his proposals four or five times, Louverture replies wearily that he has heard the same proposal at least nine or ten times. Finally, that is, near the end of their exchanges, he commands: "You must go. To respect the word of honor I have given you, I have no wish to tell commissaire Raimond the propositions you have made to me." When Sonthonax demands letters of "felicitation" to carry back to France—that is, good recommendations, Louverture agrees: "I will give you everything you wish; because I view your departure as absolutely necessary to the health of the Colony." The last words are, inevitably, Louverture's: "Leave quickly ... I promise that this exchange will remain between us ... If there is any trouble, and you in bad faith fail to fulfill the promise you have made me, I will reveal everything and put you on board ship by force." He backs his decision with a Creole proverb delivered in a Creole-French dialect Haitian and non-Haitians used by the 1790s:

> Je vais vous répondre comme les créoles disent; les créoles disent: "Yon cochon qui déjà mangé poule, vous borgné yon yeux li, vous borgné l'autre yeux li; ça pas empêché li quant li passé côté poule, il va cherché mangé li toujours."[57]

If ever there was a speech act, this is it. Choosing here to put aside the elegant French that Sonthonax said he could not possibly have written or spoken, Louverture compares his French adversary to a pig who keeps eating chickens: "if you are blind with one eye when the pig eats a chicken and then blind with the other eye, that will not stop it [pig] when it passes a chicken, it [pig again] will always look to eat chicken."

Louverture's dialogue was an extraordinary gamble, call it a bet against time, at a moment (like one of many) when his rise to power as a Black Haitian had sharpened French suspicions that he might turn on them. To suggest, even as a condition contrary to fact, that he might do just that makes this risk explicit, in order to deny it. Here, I suggest we meet the Louverture-Raynal story from its future, when a prediction is no guarantee. What lay ahead was a perilous time, and a futurity that depended on tactical maneuvers as alert and secretive as his military campaigns.

Conclusion

As a public Romantic subject in the volatile image and print culture that he still inhabits, Louverture offers a different model for reading Romanticism as a desiring machine directed toward a revolutionary futurity. He invites us to rethink how Romantic writers and protagonists calculate odds and impossibilities in the folds of narratives. Proximate, akin and yet not, the differences between Louverture and other Romantic subjects (public vs private; fictional or not) specify the fault lines that mar or make Romantic subjects.

How Louverture animated the public and textual space of his life and times also invites us to rethink what it means to be a Romantic subject. Louverture is not a subject who stands outside time, impervious to its impersonations. He is neither Benjamin West's painting of a Welsh Bard gesticulating from a high (and safe) promontory against an invading English army, nor a poet singing in solitude. Louverture matters for Romanticism as a European and global phenomenon because he invites an uneasy return to those Romantic subjects whose revolutionary desires we celebrate or dismiss when they stumble or fail.

For Louverture political freedom was always an uncertain horizon, existing or shimmering somewhere between prophecy, with its providential eye on the future, and a speculative futurity marked by hazards, the flip side of the opportunities that arise from contingency. Like other Romantic heroes and poets who struggle with getting to the future, he reckoned with what might happen should the Revolution run amok. In public he insisted that the Haitian Revolution would continue after his death, that it could not be stopped. At other moments, he predicted he would be destroyed, and wondered whether slavery would return to Haiti. In his relentless campaigns in the field and on the page, he was a Romantic subject who desires revolution, but he also understood that prediction is never, could never be, a sure bet. That he did so in public and in print as a formerly enslaved Black subject makes visible the perilous character of Romantic subjects.

Across these registers Louverture is Romanticism's two-hearted subject: a public voice acting on his own public stage, seeking to ensure his own ends. He conducted this project, a Caribbean and Black reply to eighteenth-century projects that speculated on making a profit in the New World, in the open or at least in print, even if what he said or is said to have said was spoken in secret or in a room with only a single, unidentified witness. That he failed in the end is part of the story but it is not the whole story. Why it is not has everything to do with other Romantic protagonists who also fail. For them and for him, what matters is how they meet contingencies that stand between them and the futures they imagine or predict. Those contingencies may be, as they were for Louverture, what happened in the revolutionary place and time where he became a public Romantic subject, or they may be narrative impediments in fictional worlds with prophetic ambitions. Either way, how these Romantic subjects take on contingencies (or do not) is more telling than whether they succeed or fail. Reading for contingency in this way matters for how we read Romanticism now. It also matters for modern subjects.

Charles Taylor's claim that the modern self begins as an interior Romantic self-consciousness misses the mark. To the contrary, Schiller's insistence that contingency may make or break what it means to become a subject invites attention to the ethical and imaginative complexity at issue in becoming public as well as private subjects. Romantic and modern subjects, whether public or private and avowedly fictional, are not only or always interior beings. Rather, as Louverture's career and writing invite us to recognize, some are subjects whose future belongs to the public spaces where action and writing are the work at hand. So understood, Toussaint Louverture is the Romantic subject we need now, not because he is at every turn the heroic figure we hope will appear, but because he stages the relation between becoming a subject and living in a contingent world.

Notes

1 Paul Youngquist and Grégory Pierrot, *An Historical Account of the Black Empire of Hayti*, ed. Marcus Rainsford (Durham: Duke University Press, 2013), li.

2 Lord Byron, *Don Juan*, ed. Jerome J. McGann (Oxford: Oxford University Press, 1986), 1:1–4, 378.

3 Recent historians have assessed Louverture's actions and declarations on these and other occasions. They include: Philippe R. Girard, *Toussaint Louverture: A Revolutionary Life* (New York: Basic Books, 2016), 1–48, 109–247; David P. Geggus, *Haitian Revolutionary Studies* (Bloomington: Indiana University Press, 2002), 5–29, 55–151; Laurent Dubois, *Avengers of the New World* (Cambridge, MA: Harvard University Press, 2004); and Srinivas Aravamudan, *Troicopolitans* (Durham: Duke University Press, 1999).

4 Ian Balfour observes that Romantic prophecy does not necessarily have much to do with prediction in *The Rhetoric of Romantic Prophecy* (Stanford: Stanford University Press, 2002), 3.

5 Girard, *Louverture: A Revolutionary Life*, 153.

6 Girard, *Louverture: A Revolutionary Life*, 61 (*lieu dit*) and Girard, trans. and ed., Toussaint Louverture, *The Mémoire of Toussaint Louverture* (Oxford: Oxford University Press, 2014), 48–9; Girard, *Louverture: A Revolutionary Life*, 244 reports what Louverture said as he boarded ship for France; John Walsh quotes another version of this declaration in *Free and French in the Caribbean: Toussaint Louverture, Aimé Césaire and the Loyal Opposition* (Bloomington: Indiana University Press, 2013), 334; the earliest account of what Louverture may have said may be François-Joseph-Pamphile de Lacroix *Mémoires pour servir à l'histoire de la révolution de Saint-Domingue*, 2 vols. (Paris: Pillet, 1819), 1:340.

TOUSSAINT LOUVERTURE

7 David P. Geggus, "Underexploited Sources," in *Haitian Revolutionary Studies* 43–54; Geggus, "Changing Faces of Toussaint Louverture," https://www.brown.edu/Facilities/John_Carter_Brown_Library/exhibitions/toussaint/pages/iconography.html accessed May 25, 2020; Girard notes these aspects of Louverture's life and career in *Louverture: A Revolutionary Life* 41, 45, 54, 126, 219, 220, 222.

8 Girard, "Quelle langue parlait Toussaint Louverture? Le mémoire du fort de Joux et les origines du kreyòl haïtien," *Annales. Histoire, Sciences Sociales*, 68:1 (January–March 2013): 109–32; Girard, *Toussaint Louverture: A Revolutionary Life*, 22–4, 126–7, 239.

9 My analogy between Louverture and maroon communities does not assume that those communities contributed to the Haitian uprisings that in effect began the revolution. Geggus has argued against claims for maroon involvement in *Haitian Revolutionary Studies*, 69–80, and "Saint-Domingue, le marronage et la révolution haïtienne," in *Societes marrones des Ameriques*, ed. Jean Moomou (Matoury-Guyane: Ibis Rouge Éditions, 2015), 127–38.

10 Girard assesses Louverture's literacy, use of secretaries and lists some of his most significant printed works in *Louverture: A Revolutionary Life*, 126, 171, 304–6.

11 Wim Klooster, *Revolutions in the Atlantic World: A Comparative History* (New York: New York University Press, 2009), 84.

12 David Alff discusses the speculative, future-oriented logic of projects in *The Wreckage of Intentions: Projects in British Culture, 1660–1730* (Philadelphia: University of Pennsylvania Press, 2017), 114–42.

13 Achille Mbembe, *Critique of Black Reason* (Durham: Duke University Press, 2017), 5, 16.

14 Charles Taylor, *Sources of the Self: The Making of the Modern Identity* (Cambridge, MA: Harvard University Press, 1989), 422.

15 Balfour, *Rhetoric of Romantic Prophecy*, 1–18.

16 C. L. R. James, Preface to the first edition, *The Black Jacobins*, 2nd ed. rev. (New York: Vintage Books, 1989), x.

17 Christina Lupton, "Contingency, Codex, the Eighteenth-Century Novel," *ELH* 81, no. 4 (2014): 1186–7; Lupton, *Reading and the Making of Time in the Eighteenth Century* (Baltimore: Johns Hopkins University Press, 2018), 99.

18 Lupton, *Reading and the Making of Time*, 102–4.

19 Friedrich Schiller, *On the Aesthetic Education of Man*, trans. Elizabeth M. Wilkinson and L. A. Willoughby (Oxford: Clarendon Press, 1967), 45–7, 71.

20 Schiller, *Aesthetic Education*, 97, 111, 173, 189, 209.

21 Schiller, *Aesthetic Education*, 73.

22 Paul de Man, *Rhetoric of Temporality* (New York: Columbia University Press, 1984), 265.

23 Schiller, *Aesthetic Education*, 73, 80, 150.

24 Novalis, Blüthenstaub, "in Band 2: *Das philosophisch-theoretischer Werke, Tageblücher und Briefe*, ed. Hans-Joachim Mähl and Ricard Samuel (Munich: Carl Hanser Verlag, 1978), 227–9; English, "Pollen," in *The Early Political Writings of the German Romantics*, ed. Frederick E. Beiser (Cambridge: Cambridge University Press, 1996), 12, 14, 17, 20–2.

25 Alain Badiou, *Theory of the Subject*, trans. Bruno Bosteels (London: Bloomsbury, 2009), 286; French text, *Théorie du Sujet* (Paris: Éditions du Seuil, 1982), 302; Emily Rohrbach assesses Romantic versions of the future anterior in *Modernity's Mist: British Romanticism and the Poetics of Anticipation* (New York: Fordham University Press, 2016), 1, 5.

26 Badiou, *Theory*, 179, 259; French text 195, 275.

27 Badiou, *Being and Event*, trans. Oliver Feltham (New York: Bloomsbury, 2005), 416; French, Badiou, *L'être et l'événement* (Paris: Editions du Seuil, 1988), 433.

28 Badiou, *Being and Event*, 414, 416–18; French, Badiou, *L'être et l'événement*, 432–4.

29 Niklas Luhmann, *Social Systems*, trans. John Bednarz, Jr. with Dirk Baecker (Stanford: Stanford University Press, 1995), 104–5.

30 Ralph Korngold, *Citizen Toussaint* (London: Victor Gollancz, for the Left Book Club, 1945), 92. Versions of this story recirculate in the print record and beyond. See, for example, John S. Brown and Wendell P. Woodring, *Haiti: General Descriptive Data* (Washington, DC: Government Printing Office, 1924), 29; Anonymous, *Agricultural Progress in Haiti: Summary Report, 1944–1949* (Washington, DC: Institute of Inter-American Affairs, 1949), 1; Selden Rodman, *Haiti The Black Republic: the Complete Story and Guide*, new rev. ed. (New York: Devin Adair, 1954), 3; Jerome R. R. Adams, *Latin American Liberators and Patriots from 1500 to the Present* (New York: Random House, 1991), 15; a sample GMAT question https://gmatclub.com/forum/after-queen-isabella-asked-admiral-columbus-to-describe-the-island-of-82536.html#p618576; and a photo of the national flag of Haiti as a crumpled sheet of paper, dated February 11, 2019. https://www.alamy.com/national-flag-of-haiti-on-crumpled-paper-flag-printed-on-a-sheet-flag-image-for-design-on-flyers-advertising-image342190764.html.

31 Philippe Girard, *Louverture: A Revolutionary Life*, 34, quoting Jean-Baptiste Lemonnier-Delafosse, *Seconde campagne de Saint-Domingue du décembre 1803 au 15 juillet 1809, précédée de souvenirs historiques et succints de la première campagne* (Le Havre: Brindeau, 1846); Korngold quotes the same passage in *Toussaint*, 172, but cites Lacroix's *Mémoires*.

32 Girard, *Louverture: A Revolutionary Life*, 220.

33 Kathryn Yusoff, *A Billion Black Anthropocenes or None* (Minneapolis: Minnesota University Press, 2019), xi.

34 Girard, *Louverture: A Revolutionary Life*, 67, 124–8.

35 Girard, *Louverture: A Revolutionary Life*, 141 (Spanish gifts to Louverture) 298, n. 35; 249–50 (Napoleon's refusal to read Louverture's *Mémoire*).

36 Serres describes "noise" variously in *Genesis*, trans. Genevieve James and James Nielson (Ann Arbor: University of Michigan Press, 1995): as multiples that conceptual categories do not recognize 23–4; as the murmuring of as yet indiscernible forces prior to the formations of atoms and other particles of the cosmos 4–5.

37 Serres and Bruno Latour, *Conversations on Science, Culture, and Time*, trans. Roxanne Lapidus (Ann Arbor: University of Michigan Press, 1995), 60. Jane Bennett and William Connolly offer a luminous analysis of Serres on noise and a crumpled handkerchief in "The Crumpled Handkerchief," in *Time and History in Deleuze and Serres*, ed. Bernd Herzogenrath (New York: Bloomsbury, 2012), 60.

38 Guillaume-Thomas-François Raynal, *Histoire philosophique et politique des établissements et du commerce des Européens dans les deux Indes*, 7 vols. (A La Haye: n.p., 1774), Book XI, 4:226–7. Spartacus was a Thracian gladiator whom the Romans had enslaved. He led a slave revolt that the Roman general Crassus crushed in 71 BC; Louis-Sébastien Mercier, *L'An deux mille quatre cent quarante, Rêve s'il en fût jamais* (Londres, 1772), 154–8.

39 Abbé Raynal, *A Philosophical and Political History of the Settlements and Trade of the Europeans in the Two Indies, 5 vols.* (London: T. Cadell, 1776), Book XI, 3:466.

40 Lupton emphasizes the nested character of the print record in "Immersing the Network in Time: From the Where to the When of Print Reading," *ELH* 83, no. 2 (2016): 302.

41 Marlene Daut quotes several contemporary versions of the Black Spartacus/Louverture legend in *Tropics of Haiti: Race and the Literary History of the Haitian Revolution in the Atlantic World 1789–1865* (Liverpool: Liverpool University Press, 2015), 49–56. Marcus Rainsford transmits the Louverture/Raynal legend to English readers in *An Historical Account of the Black Empire of Hayti*, 152, 311 n. 293. I cite here only a few recent modern discussions of this legend: James, *Black Jacobins*, 24–5; Grégory Pierrot, *The Black Avenger in Atlantic Culture* (Athens: University of Georgia Press, 2019), 100–2; Srinivas Aravamudan, *Tropicopolitans: Colonialism and Agency* (Durham: Duke University Press, 1999), 300–2; Deborah Jenson, *Beyond the Slave Narrative: Politics, Sex, and Manuscripts in the Haitian Revolution* (Liverpool: Liverpool University Press, 2011), 48–9.

42 James, *Black Jacobins*, 91.

43 Louis Dubroca, *La vie de Toussaint-Louverture, chef des noirs insurgés de Saint-Domingue* (Paris: Dubroca, 1802), 16. Quoted by Daut, *Tropics*, 54.

44 Cousin d'Avallon, *Histoire de Toussaint L'Overture, chef des noirs insurgés de Saint-Domingue* (Paris: Pillot, 1802), 36–7. Quoted by Daut, *Tropics*, 55.

45 Pamphile de Lacroix, *Mémoires* 1:405. Quoted by Daut, *Tropics* 55–6.

46 Anonymous correspondent, *Le Moniteur ou La Gazette nationale* (1799), 585 bis.

47 Louverture, "Constitution de 1801," Titre II, Articles 3, 4, and 5. http://thelouvertureproject.org/index.php?title=Haitian_Constitution_of_1801_(French).

48 Jenson, *Beyond the Slave Narrative*, 48–9, 73.

49 Colonel Charles Malenfant, *Des colonies, particulièrement de celle de Saint-Domingue: mémoire historique et politique* (Paris: Audibert, 1819), 94–95n; quoted in: Victor Schoelcher, *Vie de Toussaint Louverture* (1889 rpt.; Paris: Éditions Karthala, 1982), 395; James, *Black Jacobins*, 260–1 and Girard, *The Slaves Who Defeated Napoleon: Toussaint Louverture and the Haitian War of Independence 1801–1804* (Tuscaloosa: University of Alabama Press, 2011), 25.

50 Girard, *Louverture: A Revolutionary Life*, 166.

51 Daut, *Tropics of Haiti*, 49–72; Girard, *Slaves* 351 n. 78; Girard, *Louverture: A Revolutionary Life*, 67, 155, 159, 176–7.

52 Louverture's Haitian contemporary, Médéric-Louis-Élie Moreau de St. Méry, created or codified a racial hierarchy keyed to skin color, from fully white through 110 shades of blackness in his *Description topographique, physique, civile, politique et historique de la partie française de l'isle Saint-Domingue, 3 vols.* (Philadelphia: chez l'auteur, au coin de Front & de Callow-Hill Streets, 1797), 1: 17–114. St. Méry acknowledged the problems of misattribution that plagued his classification: skin color might, or might not, convey the degree of inherited "black blood." Doris Lorraine Garraway provides a richly contextual and theoretical account of St. Mery's argument and career in "Race, Reproduction and Family Romance in Moreau de St. Méry's *Description ... de la partie française de l'isle Saint-Domingue*," *Eighteenth-Century Studies* 38, no. 2 (Winter 2005): 227–46.

53 Girard, *Louverture: A Revolutionary Life*, 169.

54 Louverture, *Extrait du rapport adressé au Directoire exécutif par le citoyen Toussaint Louverture, général en chef des forces de la République Française à Saint-Domingue Septembre 4, 1797* (Cap Français: September 4, 1797), d. 961 AF/III, 210, AN. Girard, *Louverture: A Revolutionary Life*, 16–170 and 301 n.15 tracks the archival history of Louverture's *Extrait* and Sonthonax's efforts to clear himself to members of the French Directory first in a letter to Bauvais (August 18, 1797) fr. 8988, BNF and then in a formal appeal to the Directory: "Toussaint ne parle," (January 30, 1798) AF/III, 210, AN. Jenson assesses Louverture's management of dramatic gesture and occasion in *Beyond the Slave Narrative* 47, 70–4.

55 Jenson, *Beyond the Slave Narrative*, 5–23.

56 Louverture, *Extrait*, 5.

57 Louverture, *Extrait*, 35.

4

Seeing into the Very Bones: C. L. R. James and William Wordsworth on Figure, Personhood, and Revolutionary Discourse

Brian McGrath

I borrow my title from a rather enigmatic figure C. L. R. James uses in the preface to *The Black Jacobins* to describe his historical method. Writing in the context of ongoing revolution and social upheaval in the 1930s, James suggests that "The violent conflicts of our age enable our practiced vision to see into the very bones of previous revolutions more easily than heretofore."[1] The present makes the past legible. One understands previous revolutions differently when one is surrounded by violent conflict, which trains the historian's eye and improves the historian's vision. By referring to the bones of previous revolutions, James reminds readers that revolutions and counterrevolutions often turn violent and reduce living bodies to mere bones. But with the figure James does more than allude to the violence of revolution, for the historian's task is not only to see the bones left by previous conflicts, bones standing figuratively for all acts of violence that accompany political and social change. For James the task of the historian is to see "into" the bones of previous revolutions, so not *see* but *see into*, where James's use of the preposition grants previous revolutions something like a skeletal body. With this figure, the historian's task is like the radiologist's: to write history one must see into the bones of a personified or anthropomorphized revolution. James's use of the hedge *very* makes more pronounced the figure, as the historian does not see into bones but into the *very* bones. The intensifier makes the challenge less literal and more difficult. In subtly granting previous revolutions bones, a skeletal body, James shows how the work of the historian depends on the power of figuration, depends on animating tropes like personification and anthropomorphism familiar to poets.[2]

In the next sentence of the preface, James self-consciously alludes to the writing of one of the most famous British Romantic poets, William Wordsworth, but does not name him, referring instead to "a great English writer," where "English" may stand for White. "Yet for that very reason," continues James, "it is impossible to recollect historical emotions in that tranquility which a great English writer, too narrowly, associated with poetry alone."[3] James offers a historical method that depends on figurative vision (seeing into the very bones of previous revolutions) in direct contrast to Wordsworthian poetics, as Wordsworth famously describes poetry as emotion recollected in tranquility in his preface to *Lyrical Ballads*. The violent conflicts of the present age enable a vision that depends on figure, perhaps even a vision *for* figures; if living amidst conflict makes it easier for historians to see into the bones of previous revolutions, then tranquility does not, for James, lead to the sort of vision required to write revolutionary history.

This essay takes up James's invitation to read his history of Toussaint Louverture and the San Domingo Revolution alongside Wordsworth's writing in general and Wordsworth's poem "To Toussaint L'Ouverture" in particular.[4] As I will go on to show, both James and Wordsworth worry about personification's power and yet both turn to animating figures in their different responses to Louverture's revolutionary history. To advance *The Black Jacobins*, James turns to the figure of an embodied revolution. In his sonnet "To Toussaint L'Ouverture," which he wrote in response to news of Louverture's capture, Wordsworth grants natural entities animate personhood, asserting that air, earth, and skies will advance a revolutionary cause even after Louverture's death. His legacy will be a nature personified. Figure will be his legacy.

Likes James's preface, Wordsworth's poem is densely figurative. Personifications proliferate. Wordsworth begins the poem with an apostrophe and then after asserting that air, earth, and skies will work for Louverture suggests that the breathing of the common wind will not forget him and that henceforth his friends will be exultations, agonies, love, and Man's unconquerable mind. Careful readers of Wordsworth's poem have understood Wordsworth's closing tangle of personifications as a retreat from political action into abstracted nature. In what follows, though, I take seriously the ways the poem's many personifications throw into doubt the given-ness of personhood. As James grants previous revolutions bones, Wordsworth transforms exultations, agonies, and love, and perhaps most conspicuously the abstract concept of "Man" itself, into friends. I place James's *The Black Jacobins* and Wordsworth's "To Toussaint L'Ouverture" in the context of the Haitian Revolution's indictment of Enlightenment definitions of person, the assumed given-ness of which was used repeatedly by white Europeans to deny personhood to enslaved and formerly enslaved persons, those excluded from the European definition of "Man" and deemed less than human. As they work to respond to the revolution's demand for more capacious ideas of person and personhood, both texts identify a key role for figure, which is not, in the case of Wordsworth's poem, to suggest that personification is in any simple way revolutionary action. I am, however, interested in the ways these densely figurative texts recognize personhood as an effect of language and not a natural given. If personhood is an effect of language, then it can be reimagined (a chance that may inspire hope as well as worry, for if discursive definitions of personhood can be expanded, they can also be narrowed). In their own ways, both *The Black Jacobins* and "To Toussaint L'Ouverture" recognize the importance of personification to personhood, however complicated, and write Haiti's legacy with repeated turns to literary figures.

To recognize the importance of personification to personhood is, as Angela Naimou writes in *Salvage Work*, to recognize the legal person as a legal fiction. The word "person," Naimou notes, is drawn from the Latin *persona*, which refers to the mask worn by classical actors on stage to amplify the actor's voice: "Individual political rights depend on giving the abstract figure of the person a human face and voice."[5] If person is a figure, then the workings of figure offer no retreat from the workings of politics. Instead, and as Barbara Johnson suggests, "the study of rhetoric has everything to do with human politics," by which she means not only politics among humans but also the politics of who gets to count as human, as having a voice, who is recognized as having the right to claim the rights of personhood.[6] "The very essence of a political issue," Johnson continues, "hinges on the structure of figure."[7]

James begins a lecture from 1971 titled "How I Would Rewrite *The Black Jacobins*" with an early moment in the book when he quotes a white European traveler's description of what James in 1971 calls "a gang of slaves at work."[8] The author of the quote, Justin Girod-Chantrans, focuses on the ways the enslaved men and women of the labor crew strain themselves in the sun. "Today I would not do that," continues James: "I would write descriptions in which the black slaves themselves, or people very close to them, describe what they were doing and how they felt about the work they were forced to carry on ... I would want to say what we had to say about how we were treated, and I know that that information exists in all the material."[9] Instead of quoting Girod-Chantrans, James would search the archive for what enslaved persons had to say about how they were treated, giving voice back to the Black bodies Girod-Chantrans sees but does not hear. To quote Girod-Chantrans is to let those who had a voice continue to speak (and reproduce only some names from the historical archive). Speaking in 1971, James is sure that other names and other voices exist in the historical archive. He is not wrong, but in more recent years scholars have begun to question the archive. To tell the story of young Black women in the early twentieth century and to learn from what these women knew about Black life, Saidiya Hartman describes in her recent book *Wayward Lives, Beautiful Experiments* how she "pressed at the limits of the case file and the document, speculated about what might have been," imagined and amplified moments when vision and dreams seemed possible.[10] All of the characters and events are real, but at key moments, Hartman reports, she had to break open the archival documents to produce what she calls "a dream book for existing otherwise."[11] Quoting Hortense Spillers, Christina Sharpe describes the experience of the archive in more general terms in *In the Wake*: "Again and again scholars of slavery face absences in the archives as we attempt to find 'the agents buried beneath' the accumulated erasures, projections, fabulations, and misnamings."[12] And Sharpe explains how scholars of slavery, anti-Blackness, and Black life trying to make sense of silences and absences get wedged in the partial truths of the archive. "The methods most readily available to us," she continues, "force us into positions that run counter to what we know," and, more pointedly, are often in the service of larger destructive anti-Black systems of power.[13] With this history in mind, and as she develops a method for encountering a past that is not past, as the effects of slavery continue to shape the present, Sharpe thinks with and through a metaphor, the metaphor of the wake "in the entirety of its meanings (the keeping watch with the dead, the path of a ship, a consequence of something, in the line of flight and/or sight, awakening, and consciousness)."[14] Inhabiting and even rupturing this figure makes possible, argues Sharpe, a mode of work, *wake work*, for imagining a future for Black lives.

In focusing on texts by James and Wordsworth, I focus not only on slightly earlier texts but also texts that exhibit great wariness of figure and explore its limitations, specifically the limitations of personification; and yet at key moments in their different attempts to write the story of Toussaint Louverture—even though, and unlike the young Black women Hartman writes about, Louverture is present in the archive—both James and Wordsworth are drawn to figure, specifically animating figures that throw into question the given-ness of a concept like person.

That Tranquility

The Black Jacobins was one of the first histories of the San Domingo and Haitian Revolution to take seriously the perspective of the enslaved person, insisting on slavery as a modern capitalist institution while simultaneously displacing the importance of Europe for any consideration of the future of revolutionary history. As David Scott writes in *Conscripts of Modernity*, James's preface is a profound reflection on the idea of the writing of history, "the problem of the representation of the past in the present and the problem of the historian's relation to that practice of historical representation."[15] The historian does not write calmly of the past but engages the past for the sake of the present.

In alluding to Wordsworth's preface in his own, James draws a marked contrast between his revolutionary approach to history, a history very much addressed to his present moment, and Wordsworth's aesthetic approach to poetry, his retreat, at least for James, from history into aesthetics. By alluding to Wordsworth indirectly, substituting "great English writer" for the proper name, James connects Wordsworth's definition of "poetry" and, accusingly, England's response to events in San Domingo and later Haiti to England's response to events in the 1930s.

The passage from Wordsworth's preface is so well known that James need only allude to it. "I have said," writes Wordsworth, "that Poetry is the spontaneous overflow of powerful feelings; it takes its origin from emotion recollected in tranquility."[16] James returns to a moment in Wordsworth's preface that is already, in a way, a return, as Wordsworth himself indicates with the phrase "I have said." Wordsworth introduces the term tranquility to prevent misunderstanding and qualify any too-easy association of poetry with spontaneity. But even in the earlier use of the phrase "spontaneous overflow" Wordsworth similarly qualifies the assertion, explaining that poems require long and deep thought.[17] Wordsworth's attention to poetic discourse, especially his focus on rhyme and meter, leads him, upon reflection, from the phrase *deep thought* to the word *tranquility*. James objects to Wordsworth's second thought. Pathetic situations and sentiments, explains Wordsworth, especially those "which have a great proportion of pain connected to them, may be endured in metrical composition, especially in rhyme."[18] Wordsworth works in the tension between language closely resembling the language of real life and the music of harmonious metrical language, which places the reader at some minimal remove from the situation and, therefore, makes pain more endurable. James recognizes that history is an art as well as a science but offers a slightly different sense of art's importance. The mission of history, of the art of history, is not to make pain more endurable. *The Black Jacobins* is of its moment and full of fever and fret. The pain of the present should be conveyed in and through the past.

For James tranquility is an escape, as one wraps oneself in ideology to shield oneself from the emergencies of history. With the allusion to that great English writer, James unites Wordsworth and England, but James is perhaps less interested in the specifics of Wordsworthian tranquility as it plays out in poetry than in what tranquility has become in James's present, in the 1930s. To celebrate tranquility in an age so full of violent conflict is a sign, for James, that the status quo is working for one. Only some can afford to be tranquil under these conditions. James expands on his sense of tranquility in the next—and final—paragraph of the preface, in which he pointedly describes the social mission of history: "Tranquility to-day is either innate (the philistine) or to be acquired only by a deliberate doping of the personality."[19] Those able to achieve a condition of tranquility deny their own historical moment either by taking no interest in it or actively working to ignore it. James associates tranquility with the philistine (a commonly used but still richly complicated figure for the uneducated or unsophisticated) or with the drug user, it would seem, or someone who sacrifices personality to purchase tranquility. The *OED* suggests that the use of philistine to refer to an uneducated or unenlightened person, one indifferent to art and culture, emerges in the early nineteenth century, with Romanticism. And for years scholars of Romanticism have similarly worried Romantic Ideology. Is Romanticism a revolutionary project or an escape from history, a celebration of human rights or a deliberate doping of the personality? Does Romanticism form a national identity (a white national identity) or do the texts contribute resources that work against nationalist and imperialist projects? These questions have received renewed focus thanks to the work of the Bigger 6 Collective (@Bigger6Romantix), an effort to decolonize Romanticism, as well as the scholarship of Manu Samriti Chander, Deanna Koretsky, and Patricia Matthews, among many others.[20] James, who discusses the importance of white Romantic poets to his early education, does not answer these questions in his preface in any straightforward manner, as he turns away from Wordsworth (or at least a certain version of Wordsworth) to Keats, so not away from Romanticism toward something else but from one white Romantic poet to another.[21]

In contrast to Wordsworth's "tranquility" James embraces fever and fret, borrowing a phrase from Keats's "Ode to a Nightingale."[22] James continues his concluding paragraph: "It was in the stillness of a seaside suburb that could be heard most clearly and insistently the booming of Franco's heavy artillery, the rattle of Stalin's firing squads and the fierce shrill turmoil of the revolutionary movement striving for clarity and influence. Such is our age and this book is of it, with something of the fever and the fret."[23] With his image of the tranquil seaside suburb James suggests at one and the same time that the literal quietness of the seaside suburb (the relative absence, in other words, of much competing noise) helps make the booming of artillery more audible; and, more metaphorically, that the relative stillness of the suburbs anticipates the violence necessary for revolution, as if the heavier the stillness the more shrill the turmoil necessary to break it, a stillness in no small part, James implies, Romanticism's legacy. In the stillness of the seaside suburb, it takes a lot to ignore the boom, rattle, and fierce shrill of turmoil. James writes neither in literal nor metaphorical stillness. He cannot choose but hear. *The Black Jacobins* is very much a book "of our age" and full of "fever and fret," and with this sentence James again draws on Romantic figures, as "our age" and "fever and fret" evoke the title of William Hazlitt's most successful book (*The Spirit of the Age*) and John Keats's "Ode to a Nightingale": "Fade far away, dissolve, and quite forget / What thou among the leaves hast never known, / The weariness, the fever, and the fret."[24] Given the context of the line, it would be possible to lump Keats in with Wordsworth and so associate Romanticism in general with escapist fantasies, as Keats's speaker longs to forget the very fever and fret to which James holds fast. In using Keats to counter Wordsworth, though, James suggests a reading of Keats's poem. When the speaker is tolled back to himself and so does not fly with the nightingale, he returns to the fever and the fret. James finds in one Romantic poet (Keats) the language to counter another (Wordsworth). If Romanticism struggles with history, James, as historian, finds himself struggling with Romanticism as he begins *The Black Jacobins*.[25]

From Volcanos to Bones

Though James uses Wordsworth's poetics to articulate his historical method, in their individual prefaces both question the power of personification. Wordsworth explains quite famously in the preface to *Lyrical Ballads*: "I have endeavoured utterly to reject [personifications] as a mechanical device of style."[26] Earlier in his own preface, and in describing the purpose of history and of history writing, James first objects to historians who have been more artists than scientists (from Tacitus to Macaulay, from Thucydides to Green): "They wrote so well," writes James, "because they saw so little," as if writing well were incompatible with seeing much.[27] But James then objects to historians only interested in science and structure, who tend to "a personification of ... social forces" and turn "great men" into "merely or nearly instruments in the hands of economic destiny."[28] In a line that gives Fred Moten his opening in *Black and Blur*, James continues: "As so often the truth does not lie in between."[29] "Great men make history," continues James, "but only such history as it is possible for them to make," echoing Marx's famous line from *The Eighteenth Brumaire of Louis Bonaparte*.[30] James writes in tension with a version of historical inquiry that embraces art at the expense of science as well as with a version of historical inquiry that too rigidly embraces science. This later version of inquiry, perhaps paradoxically, depends on figure, the power of personification, as historians confuse persons, "great men," for personifications. James is after a particular kind of vision.

At this point and after taking issue with available historical methods, the preface becomes densely figurative as James invokes the metaphor of revolutions as volcanic and then describes his own historical method as seeing into the very bones of previous revolutions. Searching for a proper figure that raises but does not resolve the tension between available forms of historical inquiry, a figure that does not allow the historian to rest comfortably in the between, James begins with a metaphor familiar to aesthetic discourse:

> In a revolution when the ceaseless slow accumulation of centuries bursts into volcanic eruption, the meteoric flares and flights above are meaningless chaos and lend themselves to infinite caprice and romanticism unless the observer sees them as projections of the sub-soil from which they came. The writer has sought not only to analyse, but to demonstrate in their movement, the economic forces of the age, their moulding of society and politics, of men in the mass and individual men; the powerful reaction of these on their environment at one of those rare moments when society is at boiling point and therefore fluid.[31]

Here, James uses the word "romanticism" in a generally negative sense, invoking an image drawn from the discourse of the sublime and imagining the historian moved by the meaningless chaos of eruption. Though the eruption may inspire imaginative writing, the sublime experience of meteoric flares will not lead to proper historical analysis. Kant includes volcanic eruptions in his list of sublime objects in his *Critique of the Power of Judgment*.[32] As David McCallam explores in an essay on volcanic metaphors, the image of the volcano shifts from aesthetic to revolutionary discourse in the eighteenth century with the help of Edmund Burke.[33] Unlike one beholden to Romanticism, attentive to flares and flights and aesthetic experience, James analyzes the movement of economic forces, the projections from the subsoil. One must, explains James, take an interest in what is not yet visible.

But perhaps because volcanic metaphors are common in revolutionary discourse, James moves to a second metaphor: the historian as radiologist looking into the bones of previous revolutions. In his *History of the Russian Revolution*, translated into English in 1932 and a model for *The Black Jacobins*, Leon Trotsky identifies a series of worn-out metaphors, including any association of revolution with volcanic eruption: "Physical analogies with revolution come so naturally that some of them become worn-out metaphors: 'volcanic eruption,' birth of a new society,' 'boiling-point'."[34] Countering the aestheticist Romantic who admires meteoric flares, James first embraces worn-out metaphors, including the idea of society at a boiling point, but then quickly substitutes another image, as if acknowledging that the historian has to do something other than investigate the subsoil: "The violent conflicts of our age enable our practised vision to see into the very bones of previous revolutions more easily than heretofore."[35] James moves the reader from a geological to a medical metaphor, from a worn-out volcanic metaphor to a stranger and therefore more striking one: the revolution as skeletal body. Though the focus on analyzing what is beneath the surface or skin remains consistent, James, writing against structuralist historians who miss the person for the personification, brings back into his discourse the idea of the human, or the nearly human, the biological, skeletal animal. The transition from subsoil to bones requires animating tropes like anthropomorphism and personification. And as James makes this switch from one metaphor to another he draws upon Romantic poets, alluding to Wordsworth's preface and borrowing from Keats's poem in his preface's concluding paragraphs, drawing upon writers that similarly raise complicated questions about the power of animating figures in the rhetoric of personhood.

And Take Comfort

James describes as the main theme of *The Black Jacobins* "the transformation of slaves ... into a people,"[36] which is not possible without similarly transforming the very idea of and legal definition for *persons*. His primary interests are legal and historical but his sometimes densely figurative language showcases the importance of rhetoric to legal personhood.[37] When Wordsworth writes of the Revolution in San Domingo and of Toussaint Louverture, he too stages his intervention through repeated use of animating figures. James cannot begin *The Black Jacobins* without Wordsworth (without some encounter with Wordsworth) and like James Wordsworth focuses on the figure of Louverture in his most explicit writing on the Revolution, addressing him via apostrophe in a poem first published in February of 1803 in the *Morning Post*, during the time of Louverture's imprisonment (he was imprisoned in the summer of 1802 and died in April of 1803), and revised for publication in *Poems, in Two Volumes* (1807) and then repeatedly throughout his career.

Responses to Wordsworth's poem are mixed. On the one hand, as David Geggus remarks, Wordsworth's sonnet is one of the few texts by a white English Romantic writer that responds at all, let alone with sympathy, to the San Domingo Revolution.[38] James's criticisms aside, Wordsworth engaged more directly with historical events unfolding in San Domingo than most of his contemporaries. On the other hand, as Srinivas Aravamudan and others have argued, the poem also substitutes poetic abstraction for material reality, as slavery and revolution give way, poetically, to air, earth and skies, exultations, agonies, and love.[39] In other words, and in various ways one finds discomfiting, the poem translates Louverture into an example of

104   HAITI'S LITERARY LEGACIES

human spirit and preaches patience in response to horrific violence. The version of the poem first published in 1803 reads:

> Toussaint, the most unhappy Man of Men!
> Whether the rural Milk-maid by her Cow
> Sing in thy hearing, or thou liest now
> Alone in some deep dungeon's earless den,
> O miserable Chieftain! where and when
> Wilt thou find patience? Yet die not; do thou
> Wear rather in thy bonds a cheerful brow:
> Though fallen Thyself, never to rise again,
> Live, and take comfort. Thou hast left behind
> Powers that will work for thee; air, earth, and skies;
> There's not a breathing of the common wind
> That will forget thee; thou hast great allies;
> Thy friends are exultations, agonies,
> And love, and Man's unconquerable mind.[40]

The poet-speaker does not express anger at Louverture's betrayal and capture (as the hoped-for revolution is endangered and Napoleon's efforts to reinstate slavery in the colony furthered); instead, what's needed most is patience: "where and when / Wilt thou find patience?" And for these opening lines readers are, I think, right to question the poem's commitment to historical reality. As Aravamudan suggests, the poem leaves a "whiff of poetic embarrassment," as nature is substituted for tropical oppression.[41] Turning away from the revolution's human costs, Wordsworth, Charles Forsdick argues, "inaugurate[s] a representational tradition ... from which the fully incendiary implications of Toussaint are persistently absent."[42]

Indeed, the differences are plain between Wordsworth's poem and the conclusion to James's play, *Toussaint Louverture*, first performed in London in 1936, two years before the publication of *The Black Jacobins*. For many readers, Wordsworth's suggestion that Louverture "has left behind/Powers that will work for [him]" is emptied of significance when those powers are identified as air, earth, and skies—none of which can easily organize a prison-break. By contrast, James's play concludes with Dessalines's learning of Louverture's death. And with word of Louverture's death, Dessalines knows that he was deceived and that the Revolution must enter a bloodier phase. In other words, the "powers that will work" for Louverture after his death are not air and earth and skies but swords and muskets: "now see," says Dessalines, "what the treacherous dogs have done. See what they want to do. But we shall avenge Toussaint. French blood in torrents shall flow."[43] Wordsworth's turn to air, earth, and skies in 1803 is also a turn away from swords and muskets and blood, as Nature stands in for (and so fends off the need for) human violence; in this way Wordsworth removes from the scene

SEEING INTO THE VERY BONES   105

of revolutionary history the whiff of flesh and blood and bone. Dessalines's metaphor, "blood in torrents," reverses Wordsworth and substitutes human violence for Nature, as blood flows like a mountain stream.

Over the next twenty years, Wordsworth revised the sonnet, altering the opening lines and softening the image of Louverture imprisoned:

> Toussaint, the most unhappy of men!
> Whether the whistling Rustic tend his plough
> Within thy hearing, or thy head be now
> Pillowed in some deep dungeon's earless den;
> O miserable Chieftain! where and when
> Wilt thou find patience?[44]

Where Toussaint in the 1803 version is *alone* in a dungeon, in the later version he is *pillowed*, minimizing the pain of imprisonment. As Joshua Stanley notes, the original image of the milk-maid recalls an image from *The Prelude*, where Wordsworth and a friend happen upon a hunger-bitten girl in France walking a heifer. At the sight, writes Wordsworth, "my friend / in agitation said, 'Tis against *that* / which we are fighting,'" by which the friend means poverty: "I with him," continues Wordsworth, "believed/ Devoutly that a spirit was abroad / Which could not be withstood, that poverty, / At least like this, would in a little time / Be found no more."[45] When Wordsworth revises the poem he substitutes a more generically pastoral figure, the whistling rustic, for one, the milk-maid, that he at least associates with revolution and social justice.

Can You Hear Me Now?

Though Wordsworth changes the singing milk-maid to a whistling rustic, he maintains the dominant rhetorical structures of the poem. He moves through a series of animating figures, beginning the poem abruptly with an apostrophe, animating "Toussaint" at the very moment that he is in the process of being reduced to an object. Through the power of apostrophe, the poet makes present one who is absent, makes live one feared dead, and draws him to England from his prison in France through the power of poetic address. But the poem then immediately raises as a question whether Louverture can hear. Indeed, one striking feature of Wordsworth's poem is his almost relentless use of figures frequently associated with the rhetoric of personhood: apostrophe, anthropomorphism, and even personification (this despite Wordsworth's well-known rejection of personification in his preface to *Lyrical Ballads*), as the poem builds from apostrophe to personification. The poem foregrounds the importance even as it throws into question the power of figure in revolutionary discourse, especially a revolutionary discourse that aims to secure legal personhood for those considered non-persons by colonial powers.

Poetry, maybe especially Romantic poetry, is full of apostrophes, and as Jonathan Culler and Barbara Johnson have explored, poets employ apostrophe as a way of figuring poetic power.[46] Through apostrophe the poet figures himself or herself as one capable of giving life to inanimate objects, as apostrophe recalls the power of language to make present the absent and animate the inanimate. Johnson, for instance, takes as a motivating example Percy Shelley's "Ode to the West Wind," where the poet-speaker laments his near inanimacy; he grants life through the power of apostrophe to the wind and then asks that the wind grant him an animacy he fears he has lost. The poet animates the wind, turns it into an interlocutor, and thereby proves his poetic power.

Though Wordsworth revises his poem, he keeps the apostrophe and in both versions the question posed by the poem is whether the putative addressee can hear, can hear the song of the milk-maid or the whistling of the rustic. These figures within the poem are also figures for the poetic utterance itself. As Carmen Faye Mathes writes, these figures "suggest self-consciousness ... about listening's limits."[47] In both versions, the poem offers an apostrophe and then quickly challenges the apostrophe's rhetorical power. Instead of assuming that the addressee can hear the apostrophic utterance, Wordsworth stages it as a question. If "Toussaint" cannot hear the milk-maid's song or the rustic's whistling, can he hear the speaker's call, can he hear Wordsworth's poem? And what is true of Toussaint "in" the poem, figuratively speaking, is true as well of Wordsworth's reader "outside" the poem, the reader of the *Morning Post*.

In these opening lines, Wordsworth comments on the figure of apostrophe, which positions the reader as if overhearing the utterance. The poet-speaker turns away from any present audience to address an absent or inanimate entity. Here in "To Toussaint L'Ouverture" Wordsworth turns away from his *Morning Post* audience to address Louverture, situating the reader in the position of someone overhearing the address. There is a high degree of poetic self-consciousness in this opening, as Wordsworth addresses an absent addressee, who needless to say did not have access to the *Morning Post*, and then wonders if the absent addressee can hear. Readers of the *Morning Post*—the present, literal audience—are positioned as if overhearing the poet's call, just as Louverture, in the poem, is positioned as if overhearing the milk-maid's song. And so, just as the opening lines question whether Louverture can overhear another's utterance, the poem raises the equally challenging question: can readers of "To Toussaint" hear the poet's call?

The poem only figuratively offers comfort to Louverture; its literal existence offers comfort to Wordsworth's readers who might feel distraught at his capture and the threat his capture poses to revolutionary potential. But given that Wordsworth's absent addressee is only maybe able to hear a song (for only maybe can "Toussaint" hear the milk-maid), so too is Wordsworth's more literal addressee, the reader of the *Morning Post*, only maybe able to hear this song, this statement of support for Toussaint Louverture and the Revolution he fostered. The poem, in other words, asks: can you hear me now? And in this way the poem raises a question about what poetry can do in the wake of revolution.

Thy Friends Are Exultations

In the preface to *The Black Jacobins*, James objects to historians' reliance on personification and then moves toward his own anthropomorphic figure for revolutionary history, seeing into the bones of previous revolutions. In the opening lines of "To Toussaint L'Ouverture," Wordsworth questions the power of apostrophic address but, like James, does not retreat or withdraw from figure. Even if one rightly takes readers of the *Morning Post* as Wordsworth's primary audience in 1803, the poem begins by introducing the very likely possibility that it will fall on deaf ears; the poem grants a dungeon ears only to take them away, an example of something like apophatic anthropomorphism. This gentle undercutting of rhetorical power is made more overt with the empty, pedantic command that follows: "O Miserable Chieftain ... die not." Here, "die not" shows up the inadequacy of language to effect the desired change (or, more precisely, prevent an unwanted change). But with this facile imperative Wordsworth increases the pressure he puts on rhetoric. If the poem opens with a question about the effectiveness of rhetoric (by staging the fiction of apostrophe most explicitly), the next chance for rhetoric is the imperative command: don't die! The command expresses Wordsworth's own pain and anticipatory mourning but only serves to undercut the power of speech (or the power of such speech acts) to bring about a desired reality.

With repeated failures, the poem continues to reach toward more figures. The imperative command is followed by the lines of the poem that have formed the basis for many critical readings. The poet turns to air and earth and skies and the common wind to make of the elements personified and anthropomorphized entities capable of working to advance Louverture's cause. The poet offers "Toussaint," his imagined reader, the comforts of fiction and figure, which is also to say that he offers the same to his literal reader. But just as Wordsworth questions the efficacy of apostrophe, here too he questions the efficacy of figures. One can hear in "air, earth, and skies" something like "errors and sighs," as if the very language of the poem in ramping up rhetorical power makes rhetorical power indistinguishable from errors and sighs.

It is conventional enough for poets to question their own power, and so transform weakness into a triumph of self-consciousness, but in the context of a poem about a man who worked to transform the enslaved into persons, the appearance in the poem of figures that expand and challenge who or what can be identified as a person, who or what can claim the right to personhood, is strikingly relevant. The sestet remains relatively unchanged after initial publication, and with the sestet the poet switches from apostrophe to more straightforward anthropomorphism. And the poem concludes with lines that come so very close to personification: "Thy friends are exultations, agonies, / And love, and Man's unconquerable mind." The lines do more than simply suggest that those who exalt Toussaint or agonize over his treatment and express love for him are his friends. Compression turns exultations, agonies, and love into friends and so, however minimally, personifies them, transforming something a person might feel (love, for instance) into something like a person.

The possible failure of apostrophe to accomplish the impossible (which is, of course, also the power of apostrophe to accomplish in the realm of fiction what cannot be accomplished in the world of the real, which Fredric Jameson describes as ideology); the possible failure of apostrophe in "To Toussaint L'Ouverture" leads Wordsworth to further animating figures, anthropomorphisms and personifications. Like James's preface, Wordsworth's poem is a dense weave of figures, as the poem explores the limitations of and possibilities for rhetoric in the future for personhood. At one and the same time Wordsworth retreats into figure (adding figure to figure and so constructing for himself and others a comforting fiction) but also shows up the ways figure resists such retreat. If the poem retreats into figure, then it does so only by expanding the concept of person to include non-persons, filling the world with persons. And given that Wordsworth writes the poem in response to the possible failure of a revolution to expand the concept of personhood to include the formerly enslaved, the retreat into figure is no simple retreat. The recompense personification offers is certainly not abundant, but as an investigation into the power of animating figures like the concept of "Man" itself, the poem explores the ways political structures hinge on rhetorical ones.

The Progress of Poetry?

Prompted by passion, Wordsworth personifies passions and expands the category of person. Is a certain confusion over personhood in 1802—at least for Wordsworth's white audience—necessary for the revolution to proceed? Is the fight for personhood possible without personification? These questions are raised to a particular pitch at the end of the poem as Wordsworth alludes to Thomas Gray's "The Progress of Poesy" with the closing phrase "Man's unconquerable mind," for Gray is the very poet Wordsworth uses in the preface to exemplify how not to personify. In this way, "To Toussaint

L'Ouverture" is strangely entangled with the preface to *Lyrical Ballads*, as Wordsworth rewrites in the context of revolution his earlier statement on poetic discourse.

Gray's poem offers a nationalist story of poetry's development from Greece to Britain. The phrase to which Wordsworth is drawn and that he includes in "To Toussaint L'Ouverture" appears in the middle of Gray's poem, as Gray transitions from describing poetry's power to curb violence to celebrating the future of poetry in Britain. Gray's nationalist project is veined with racist discourse, as the poet-speaker imagines two similarly distant but opposed places in the story of poetry's development, "ice-built mountains" and "Chili's boundless forests," combining metaphors of natural scarcity with metaphors of natural abundance.[48] Gray imagines "shaggy forms" roaming over the mountains and a "savage youth" in Chile who repeats the "feather-cinctured" chief. The presence of Poesy—who "deigns" to hear the loose numbers wildly sweet—is proof of a universal unconquerable mind, and the unconquerable mind proof of Freedom's holy flame. Poesy's power cannot wane for it inspires even shivering natives and savage youths. Its full power in now headed to Britain, suggests Gray's poem.

In drawing on the poem, Wordsworth risks placing Louverture in the position of Gray's shaggy form, shivering native, or savage youth, making of him proof of Man's unconquerable mind (and so similarly enlisting Louverture in a white, nationalist project). As Alexander G. Weheliye has recently written in *Habeas Viscus*, generalizing projects in Western European literature celebrate a "Man" almost always white.[49] Weheliye draws on the work of Sylvia Wynter, who argues that the struggle of our times is the struggle against the overrepresentation of "Man," as the figure of Man emerges in rationalist discourse to legitimate the subordination of the world and well-being of racialized others: "one cannot 'unsettle' the 'coloniality of power' without a redescription of the human outside the terms of our present descriptive statement of the human, Man, and its overrepresentation."[50]

Wordsworth transforms Louverture into a figure for and proof of "Man's unconquerable mind" and finds in the sort of poem he otherwise rejects for artistic reasons support for his ideological position. From the first line, Wordsworth's poetic gesture is on the side of inclusion as Wordsworth recognizes Louverture's humanity, if only barely, as Paul Youngquist notes, calling "Toussaint" the "most unhappy Man of Men."[51] But the turn to Gray at the end of the poem does not fit easily with this abstracted, generalizing impulse. "Man's unconquerable mind" is set off from the list of Louverture's "friends" by the additional conjunction, one necessitated by the poem's regular meter: "And love, and Man's unconquerable mind." Like exultations, agonies, and love, "Man's unconquerable mind" is a friend to Louverture but unlike exultations, agonies, and love, all of which are expressed by Wordsworth's imagined reader and so taken as signs of support for Louverture's cause, the additional *and* makes of "Man's unconquerable mind" almost an after-thought. Where meter, according to Wordsworth's preface, is to make pain endurable, here it results in a challenge to the abstracted generalization of Man the poem offers in celebratory conclusion. The poem concludes with the image of a minimally personified unconquerable mind, Man's unconquerable mind, supporting Louverture as friend. With the reference to Man's unconquerable mind, the poem repeats the racialized ideology present in Gray's poem; but in calling Man's unconquerable mind a "friend," the poem distances itself from the very same figure and reflects on that racialized ideology. In other words, and as Kristen Mahlis suggests, the poem ignores that "the unconquerable mind of man is as much the author of slavery as its opponent."[52] But by personifying Gray's figure and making Man's unconquerable mind a "friend," Wordsworth introduces distance between Louverture and "Man" at the very moment the poem seems otherwise to assert identity. Wordsworth's personification throws into doubt the honesty of a concept like "Man." If Louverture is the most unhappy Man of men, then he is included in the idea of Man (if only at the limit). If "Man's unconquerable mind" is Louverture's friend, only his friend, then he is excluded from the figure; he is merely adjacent to and not a member of the category. Whether Wordsworth intends to or not, the subtle personification of Man challenges the self-evidence of Man as concept and category. The poet's commitment to the work of animating figures shows up their potential to craft and complicate a generalized abstraction.

In "To Toussaint L'Ouverture," Wordsworth returns to the writing of Gray to think through questions about personification, now in the context of revolutionary struggle for personhood. In making of Man's unconquerable mind a friend, Wordsworth personifies a personification, and so calls attention to a deceptively simple fact: the general concept of "Man" has always been a personification. While awareness of this fact does not make the figure any less powerful, violent, or potentially corrosive, if the figure is made to function it can be made to function differently; if it is made to function, its most corrosive functions can be unmade.

Flesh and Blood and Bone

In this essay I have read my primary texts in a reverse chronological order, James's preface to *The Black Jacobins* first, Wordsworth's sonnet second. In reading "To Toussaint L'Ouverture" alongside and after *The Black Jacobins* I have tried to make newly legible Wordsworth's investigations into the power of animating figures, as the poem proceeds from apostrophe to personification. In the light of Louverture's revolutionary challenge to the prevailing Enlightenment definition of human person, one that generalized a concept of Man in order to exclude enslaved persons, Wordsworth's poem challenges the given-ness of Man, shows the limits of the concept, and

SEEING INTO THE VERY BONES   111

demonstrates some of the various ways personhood itself is constructed, crafted, made. There may be no personhood without a poetics (from the Greek for "to make"), and for this reason there may yet be hope for future revolutions. James's rejection of Wordsworthian "tranquility" is clear in *The Black Jacobins*, but James is never more Wordsworthian than when he, like Wordsworth, rejects personification to differentiate his historical method from others. To conclude this essay, I return to James's preface, for James's resonance with Wordsworth exceeds Wordsworth's sloganeering about "tranquility."

When James turns his 1936 play *Toussaint Louverture: The Story of the Only Successful Slave Revolt in History* into his 1938 history *The Black Jacobins: Toussaint L'Ouverture and the San Domingo Revolution*, he moves Louverture's name to the second part of the title.[53] James was in part inspired to write about Louverture because white historians systematically refused to recognize not only the importance of the Haitian revolution to Enlightenment history but also Louverture's unique, compelling, and very human character. *The Black Jacobins* aspires to present Louverture as a fully realized, and so complicated, historical actor and he is, as David Scott argues, the Romantic hero of the book.[54] But as James writes in the preface, "Toussaint did not make the revolution. It was the revolution that made Toussaint."[55] Throughout the book, James attempts to work out this relationship between historical actors and social and economic forces, this relationship between persons and personifications. The second sentence of the quote above ("It was the revolution that made Toussaint"), by granting a minimally personified revolution the power to make Louverture already anticipates the broader questions James pursues in *The Black Jacobins*. Who or what gets to be the subject of a sentence, who or what the object? In this instance, the grammatical subject of the sentence, "it," is not the same as the logical subject ("revolution"), and neither are human subjects. James's sentence demonstrates how common it is to personify abstractions in English and how difficult it can be to stop. Questions about agency are entangled with questions about personification, as James shows in the next paragraph, and such personifications trouble James because he does not want to reduce Louverture to an object of history. If Louverture can be reduced to an object of historical processes as easily as he can be made the direct object of a sentence, then his fight for personhood has failed. To continue that fight, James rescues the person from the personifications of historians, but even that, to paraphrase James, is not the whole truth.

Like Wordsworth, James rejects personification but then turns toward an embodied figure to close his preface. In the preface to *Lyrical Ballads*, and after rejecting personification, Wordsworth explains his wish "to keep [his] reader in the company of flesh and blood,"[56] replacing the language of men—and so, by extension, the language of Man—with a figure neither fully human nor inhuman.[57] As Wordsworth turns from personification to "flesh and blood," James turns from personification to the "very bones of previous revolutions," the use of the genitive granting revolution a body. James dislikes the ways historians imagine an economic destiny with hands but counters by granting previous revolutions "bones," bones the historian sees into.

In drawing on this figure James may have in mind a passage from the 1804 Haitian Declaration of Independence, where Jean-Jacques Dessalines suggests that if the new Haitians fail to avenge the victims of colonial power, the bones of the dead will expel them from shared tombs: "Descendres-vous dans la tombe sans les avoir vengés? Non, leurs ossements repousseraient les vôtres" (Will you be granted entry to shared tombs if you have not avenged them? No, their very bones will expel yours).[58] Dessalines animates the bones, granting them an imagined, future agency. In *Beyond the Slave Narrative*, Deborah Jenson contrasts Louverture's defensive and arguably pre-Romantic rhetorical identifications with Dessalines's critical reappropriations of political tropes and figures. "There is a fluid, sustained, and critical structure of metaphor in the major Dessalinian texts, regardless of secretarial signature," writes Jenson: "Dessalines generally was attentive to established political tropes, but rather than reiterating them, he recast them so that they were simultaneously appropriated and critiqued."[59] Perhaps from Louverture's failure, Dessalines learns something about the power of figurative language.

In following James's invitation in the preface to *The Black Jacobins* to read him alongside Wordsworth, I have tried to make newly legible not only James's struggle with the general ideologies frequently associated with Romanticism but also his rigorous investigations into the power of figure, the power of personification, as well as the power of more enigmatic figures like the bones of a revolution. In response to the failure of Enlightenment Man to recognize Black personhood, texts like *The Black Jacobins* and "To Toussaint L'Ouverture" offer readers, the fevered and fretful, a chance to articulate poetic methods of critical inquiry that do not leave unacknowledged the difficulty of determining what a person is while, at the same time, acknowledging the importance of personhood to future revolutionary action.

Notes

1 C. L. R. James, *Black Jacobins: Toussaint L'Ouverture and the San Domingo Revolution*, 2nd ed., rev. (New York: Viking, 1963), xi.

2 For careful disambiguation of rhetorical terms like personification and anthropomorphism, see Barbara Johnson, *Persons and Things* (Cambridge, MA: Harvard University Press, 2008), especially 3–26.

SEEING INTO THE VERY BONES

3 James, *Black Jacobins*, xi.

4 James refers to the French colony of Saint-Domingue by its contemporaneous English name of San Domingo and I will follow his practice throughout this chapter.

5 Angela Naimou, *Salvage Work: U.S. and Caribbean Literatures amid the Debris of Legal Personhood* (New York: Fordham University Press, 2015), 19.

6 Barbara Johnson, *A World of Difference* (Baltimore: Johns Hopkins University Press, 1987), 6.

7 Johnson, *A World of Difference*, 184. As Sara Guyer writes, "Insofar as politics is a matter of power, and power is a matter of violence, the essence of any political issue is the question of life and death, of *the power over life and death*, and this is where poetry (or figural language) comes into the picture," Sara Guyer, *Reading with John Clare: Biopoetics, Sovereignty, Romanticism* (New York: Fordham University Press, 2015), 14.

8 C. L. R. James, "Lectures on *The Black Jacobins*," *Small Axe* 8 (September 2000): 65–112, 99.

9 James, "Lectures," 99.

10 Saidiya Hartman, *Wayward Lives, Beautiful Experiments: Intimate Histories of Riotous Black Girls, Troublesome Women, and Queer Radicals* (New York: W. W. Norton, 2019), xiv–xv.

11 Hartman, *Wayward Lives*, xv.

12 Christina Sharpe, *In the Wake: On Blackness and Being* (Durham: Duke University Press, 2016), 12.

13 Sharpe, *In the Wake*, 12.

14 Sharpe, *In the Wake*, 17–18.

15 David Scott, *Conscripts of Modernity: The Tragedy of Colonial Enlightenment* (Durham: Duke University Press, 2004), 34.

16 William Wordsworth, *The Major Works, including* The Prelude, ed. Stephen Gill (Oxford: Oxford University Press, 2000), 611.

17 The earlier appearance of the phrase is on page 598 of *The Major Works*.

18 Wordsworth, *The Major Works*, 610.

19 James, *Black Jacobins*, xi.

20 See for instance Manu Samriti Chander, *Brown Romantics: Poetry and Nationalism in the Global Nineteenth Century* (Lewisburg, PA: Bucknell University Press, 2017); Deanna Koretsky, "Habeas Corpus and the Politics of Freedom: Slavery and Romantic Suicide," *Essays in Romanticism* 22, no. 1 (2015): 21–33, and *Death Rights: Romantic Suicide, Race, and the Bounds of Liberalism* (Albany: SUNY Press, 2021); and Patricia A. Matthew, "Jane Austen and the Abolitionist Turn," *Texas Studies in Literature and Language* 61, no. 4 (Winter 2019): 345–61.

21 Chander's *Brown Romantics* follows a similar narrative arc, which is not to suggest that Chander was necessarily influenced by James. But after discussing the work of colonial poets Henry Derozio, Egbert Martin, and Henry Lawson,

who both echo and challenge the tropes of white Romantic poets, Chander concludes with a discussion of Brown Keats.

22 Readers of *Black Jacobins* have noted the presence of Keats as well as Wordsworth in James's preface. See Scott, *Conscripts of Modernity*, 24. See also Christian Høgsbjerg, "'The Fever and the Fret': C. L. R. James, the Spanish Civil War and the Writing of The Black Jacobins," *Critique* 44, nos. 1–2 (2016): 161–77, 162.

23 James, *Black Jacobins*, xi. On the immediate context, see Høgsbjerg, "The Fever and the Fret."

24 John Keats, *Keats's Poetry and Prose*, ed. Jeffrey N. Cox (New York: Norton, 2009), 458.

25 James writes elsewhere of the power of Romanticism, referring for instance to Romanticism as one of the most fascinating problems in the world in his 1931 article "The Problem of Knowledge." See Christian Høgsbjerg, *C.L.R. James in Imperial Britain* (Durham: Duke University Press, 2014), 162.

26 Wordsworth, *The Major Works*, 600.

27 James, *Black Jacobins*, x.

28 James, *Black Jacobins*, x.

29 James, *Black Jacobins*, x. Fred Moten, *Black and Blur* (Durham: Duke University Press, 2017), 1–27.

30 Karl Marx, *Later Political Writings*, ed. and trans. Terrell Carver (Cambridge: Cambridge University Press, 2006), 32. See also Scott, *Conscripts of Modernity*, 38.

31 James, *Black Jacobins*, x–xi.

32 Immanuel Kant, *Critique of the Power of Judgment*, trans. Paul Guyer and Eric Matthews (Cambridge: University of Cambridge Press, 2000), 144.

33 David McCallam, "The Volcano: from Enlightenment to Revolution," *Nottingham French Studies* 45, no. 1 (Spring 2006): 52–68.

34 Leon Trotsky, *History of the Russian Revolution*, trans. Max Eastman (Chicago: Haymarket Books, 2008), 819.

35 James, *Black Jacobins*, xi.

36 James, *Black Jacobins*, ix.

37 In recent years, literary scholars have taken sustained interest in the ways literary texts reimagine the difference between persons and things, persons and non-persons, a tradition that includes Wordsworth's writing. My thinking on these questions has been shaped by Barbara Johnson's work, especially *Persons and Things*. Other exceptional work more focused on the eighteenth century includes Clifford Siskin, "Personification and Community: Literary Change in the Mid and Late Eighteenth Century," *Eighteenth-Century Studies* 15, no. 4 (Summer, 1982): 371–401; Jonathan Lamb, *The Things Things Say* (Princeton: Princeton University Press, 2011); and Heather Keenleyside, *Animals and Other People: Literary Forms and Living Beings in the Long Eighteenth Century* (Philadelphia: University of Pennsylvania Press, 2016).

On the question of personification and legal personhood, I am particularly indebted to Monique Allewaert's *Ariel's Ecology: Personhood and Colonialism in the American Tropics, 1760–1820* (Minneapolis: University of Minnesota Press, 2013) and Angela Naimou's *Salvage Work: U.S. and Caribbean Literatures amid the Debris of Legal Personhood* (New York: Fordham University Press, 2015).

38 David Geggus, "British Opinion and the Emergence of Haiti, 1791–1805," in *Slavery and British Society 1776–1846*, ed. James Walvin (New York: Macmillan Press, 1982), 123–49.

39 Srinivas Aravamudan, *Tropicopolitans: Colonialism and Agency, 1688–1804* (Durham: Duke University Press, 1999), 310–12. See also Mary Kelly Persyn, "The Sublime Turn Away from Empire: Wordsworth's Encounter with Colonial Slavery, 1802," *Romanticism on the Net* 26 (2002); Charles Forsdick, "Situating Haiti: On Some Early Nineteenth-Century Representations of Toussaint Louverture," *International Journal of Francophone Studies* 10, no. 1+2 (2007): 17–34; Kristen Mahlis, "Signifying Toussaint: Wordsworth and Martineau," *European Romantic Review* 22, no. 3 (2011): 331–7; Joshua Stanley, "Wordsworth and 'the most unhappy man of men': Sentimentalism and Representation," *European Romantic Review* 26, no. 2 (2015): 185–204; Carmen Faye Mathes, "Listening Not Listening: William Wordsworth and the Radical Materiality of Sound," *European Romantic Review* 28, no. 3 (2017): 315–24.

40 Wordsworth, *The Major Works*, 282.

41 Aravamudan, *Tropicopolitans*, 311–12.

42 Forsdick, "Situating Haiti," 29.

43 C. L. R. James, *Toussaint Louverture: The Story of the Only Successful Slave Revolt in History (A Play in Three Acts)*, ed. Christian Høgsbjerg (Durham: Duke University Press, 2013), 132.

44 On various versions of the poem, see William Wordsworth, *"Poems in Two Volumes," and Other Poems, 1800–1807*, ed. Jared Curtis (Ithaca: Cornell University Press, 1983), 160–1.

45 Wordsworth, *The Major Works*, 522. See Stanley, "Wordsworth and 'the most unhappy man of men,'" 190.

46 For example, see Barbara Johnson, *A World of Difference*, 184–200; and Jonathan Culler, *Theory of the Lyric* (Cambridge, MA: Harvard University Press, 2015), 186–243. For more on interpretive difficulties raised by apostrophe, especially in the context of historical poetics, see the recent exchange between Paul Fry and Virginia Jackson: Paul Fry, "The New Metacriticism and the Fate of Interpretation," *Modern Language Quarterly* 81, no. 3 (2020): 267–87; Virginia Jackson, "Historical Poetics and the Dream of Interpretation: A Response to Paul Fry," *Modern Language Quarterly* 81, no. 3 (2020): 289–318.

47 Mathes, "Listening Not Listening," 322.

48 *The Poetical Works of Gray and Collins*, ed. Austin Lane Poole (Oxford: Oxford University Press, 1926), 48–9. All quotations are taken from the second stanza of the second part of the poem.

49 Alexander G. Weheliye, *Habeas Viscus: Racializing Assemblages, Biopolitics, and Black Feminist Theories of the Human* (Durham: Duke University Press, 2014). Weheliye argues that even more recent discourses of bare life and biopolitics associated with the work of Giorgio Agamben and Michel Foucault, discourses that emerged to challenge the supposedly transparent and universal conception of Man in the late-twentieth century, also underscore it by placing "racial difference in a field prior to and at a distance from conceptual contemplation" (7). In other words, Agamben and Foucault risk repeating the very sorts of abstraction and generalization that they may otherwise wish to challenge.

50 Sylvia Wynter, "Unsettling the Coloniality of Being/Power/Truth/ Freedom: Toward the Human, After Man, Its Overrepresentation—An Argument," *CR: The New Centenial Review* 3, no. 3 (Fall 2003): 257–337, 267.

51 In "Black Romanticism: A Manifesto," Paul Younquist notes that from the first line of the poem Toussaint is "Man at its most liminal, least human, most unhappy" (9). *Studies in Romanticism* 56 (Spring 2017): 3–14.

52 Mahlis, "Signifying Toussaint," 334.

53 On the relationship between drama and history, see Rachel Douglas, *Making The Black Jacobins: C. L. R. James and the Drama of History* (Durham: Duke University Press, 2019).

54 Scott, *Conscripts of Modernity*, 74.

55 James, *Black Jacobins*, x.

56 Wordsworth, *The Major Works*, 600.

57 For an extended reading of this figure in the context of bare life, see Sara Guyer, *Romanticism After Auschwitz* (Stanford: Stanford University Press, 2007), 46–70.

58 Quoted in Deborah Jenson, *Beyond the Slave Narrative: Politics, Sex, and Manuscripts in the Haitian Revolution* (Liverpool: Liverpool University Press, 2011), 96. For more on the figure of bones in the Haitian Revolution, see also Tanya L. Shields, *Bodies and Bones: Feminist Rehearsal and Imagining Caribbean Belonging* (Charlottesville: University of Virginia Press, 2014). I thank Deborah Elise White for drawing my attention to the figure of bones in the Haitian Declaration of Independence.

59 Jenson, *Beyond*, 90. For more on the contrast, see also page 56.

5

Unavowed Community in Kleist's *Betrothal in San Domingo*

Kir Kuiken

Written shortly before his suicide in 1811, Heinrich von Kleist's *Betrothal in San Domingo* constitutes one of the first literary responses to the Haitian Revolution in European Romanticism. As such it registers elements of the political earthquake that constituted that event for Europeans. While Kleist's *Betrothal* is undoubtedly permeated by the racialist categories that underpinned the colonial slave system, it also registers something that I call, following Benjamin, the Haitian Revolution's "shock effect:"[1] the novella indexes and is itself informed by the Revolution's dislocation of a specific set of aesthetic and political coordinates. For European observers of the Haitian Revolution, particularly those under a French authority which had long ago ceased to be the vanguard of the ideals that had given the *French* Revolution its purpose, Haiti represented something of a riposte to European exceptionalism. It at once suggested that the emancipatory promise of revolution had changed hands and that this shift had, at least potentially, revised the nature of that promise—its scope and application. If Kant had in 1797 interpreted the French Revolution not in terms of its actuality but in terms of the enthusiasm for its *promise*,[2] the Haitian Revolution could be said to have re-concretized that promise—albeit in ways that were not exactly greeted with the same enthusiasm. The Haitian Revolution, unlike the French one, provoked profound questions about the nature of the collectivity capable of giving itself its own newfound sovereignty—questions that, as Andreas Gailus suggests, pertained to the "subject of the revolution": "Who belonged to the 'we' in whose name the ideas of freedom, equality and fraternity were pronounced?"[3] In what follows I argue that Kleist's *Betrothal* presents the effect of this shock most of all in the way that it intertwines the problem of promising or avowal (the "*Verloben*" of its title translated in English as "betrothal") with the question of community.

Scholarship on Kleist's *Betrothal in San Domingo* revolves around two main tendencies: on the one hand, starting with Sander Gilman's seminal essay on the aesthetics of blackness in Kleist's novella, critics have focused on the politics of race and slavery which are crucial to the novella's setting during the final period of the Haitian Revolution's push toward an independent state; others read *Betrothal* within a set of concerns about political sovereignty and the epistemology of language that characterizes much of Kleist's other literary production.[4] Joshua Gold argues, for example, that "the Haitian Revolution caught Kleist's attention not because of his interest in race (which the text may or may not faithfully reflect), but because race, a domain that has in the modern era inspired intellectually spurious speculation on the necessary continuity between physical appearance and psychology, furnished him with a figure of interpretation."[5] This essay offers another possible explanation for the novella's setting: its belated attempt to register the Haitian Revolution's radical and unprecedented historical significance.[6] That significance, for Kleist, had to do with the fact that the Haitian Revolution represented an example of the overthrow of French colonial power, which was then at its height.[7] That it was former slaves that had liberated themselves from French occupation, however, as opposed to a Germany mostly acquiescent to French rule, was not immaterial.

As problematic as they sometimes are, the depictions of race and slavery in *Betrothal* cannot fundamentally be distinguished from the novella's exploration of the nature of insurgency, the relation between language and political sovereignty, or the question of community that is often central to Kleist's work. In other words, the novella's involvement with racialized tropes—including the figure of the "tropical temptress" who "uses her sexuality ... to facilitate the brutal violence of the male revolutionaries"[8]— refracts Kleist's interest in the conditions of a community and of a sovereignty that would be different from and irreducible to the state. This doesn't seem to me to be a particularly surprising claim, given the context— occupied Prussia—in which Kleist was writing. Kleist is famously and explicitly insurrectionary: *The Battle of Hermann (die Hermmanschlacht)*[9] explores how an insurgency making use of specific guerilla tactics can turn a disparate and divided population against an occupying power. His other works frequently examine the conditions in which a collectivity mounts a resistance to a thoroughly corrupted juridical-political domain.[10]

However, in the case of *Betrothal*, the corrupted juridical–political domain in question is not French colonial power but the emerging

UNAVOWED COMMUNITY

independent Haitian state which, while predicated on the destruction of the old colonial order organized on hierarchies of race, nonetheless, in Kleist's novella, ends up reinstating a new order organized on a similar basis as an *inversion* of that hierarchy. The crucial background for the story is built on what Michael Perraudin identifies as a historically accurate albeit anachronistically situated law that required the killing of white and Creole French citizens[11] and which organizes the major tension in the novella between friend and enemy.[12] It is in this context that the "betrothal" of the title takes shape, placing the central character, a mixed-race mulatto named Toni, in existential peril once she refuses to abide by this edict. This is why I propose that the political dimension of Kleist's novella be situated in terms of the trope of the numerous star-crossed lovers that populate his other writings. Kleist's depiction of an insurgent community ranges from the macro-level of a nascent nationalism in *The Battle of Hermann*, to the micro-level of a pairing between two individuals whose very existence is incompatible with the existing juridical–political system. Yet it is only when one sees how Kleist places these two forms of community—the state and the couple—*in relation* to each other that one begins to grasp that Kleist is contrasting fundamentally different forms of community, while at the same time showing how each destabilizes the other. The prerogatives of the lovers in Kleist's novellas and plays (with the exception of *Penthilesea*) are always in conflict with the demands and prerogatives of the state.[13] The "society" of a pair of lovers, which becomes symbolic of forms of attachment that surpass the communal bonds of the nation-state, is almost always impermanent in Kleist in part because it is threatened from without by the state itself, which is usually predicated either on some form of "natural" or "spiritual" (i.e., racial or national) identification, or on a (false) abstract equality before the law. Moreover, the society of lovers is impermanent because of the fragility of what ties the lovers together in the first place: they represent a kind of degree-zero of community, a minimal relation between two that is irreducible to the state, to the social contract, or to other structures that govern collective belonging. It is in the figure of the pair of lovers that a rather different story of revolutionary "promise" emerges in Kleist's novella—one that remains decidedly *unavowed* and unavowable, and yet nonetheless proffered.

My reading of Kleist's novella draws on Maurice Blanchot's claim in *Unavowable Community* that a pair of lovers constitutes the most important example of what he calls, paraphrasing Georges Bataille, a "community of those who have no community."[14] Blanchot suggests that lovers are not just an alternative model of collectivity, but an active *contestation* of the existing constitution of the body politic: "The community of lovers—no matter if the lovers want it or not, enjoy it or not, be they linked by chance, by *l'amour fou* by the passion of death (Kleist)—has as its ultimate goal the destruction of society. There where an episodic community takes shape between two beings who are made or who are not made for each other, a war machine is set up."[15] Though this might at first sound like a retreat to the private, domestic space of individuals joined by a bond of love that is resolutely nonpolitical or that desires its own death or dissolution, it is important to remember that Blanchot begins his chapter on the community of lovers with a discussion of the events of the student uprisings in Paris in May 1968, insisting that, like the "community of lovers," the student uprising constitutes a new form of politics, one *without a determined project* and without the aim of taking over the state apparatus.[16] May 1968, according to Blanchot, produced a momentary community that, in eschewing traditional forms of sovereignty, "let a possibility manifest itself, the possibility—beyond any utilitarian gain—of a *being-together*."[17] While he describes this "being-together" in quasi-Levinasian terms as a singular relation to the other that privileges incommensurability over equality, Blanchot likewise emphasizes that the community of lovers is predicated on the motif of a *secret avowal*, the sharing of something that, because it is unknown not only to outsiders, but also to the couple themselves, cannot be verified in terms of what J. L. Austin refers to as a "felicitous" speech act.[18] Thus the titular *Verlobung* (betrothal or vow) is not quite a *Versprechen*—a promise that can be confirmed as having been made, a vow that enters the domain of speech and attestation in a context capable of ascertaining its perlocutionary force. A betrothal or *Verlobung* is not yet the performance or even the *utterance* of that speech act, as we will see. It is rather a vow to make a vow, a vow to ratify what has been promised to the other. Since traditional speech acts, particularly acts of betrothal, require the presence of a legal apparatus that would render it "felicitous," the novella gestures toward another form of "avowal" or betrothal that is *prior* to the social contract.

The "unavowed" dimension of the community of lovers, therefore, might also appear to take the form of a complete withdrawal from the space of the political, and an investment in something that eschews every form of political sovereignty because it remains "prior" to existing social relations.[19] However, in Kleist, the community of lovers is always a cipher for a *contestation* of the political as it is presently constituted, rather than the "founding" of a new politics. The "unavowable" community that they represent might be more productively understood as a differently conceived relation between the sovereign (the agency granted final authority within the political) and its ground. When Carl Schmitt defines the modern sovereign as "he who decides on the exception"[20] he makes the sovereign into a power capable of deciding the relation between norm and exception as the very basis of its own self-legitimation, where something fundamentally *outside* the law (the sovereign's own capacity to decide) grounds its very authority. Kleist, on the other hand, through the figure of the "community of lovers," contemplates an exteriority to the law that cannot be made the object of a decision. As I will argue, in Kleist, the pair of lovers performs nothing, enacts nothing, other than the overturning of a form of sovereignty predicated on its own self-authorizing mandate. In this sense, Kleist's "community of lovers" is political through and through, since it destabilizes and deracinates, through its unavowed or not-yet-felicitous avowal, social contract theories of the state and bio-political regimes reliant on the category of race or other identitarian structures. The community of lovers threatens or destabilizes these regimes, even if, in the end, those very same structures come to haunt and ultimately destroy this unavowed community once it manifests itself.

Kleist's novella is set in 1803, in the second wave of the Haitian Revolution, just prior to independence at the moment when leadership of the revolt had passed to Dessalines, who had begun a fierce military campaign to rout French forces at Port-au-Prince and cut off any possibility for the restoration of slavery on the island. A sort of fictional Dessalines, Kleist's main antagonist Congo Hoango, functions as a caricature of rebelling Black slaves. In what the novella calls an "orgy of vengeance" (*Taumel der Rache*),[21] Hoango kills his master, and claims the plantation as his own. Despite debates about the extent to which Kleist may have viewed Hoango's acts of violence as justified,[22] the novella appears initially to treat Hoango's ascendency in terms of a cycle of vengeance, a notion familiar from Kleist's other works where it is usually a sign of the corruption of the legal and political mechanisms that are supposed to administer justice. Andreas Gailus views the novella's description of Hoango's takeover of the plantation as decidedly ambiguous, caught between imagery suggestive of the establishment of a new political order and the possible repetition of the old: "Hoango's presence in the house of his master ... would be a metaphor of the failure of the revolution, its reconstitution despite the initial call for *Gleichmachung* (equality), of traditional hierarchies."[23] This reading of Hoango's actions reveals what generates the necessary conflict in Kleist's novella: coupled with the decree that all whites must be put to death, it indicates the necessary state-sanctioned friend/enemy distinction that will eventually be challenged by the lover's betrothal.

Although the possibility that Hoango's takeover of the plantation entails the reproduction or mere inversion of the old racial hierarchies dismisses Hoango's right to violence, the fact that Hoango is the first character to break a legal contract ratified under the former regime serves a larger function. After having saved his master's life and, as a result, been granted a number of privileges, Hoango nevertheless kills his master despite having been named in the master's will. In other words, Hoango rejects not only the relative privileges afforded him by the plantation regime, where a white master determines the rights or freedoms of individual slaves, but he also rejects the *entire legal framework* underpinning the structures of inheritance that perpetuate that regime—in other words, his master's will. Hoango's act of violence, therefore, takes shape within the overturning of a political order that is itself grounded in a distinct legal framework. Kleist points to this notion in one of his first descriptions of Hoango, focused on the significance of his act of killing Villeneuve, his master:

> Congo Hoango, in the general orgy of vengeance flaring up on those plantations as a result of the reckless measures of the National Convention, was one of the first to seize a gun and, mindful of the tyranny which had torn him away from his native land, he put a bullet through his master's head.

> *Congo Hoango war, bei dem allgemeinen Taumel der Rache, der auf die unbesonnenen Schritte des National-Konvents in diesen Pflanzungen auf loderte, einer der ersten, der die Büchse ergriff, und, eingedenk der Tyrannei, die ihn seinem Vaterlande entrissen hatte, seinem Herrn die Kugel durch den Kopf jagte.*[24]

Though Hoango's actions are situated in a "general orgy of vengeance," which initially suggests that he is motivated by a desire for retribution, the sentence goes on to place Hoango's acts within the context of the "reckless measures of the National Convention"—referring presumably to its decision in 1794 to abolish slavery in all French colonies. That decree in effect made the existing legal framework for slavery moot and, as a result, opened up a space in which the foundation of law could be violently contested. Hoango does precisely that by taking violent action against the "tyranny which had torn him away from his native land" in the most immediate representative of that tyranny. In other words, as Andreas Gailus has suggested, what primarily interests Kleist with regard to the Revolution is "the abyss that opens up when a cultural form of life loses its conceptual grounding."[25] I would add, however, that what also interests him is the extent to which— or the means by which—that abyss is quickly filled back in by a social order that reconstitutes itself with a vengeance, either as in *Earthquake in Chili* by the reactionary and violent return of the prior theological-political framework that had underpinned it or, as in *Betrothal*, with a new social order that simply inverts the old one.

In *Betrothal*, what follows from the initial suspension of the legal frameworks of the old order is a gradual entrenchment of the new one through the nascent state's grounding in the friend/enemy distinction, implicating everyone in the colony, and forcing everyone to choose one or the other relation to the state. Hoango is depicted not just as an example of personal vengeance, but as an active agent for the Revolution at its core: for example, when he is first introduced in the novella, he is on a mission to supply gunpowder to Dessalines. Upon his capturing of the plantation he enlists the slaves who will remain faithful to the revolutionary cause, including the two main mixed-race characters in the novella—Babekan and her daughter Toni, the product of a disavowed affair with a Frenchman. Their mixed-race status provides sufficient ambiguity concerning their allegiances and thus makes them a useful tool for luring white colonists to their death. This ruse is predicated on the inversion of prior racial hierarchies: the very same whites who had participated in the regime of slavery might be convinced that Toni and Babekan, given their liminal status, are in fact allies. The colonists' own racial categories are thus weaponized against them. However, it becomes clear that the same question of allegiance surfaces on the other side of the friend/enemy divide. While Hoango utilizes Toni's mixed-race status to his advantage, the very thing that makes her such a successful ploy is also what necessitates the implementation of a second form of the death penalty: "he [Hoango] encouraged her to allow their visitors every intimacy, except the last, which was forbidden on pain of death" (*sie ermunterte dieselbe, den Fremden keine Liebkosung zu versagen, bis auf die letzte, die ihr bei Todesstrafe verboten war*).[26] This "last intimacy" constitutes, for Hoango, a betrayal of the edict that ordains the friend/enemy distinction, because it denotes a moment when that line has presumably been crossed. But, as we will see, Toni's liminal status is problematic for both sides of this divide, and provides the novella with the main test not only of this distinction's reliability, but of the form of community capable of resisting it.

This liminality can to some extent be found on the other side of the pair of lovers as well, represented by Gustav von der Ried, a Swiss mercenary serving in the French army at Fort Dauphin, who is attempting to lead his family to safety in Port-au-Prince. The fact that he is Swiss, and therefore not French (or somewhere between French and German), places him in a similarly liminal position to Toni, overriding the fact that he is nonetheless serving in the military on behalf of Napoleonic France. Gustav's liminal status is reinforced later in the novella when we learn that he was in fact determined at one point to be an enemy of the very state in whose military he is currently serving: during his time in Strasbourg, on the border between France and Germany, he is accused of conspiring against the French revolutionary tribunal. Though this fact is revealed much later in the novella, Gustav is positioned as potentially both friend *and* enemy, since he at one point had to flee the friend/enemy distinction set up by the very same colonial power with which the slaves are at war.

Unlike the prior friend/enemy distinction based on *ideological* differences, however, Gustav is clearly aware of, and actively participates in, the friend/enemy distinction predicated on race that governs the current situation. The fact that this criterion is constructed around a visible feature intended to indicate a specific interiority means that Toni's liminality is the crucial one, marking as it does the only *ambiguous* liminality in the eyes of the state. Hers, and her mother Babekan's racial identification, is the only one that requires an act of interpretation, a decision about where to place them in the friend/enemy divide. Thus, when Gustav arrives at Hoango's plantation while he is away delivering supplies, his encounter with Babekan and Toni

124 HAITI'S LITERARY LEGACIES

is possible only because their position with regard to the edict is unclear. Gustav, seeking food and shelter for himself as well as his white family who is hiding in the woods, approaches the plantation and is initially alarmed when Babekan greets him at the door. Unable to ascertain whether or not she is friend or foe, Gustav falls back on existing racial categories to determine the attitude he must adopt toward her. In their first exchange, before Gustav can ascertain whether he has indeed arrived at a place of refuge or not—that is, before he can verify her racial status—he asks for a verbal confirmation of her identity:

> In all the darkness of a night of wind and rain somebody knocked at the back door of [Hoango's] house. Old Babekan, already in bed, rose and, only flinging a skirt around her waist, opened the window and asked who was there. "In the name of Mary and all the saints," said the stranger in a whisper, positioning himself under the window, "answer me one question before I tell you." And so saying he stretched out his hand through the darkness of the night to seize the old woman's hand, and asked: "Are you a negress?" Babekan said: "You must certainly be a white man if you would rather look this pitchblack night in the face than a negress. Come in," she added. "and have no fear. It is a mulatto who lives here and nobody else is in the house except my daughter, a mestiza."
>
> *In der Finsternis einer stürmischen und regnigten Nacht, jemand an die hintere Tür seines Hauses klopfte. Die alte Babekan, welche schon im Bette lag, erhob sich, öffnete einen bloßen Rock um die Hüften geworfen, das Fenster, und fragte, wer da sei? "Bei Maria und allen Heiligen," sagte der Fremde leise, indem er sich unter das Fenster stellte: "beantwortet mir, ehe ich Euch dies entdecke, eine Frage!" Und damit streckte er, durch die Dunkelheit der Nacht, seine Hand aus, um die Hand der Alten zu ergreifen, und fragte: "seid Ihr eine Negerin?" Babekan sagte: nun, Ihr seid, gewiß ein Weißer, daß Ihr dieser stockfinstern Nacht lieber ins Antlitz schaut, als einer Negerin! Kommt herein, setzte sie hinzu, und fürchtet nichts; hier wohnt ein Mulattin, und die einzige, die sich außer mir noch im Hause befindet, ist meine Tochter, eine Mestize!*[27]

This first encounter between Gustav and Babekan unfolds around an initial verbal oath. Asking her to confirm her racial identity "in the name of Mary and all the saints," Gustav in effect asks her to verbally confirm what he cannot otherwise *see* given the obscurity of the night. This very question gives his own racial identification away, since Babekan correctly ascertains why he is asking it. Having been assured verbally that she and Toni are of mixed race, Gustav is then confronted by Nanky, Hoango's young Black son who, awoken by the commotion of Gustav's arrival, locks the gate behind him. The sight of Nanky is Gustav's first visual confirmation that the

UNAVOWED COMMUNITY 125

plantation is in fact inhabited by Black slaves, and it is only thanks to the arrival of Toni that he refrains from escaping back into the night. By shining the light of the lantern she carries directly onto her face, Toni makes clearly visible her mixed-race status, and calms Gustav enough to convince him to enter the house.

Toni's arrival at the scene generates a series of ruses, all of them predicated on ambiguous markers of racial affiliation that force Gustav to engage in a series of acts of interpretation. But whereas his initial encounter with Babekan was based on a verbal oath or confirmation, once he enters the house his sense of trust is predicated entirely on visual appearances and on his faculty of vision. Seeing that Gustav is in fact armed, Babekan begins by (falsely) insisting that, by simply giving him shelter, they have in fact revealed their allegiances:

> "What is the meaning of the sword there under your arm? It looks ready to be used. We," she added, pressing a pair of spectacles on to her nose, "have risked our lives to offer you shelter in our house. Have you entered after the custom of your compatriots to repay this kindness with treachery?"
>
> "was bedeutet der Degen, den Ihr so schlagfertig unter Eurem Arme tragt? Wir haben Euch", setzte sie hinzu, indem sie sich die Brille aufdrückte, "mit Gefahr unseres Lebens eine Zuflucht in unserm Hause gestattet; seid Ihr herein gekommen, um diese Wohltat, nach der Sitte Eurer Landsleute, mit Verräterei zu vergelten?"[28]

This will not be the first or last time that the characters' joint awareness of the law of the land will be used as a pretext to affirm a bond of trust, predicated on the idea that since Babekan and Toni have purportedly risked their lives by providing shelter for someone designated an enemy, they too have become enemies of the state along with him. It is, however, this notion of sharing the risk of a death sentence in the name of an apparent form of hospitality that provokes Gustav's sense of faith in Babekan. When Babekan asks Gustav where his companions are so that they too can be lured to the plantation in their turn, Gustav emphatically states why he feels he can trust her with this information: "'To you' the stranger replied after a moment's thought, 'to you I can entrust myself. There is in the colour of your face a glimmer of my own colour, and it shines forth at me'" (Euch, versetzte der Fremde, nachdem er sich ein wenig besonnen hatte: Euch kann ich mich anvertrauen; aus der Farbe Eures Gesichts schimmert mir ein Strahl von der meinigen entgegen).[29] This initial appeal to a visible "shining forth" of a bond between them, grounded in white racial identity, is used by Babekan as a way of gaining Gustav's trust, not just in the sense of a shared opposition to state decrees, but in the sense of a shared racial identification. It is only because Gustav sees his own skin color

HAITI'S LITERARY LEGACIES

reflected in hers that he falls prey to her ruse. Babekan then reinforces this initial identification by suggesting that she and her daughter too are often the objects of Hoango's vengeance against white rule since, as mixed-race, they are subject to the same decree concerning whites:

> "Ah the rage and hatred," said the old woman piously. "Is it not as if the hands of a body or the teeth of a mouth were to set upon one another merely because they are not all made the same? How can I—whose father was from Cuba, from Santiago—help it that a shimmer of lightness dawns on my face when daybreak comes? And how can my daughter, conceived and born in Europe, help it that the full daylight of those parts is reflected in hers?"

> *"Ja, diese rasende Erbitterung" heuchelte die Alte. "Ist es nicht, als ob die Hände eines Körpers, oder die Zähne eines Mundes gegen einander wüten wollten, weil das eine Glied nicht geschaffen ist, wie das andere? Was kann ich, deren Vater aus St. Jago, von der Insel Cuba war, für den Schimmer von Licht, der auf meinem Antlitz, wenn es Tag wird, erdämmert? Und was kann meine Tochter, die in Europa empfangen und geboren ist, dafür, daß der volle Tag jenes Weltteils von dem ihrigen widerscheint?"*[30]

When Gustav asks explicitly whether she and Toni are "accursed" along with the Europeans, she replies by claiming she is under the same threat by Hoango as he is:

> [Hoango's] chief desire is to bring down the vengeance of the blacks upon us white and creole mongrels, as he calls us, partly in order to be rid of us, since we speak against his savage treatment of the whites, and partly so that he might appropriate what little fortune we should leave behind.

> *Und nichts wünscht er mehr, als die Rache der Schwarzen über uns Weiße und kreolische Halbhunde, wie er uns nennt, hereinhetzen zu können, teils um unserer überhaupt, die wir seine Wildheit gegen die Weißen tadeln, los zu werden, teils, um das kleine Eigentum, das wir hinterlassen würden, in Besitz zu nehmen.*[31]

Babekan engages in a series of appeals to both the racial hierarchies Gustav uses to interpret the world, and to notions of bourgeois individualism and abstract equality that Babekan uses to suggest the similarity in their situations. Her peculiar diction and emphasis on the determinate article *eines* describing the physical violence perpetrated by ostensibly neutral "hands," "bodies," and "mouths" deemphasizes the political and colonial structures that condition the violence perpetrated by individuals. Using language similar to Gustav's centered around the notion of a "light" that glimmers or shines forth through the skin, Babekan deftly uses Gustav's own racial logic to identify herself as almost-white, and therefore likewise the target of the "vengeance of the blacks" on account of her racial identification. Her own claims to "speak against the savage treatment of the whites" is meant to enlist Gustav's sense of a shared *fraternité* commensurate with an abstract equality that claims to be "blind" to race, while nonetheless being surreptitiously predicated upon it.

Underneath this ruse, of course, is Babekan's fidelity to Hoango's cause, founded on the injustices she experienced under the French judicial system. Babekan's deception, which includes convincing Gustav that bringing his family to the plantation that night would run the risk of them encountering troops of armed Black slaves, which in turn enables her to keep the group divided so as not be overpowered, relies on the newfound "trust" generated by the "shadow of kinship" (*Schatten von Verwandtschaft*)[32] that Gustav claims to recognize in Babekan and Toni. Unbeknownst to him, however, that very kinship also turns out to be the source of Babekan's enmity, despite her pledging to help Gustav's family with food and provisions "for the sake of the European, my daughter's father" (*um des Europäers, meiner Tochter Vater willen*).[33] In fact, it is this European—along with the oath he openly breaks in a French court—that becomes the motivation for her willingness to aid Hoango. This background unfolds when Toni returns to offer Gustav the meal she has prepared. He asks about Toni's place of birth, whereupon Babekan proceeds to outline the story of her daughter's origins: while on a trip to Europe with the wife of her master fifteen years earlier, Babekan had given birth to Toni, whose father was a rich merchant from Marseilles named Bertrand. This information appears initially to Gustav to reinforce the lines of "kinship" he detects in both Babekan and Toni. Having been born to a rich representative of the French government, Toni, he insists, is in fact "a rich and respectable young woman" (*ein vornehmes und reiches Mädchen*) who can "press her claims to these advantages and might hope one day at her father's hand to be introduced into more brilliant circumstances than those in which she was living now" (*daß sie Hoffnung hätte, noch einmal an der Hand ihres Vaters in glänzendere Verhältnisse, als in denen sie jetzt lebte, eingeführt zu werden!*).[34] Gustav, in other words, interprets Babekan's tale in terms of the European kinship structures he already shares with them.

However, as we soon learn, those kinship structures are the target of a *false oath* that Bertrand had taken to legally *disavow* any relation to Toni. Given his status in the French government and his desire to marry another rich (white) Frenchwoman, it is impossible for Bertrand to acknowledge having a child with a slave. While Babekan testifies truthfully that he is the father of her child, Bertrand, on the other hand, disavows her in a public oath:

M. Bertrand, when I was pregnant in Paris, because he was ashamed on account of the rich lady he wished to marry, denied in court that he was the father of my child. I shall never forget the oath he had the nerve to look me in the face and swear; a gall-fever followed it, and soon after that sixty lashes given me on the orders of M. Villeneuve which have left me consumptive to this day.

Herr Bertrand leugnete mir, während meiner Schwangerschaft zu Paris, aus Scham vor einer jungen reichen Braut, die er heiraten wollte, die Vaterschaft zu diesem Kinde vor Gericht ab. Ich werde den Eidschwur, den er die Frechheit hatte, mir ins Gesicht zu leisten, niemals vergessen, ein Gallenfieber war die Folge davon, und bald darauf noch sechzig Peitschenhiebe, die mir Herr Villeneuve geben ließ, und in deren Folge ich noch bis auf diesen Tag an der Schwindsucht leide.[35]

This betrayal, which takes the form of an oath (*Eidschwur*)—literally an "oath-swear"—that is given perlocutionary force through the imprimatur of French juridical authority, demonstrates the extent to which, in this case, the "felicity" of Bertand's speech-act is founded on a legal authority that not only wishes to maintain its monopoly on violence, leading to Babekan's merciless beating, but also makes race—a category supposedly outside the alleged neutrality of the law—the final arbiter in the case, since it is only Bertand's status as a free white that allows his false testimony to have any legal force. Though this incident in the story might appear to simply provide Babekan with the motivation to side with Hoango, Kleist's detailed description of Bertrand's betrayal is significant since it provides a counterpoint to the "oath-swear" (*Eidschwur*) that will soon take place between Gustav and Toni, and that can be read as either reaffirming Gustav's race-based understanding of "kinship," or as pointing to something else. Babekan's story suggests that the social order which recognizes Bertrand's oaths under the guise of an ostensible universality of law is nothing but a sham, a way of perpetuating war by other means. Moreover, Babekan's story orients the reading of all of the ensuing events—those leading up to the betrothal of Toni and Gustav—by focusing our attention on the conditions in which the groundlessness of the law, its establishment by direct or surreptitious violence,[36] opens up an abyss of legitimation. Essentially, the novella asks whether avowals, oaths, and testimonies are to be considered "felicitous" only if they make reference to a legal order that is itself predicated on violence. In the absence of the fiction of a rational, grounded universal order of law and justice, Gustav's and Toni's oath to each other (the titular "betrothal") takes on the role in the novella of an alternative form of oath or promise, one that can neither be recognized by the state nor, in the case of Gustav, by the lovers themselves.

In a similar vein, the novella also examines how a different conception of a moral order beyond state law also emerges as one of the ways in which the characters justify their allegiance to one of the sides of the conflict. As the conversation between Gustav, Toni, and Babekan continues, Toni inquires as to "how the whites had made themselves so detested" (*wodurch sich den die Weißen daselbst so verhaßt gemacht hätten*)[37] in Fort Dauphin. While the obvious answer is systematic oppression and the brutal regime of slavery, Gustav stresses individual culpability:

> The madness of liberation which has seized all the plantations drove the blacks and the creoles to break the chains by which they were oppressed and to be revenged upon the whites for many wrongs done them by a few reprehensible members of that race.

> *Der Wahnsinn der Freiheit, der alle diese Pflanzungen ergriffen hat, trieb die Negern und Kreolen, die Ketten, die sie drückten, zu brechen, und an den Weißen wegen vielfacher und tadelnswürdiger Mißhandlungen, die sie von einigen schlechten Mitgliedern derselben erlitten, Rache zu nehmen.*[38]

Although Gustav's explanation may sound like an attempt to exonerate himself in advance for the cruelty of slavery, in fact the point is to set up a counter-narrative to the obligations incurred by racial and state affiliations in the name of a divine order capable of judging the actions of each side of the conflict independently and from the perspective of a justice beyond law. Gustav then tells Toni the story of a female slave who, punished and then sold for failing to succumb to her master's sexual demands, discovers during the revolt where the master is sheltering from Black revolutionaries. After three years of suffering for her refusal to sexually submit, she proceeds to infect him with yellow fever through sexual relations. James Martin correctly suggests that this story, along with the one Gustav tells Toni about his former (white) fiancée Mariane, is designed to juxtapose the female slave to Toni and to manipulate her "into choosing the side of the virtuous whites in the racial conflict and thus saving and protecting Gustav's life."[39] But there is another reason: Gustav's insistence that the slave's act be read in the context of a form of divine justice, rather than an earthly one:

> The stranger, placing his napkin on the table, replied that, heart and soul, he felt there could be no justification, however tyrannous the whites had been, for an act of such base and abominable deceit. The vengeance of heaven, he said, and rose in passion to his feet, was disarmed by it, the angels themselves, outraged, sided with those who were in the wrong, and for the upholding of order, human and divine, took up their cause.

> *Der Fremde, indem er das Tuch auf dem Tische legte, versetzte: daß nach dem Gefühl seiner Seele, keine Tyrannei, die die Weißen je verübt, einen Verrat, so niederträchtig und abscheulich, rechtfertigen könnte. Die Rache des Himmels, meinte er, indem er sich mit einem leidenschaftlichen*

HAITI'S LITERARY LEGACIES

Ausdruck erhob, würde dadurch entwaffnet: die Engel selbst, dadurch empört, stellten sich auf Seiten derer, die Unrecht hätten, und nähmen, zur Aufrechthaltung menschlicher und göttlicher Ordnung, ihre Sache![40]

Importantly, the same appeal to the "vengeance of heaven" as a justice beyond law will be invoked by Babekan when she eventually discovers Toni's own deception—her attempt to protect Gustav from Hoango's vengeance after their sexual encounter: "She [Babekan] called her contemptible and treacherous and said, averting her face where she lay against the table-leg; God's vengeance, even before she had any pleasure from her shameful act, would overtake her" (*Sie nannte sie eine Niederträchtige und Verräterin, und meinte, indem sie sich am Gestell des Tisches, an dem sie lag, umkehrte: die Rache Gottes würde sie, noch ehe sie ihrer Schandtat froh geworden, ereilen*).[41] In identifying *both* acts as subject to divine vengeance the novella stresses the fact that any sense of a transcendent, heavenly authority has also become unreliable as a source of moral and political right. Since both sides can equally lay claim to it, it no longer functions as a stabilizing force of ethical behavior. The consequence, as the novella implies, is a form of responsibility based on something far more terrestrial and mundane: a fidelity, however impossible, to the other or to the other's death—an allegiance that, as we will see, entails a very different kind of ethical faith.

That faith will be focused around the nature of the "betrothal" that occurs between Gustav and Toni. Having finished his meal, Gustav retires to his room which has been prepared by Toni. What follows is a scene of seduction that involves Toni's transgression of the command to avoid sexual consummation. Soon thereafter, Hoango unexpectedly returns to the plantation and Toni is forced to maintain the ruse of her allegiance to the friend/enemy distinction: she ties Gustav to the bed while he sleeps, but at the same time seeks the aid of Gustav's family to come to rescue him. It is important to note that the exact moment of Gustav and Toni's "betrothal," or what precisely constitutes it, has achieved little critical consensus. For unlike Bertrand's oath in court, their engagement is never explicitly uttered and hence gives rise to a range of possibilities. Joshua Gold, for instance, insists that the kiss Toni gives Gustav while he sleeps is the vow (*Eidschwur*) that constitutes her unspoken oath.[42] Gailus, on the other hand, identifies two different moments of "betrothal": the first would be Gustav's focus on the sexual act itself as a "transcendental version of betrothal characterized by male narcissism and the avoidance of otherness," while the second, recognized only by Toni, is without foundation, and entails tying Gustav to the bed with the rope as a "counterreferential expression" of love entirely unmoored from existing frameworks of interpretation.[43] The reason for this proliferation of possibilities is not only that we are dealing with nonverbal gestures, but also ones that have no context in which they might be verified as "felicitous," except retroactively. However, contrary to Gailus's contention that the mutual death of the lovers entails "the death of betrothal" as the "death of the possibility of referential and intersubjective connectedness figured in the trope of 'betrothal,' "[44] the novella seems to suggest an *Eidschwur* or oath that is different from "a medium of a repetition compulsion that moves toward death and the dissolution of otherness."[45] In fact, the novella demonstrates that repetition lies *on the other side* of the betrothal, when something akin to its "felicity" is required—the same moment when Gustav, for instance, reinstitutes prior communal structures (the friend/enemy distinction) in order to interpret Toni's fidelity. Another community is thus figured by Kleist in the space of a peculiar kind of performative evoked in the unverifiable moment of Toni and Gustav's "betrothal," in which not only Gustav, but the reader too, is forced to interpret an oath that hasn't been articulated in any previously formulated language, and that has been withdrawn in advance from any determined context in which its felicity might be assured. After all, is it a performative if it has never been enunciated, yet it annuls prior avowals or oaths, and invents something unprecedented in their place?

The question of repetition and difference is in fact placed front and center in Toni and Gustav's "betrothal" since their engagement is itself framed by Gustav's account of his prior engagement to Mariane Congreve, a woman sentenced to death for her association with Gustav. Gustav is initially attracted to Toni in part because of a "faint resemblance, he could not have said with whom, which he had noticed on first entering the house" (*eine entfernte Ähnlichkeit, er wußte noch selbst nicht recht mit wem, auf, die er schon bei seinem Eintritt in das Haus bemerkt hatte*).[46] Toni's "resemblance" to Mariane owes itself this time to something other than race. Toni enters this reference to a prior *Verloben* by playing with the golden cross around Gustav's neck, a symbol of his prior betrothal to Mariane which will eventually become his betrothal-gift (*Brautgeschenk*) to Toni. The story of this prior betrothal emphasizes the similarities in the two pairs of lovers: each lover is sworn to the other in the context of a different friend/enemy distinction. Gustav, who made public remarks about the corruption of the French Revolutionary Tribunal, is denounced. Though he evades capture, Mariane does not, and is sent to the guillotine for her association with him as an enemy of the state. While Gustav attempts to save her on the scaffold by identifying himself in order to die in her place, she refuses to acknowledge him, and is beheaded in front of him. The purpose of this "repetition," however, is not a simple identification of Toni's betrothal to Gustav as equivalent to Mariane's—that reading would indeed entail, as James Martin suggests, Toni's identification with a virtuous *white* lover, in contradistinction to the treacherous Black one Gustav mistakes her for.[47] The question that marks the crucial difference between the two stories is who commits the murder: in the former case, Mariane becomes a victim of the state; in the latter, it is Gustav who becomes Toni's executioner. At stake, therefore, is not an identification between the two women, but rather Gustav's inability to recognize the unavowed betrothal between Toni and himself. What distinguishes the two "betrothals," moreover, is the difference between an enunciated and a non-enunciated oath or avowal. Unlike Mariane, whose guilt is by mere association with Gustav, and whose fidelity to Gustav is openly declared and publicly sanctioned, Toni, by having sexual relations with Gustav, places herself under threat of the same death sentence as Gustav while also being in a situation in which she is potentially imperiled by both sides of the friend/enemy distinction. The "betrothal" between Gustav and Toni, therefore, has no possibility of being recognized by anyone but themselves.

In the absence of a verifying structure or context, when the moment in which their fidelity to each other hangs over the abyss of a performative without felicity and the reconstitution of the old order of friend and enemy, the precise moment wherein each character comes to recognize him or herself as "betrothed," as given over to the other, bifurcates. For Gustav, it appears to be commensurate with the sexual act. Gustav's first response is to take the fact of their sexual encounter as proof of his own safety; what he understands about this fact pertains mostly to the assuaging of his own fears over Toni's political allegiances. By contrast, Toni's response to their sexual encounter is far less clear: holding herself and weeping on the bed, she remains inconsolable. James Martin is right to interpret her tears variously, either as a recognition of her betrayal of Gustav, or as a betrayal of Babekan (or perhaps a recognition that she has doomed herself to death).[48] What has received less attention, though, is that the tears, ambiguous as they are, uncover the motif of an *unavowed* betrothal that makes Gustav's attempt at a moment of *verbal* betrothal both assymetrical and incomplete. When he proceeds to place the "betrothal gift" of the gold cross around her neck as a sign of his own fidelity, substituting Toni for his dead betrothed Mariane, "she [Toni] only wept and would not listen to his words" (*sie in Tränen zerfloß und auf seine Worte nicht hörte*).[49] The verbal and symbolic act of betrothal in the story is offered, but is never counter-signed, by Toni who, throughout Gustav's long explanation of what he presumes to be their engagement, gives "no answer to anything he said, but only lay there among the disordered pillows, her head in her arms in a wordless grief" (*doch da sie auf alles, was er vorbrachte, nicht antwortete, und, ihr Haupt stilljammernd, ohne sich zu rühren, in ihre Arme gedrückt, auf den verwirrten Kissen des Bettes dalag*).[50] Thus, not only is there no legal framework underpinning their "betrothal," but its precise meaning and content remain clandestine even to the parties involved. The act of placing Mariane's gold cross around Toni's neck thus has another signification: it hints at a faith in the other that never gets formalized into a declaration or contract—a promise that neither lover ever directly attests to, and which is never made public or communal.

UNAVOWED COMMUNITY

133

The nature of Toni's "betrothal" to Gustav is directly framed in terms of the death sentence under which she has placed herself: she pleads with Babekan for Gustav's release on the basis first of the laws of hospitality, and then on the basis of Gustav's neutrality as a Swiss national. Babekan's response makes clear that this is no longer an option insofar as it exposes both of them to the law of the land:

> "Very well," said the old woman, suddenly appearing to give in, "let the stranger go his ways. But when Congo Hoango comes back," she added rising to leave the room, "and learns that a white man has spent the night in our house then you must answer for the pity that moved you to let him leave again despite the explicit commandment we are under."

> "—*Wohlan*," *sagte die Alte, mit einem plötzlichen Ausdruck von Nachgiebigkeit:* "*so mag der Fremde reisen! Aber wenn Congo Hoango zurückkömmt, setzte sie hinzu, indem sie um Zimmer zu verlassen, aufstand, und erfährt, daß ein Weißer in unserm Hause übernachtet hat, so magst du das Mitleiden, das dich bewog, ihn gegen das ausdrückliche Gebot wieder abziehen zu lassen, verantworten.*"[51]

The *Antwort* or response Gustav awaits from Toni, has become by the morning something for which Toni will have to answer (*sich verantworten*) to the law. When Gustav awakes the next morning, intent on telling Babekan of what had transpired the night before, Toni insists that it remain secret for reasons obvious to her, but not necessarily Gustav. And again, everything that follows the night of Toni and Gustav's sexual consummation takes place under the auspices of this unavowed betrothal that *neither lover* can attest to, or ultimately confirm, despite the fact that it binds each of them to the other. In Toni's case, this involves an unattested avowal that displaces her obligation out of the domain of hospitality to a general "stranger" (*Fremde*) and into the singularity of a betrothal to Gustav specifically: "For now, before God and her own heart, she saw the young man no longer as merely a guest to whom they had given protection and hospitality but as her betrothed" (*Denn sie sah den Jüngling, vor Gott und ihrem Herzen, nicht mehr als einen bloßen Gast, dem sie Schutz und Obdach gegeben, sondern als ihren Velobten*).[52] The singular nature of her responsibility to Gustav—"before God and her heart" over and against the general law of hospitality—likewise supersedes the generality of the law of friend and enemy. In other words, the unavowed betrothal between Toni and Gustav orchestrates a conception of obligation and of community without legal convention, and without a universality recognizable by the law.

The clandestine nature of their avowal is reconfirmed, but only— tragically—in retrospect, once the regime of racial violence reasserts itself and annuls the betrothal through Gustav's racial violence. Awakening to find himself tied up by Toni as a ruse to buy time so that she can alert his family, Gustav's faith in the unavowed betrothal to Toni is put to the test. Confronted by a situation he reads in terms of the old regime which identified Toni as the enemy, Gustav grabs a pistol from his cousin and kills her. After being told by his family of the way she risked her own life attempting to rescue him, Gustav is forced to confront his crime:

> Gustav hid his face. "Oh," he cried, without looking up, and felt the ground was opening under his feet, "is what you tell me true?" He put his arms around her and stared, torn to pieces by his grief, into her face. "Oh," Toni cried, and they were her last words, "you should not have mistrusted me." And so saying, she breathed the beautiful spirit from her body. Gustav tore his hair. "Oh that is true,-" he said, as his cousins dragged him from the corpse: "I should not have mistrusted you, for you were betrothed to me by a vow, even though we never said so"

> *Gustav legte die Hände vor sein Gesicht. "Oh!" rief er, ohne aufzusehen, und meinte, die Erde versänke unter seinen Füßen: ist das, was ihr mir sagt, wahr? Er legte seine Arme um ihren Leib und sah ihr mit jammervoll zerrissenem Herzen ins Gesicht. 'Ach,' rief Toni, und dies waren ihre letzen Worte: 'du hättest mir nicht mißtrauen sollen!' Und damit hauchte sie ihre schöne Seele aus. Gustav raufte sich die Haare. Gewiß! sagte er, da ihn die Vettern von der Leiche wegrissen; ich hätte dir nicht mißtrauen sollen; denn du warst mir durch einen Eidschwur verlobt, obschon wir keine Worte darüber gewechselt hatten!*[53]

Gustav's belated recognition—"you were betrothed to me by a vow, even though we never said so"—emphasizes too late a responsibility Gustav confronts only over the abyss, through the sense he feels of the solidity of the earth falling away beneath his feet. For Gustav, the recognition comes only when faced with the death of the other—a death he caused—in a responsibility that cannot be grounded in law, but only on the trust (*trauen*) or faith that makes the promise of another form of community possible. The *Eidschwur* or vow in Gustav's final words (he shoots himself immediately after) combines both the vow and its enunciation, which only now has become an object of certainty (*Gewiß*), and which in turn can only provide the *promise* of the *verloben* or betrothal without any exchange of words, without any confirmation, except when it comes too late.

After burying the lovers and fleeing Haiti, Gustav's family erects a monument in Europe, with the last words of the novella underscoring its memorialization of the "faithful Toni" (*treuen Toni*).[54] It is precisely this faith or trust—at once amorous and political—that Gustav lacks, despite his having bestowed a symbol of both religious and amorous fidelity on Toni as a "betrothal gift." Mariane's namesake as symbol of the French Republic and embodiment of liberty, equality, and fraternity,[55] along with the cross as symbol of faith in general, is meant to produce a form of difference and repetition, though in ways the text does not fully control. Either it allows us to read Toni as yet another white Mariane sacrificing herself for Gustav, or it opens up a context in which Toni's relationship to Gustav becomes a cipher for an unprecedented and unavowed form of community external to the distinction between "us and them" enforced by the state. The fact that this repetition echoes a prior moment during the French Revolution when Gustav's lover dies *in his place* as an enemy of the state, makes his inability to recognize Toni's fidelity within the context of the Haitian Revolution all the more egregious, since it is he—and not the state—who ends up repeating and reinstating the qualification of her as an enemy. However, despite Gustav's inability to understand or recognize a form of "betrothal" to the other that would be unannounced or unavowed, a vow with no legal grounding or sense of shared identity organizing it, the novella's ending suggests that what remains is an unprecedented relation to the singular *death* of the other. Memorializing "the faithful Toni" implies a relation to her death that, in Blanchot's words, "is the only separation that can open me, in its very impossibility, to the Openness of a community."[56] Gailus's suggestion that the monument "signals not an ultimate betrothal in death but rather the death of betrothal"[57] reads this impossibility as fatally terminal. On the contrary, the novella's ending implies that the "impossibility" of the community of lovers does not lie in their deaths, in the passion of an *amour fou*, or in the temporal disjunction of a love realized before its time. It lies, rather, in an "impossibility" that in fact "took place," as a singular, unparalleled avowal that, in its very fragility, constitutes a community that invents itself as an exception to the law, even if it does not know how to enunciate, or recognize itself.

Kleist's novella, therefore, engages with the Haitian Revolution as something more than simply a background setting for a tale of romantic love gone wrong. While it is structured by familiar tropes, including well-known racialized ones that always threaten to consign it to yet another domestication of the symbolic force of the first successful slave revolt in history, it redeploys those tropes in ways that register the Revolution's "shock-effect," its status as an unprecedented event that not only interrupts history, but enacts and inaugurates a new one. Kleist's novella does this by enacting its own fictionalizing and monumentalizing gesture that reads the Haitian Revolution, framed by the impossible community of Gustav and Toni, as an event that cannot be understood simply in terms of the universalizing history of emancipation *à la* Kant, but as the unrealized promise of "betrothal" to the other. Kleist presents the Revolution through the image of a "community of lovers" predicated on a form of solidarity or engagement that precisely *eludes* universality as well as any communalism organized around the friend/enemy distinction or around racial hierarchies.

136 HAITI'S LITERARY LEGACIES

Kleist's *Betrothal* gives us the image of a "community" attempting to enact the impossible, without knowing in advance how to do so, without prior forms of enunciation, rules, norms, or criteria that would ratify it. The novella, therefore, functions as a monumentalizing of the Revolution that leaves intact two very different visions of history: on the one hand, Gustav's (European) failure to interpret events in terms that transcend existing forms of community, and on the other, the memorialization of Toni's (Haitian) fidelity to the impossible promise of another one. In the context of the Haitian Revolution's inauguration of a genuinely postcolonial history, these two conceptions of the impossible—one that forecloses forms of collectivity irreducible to the state, and the other that is their very condition of possibility—remain to a large extent the horizon of our own political moment.

Notes

1 I draw this term from Walter Benjamin's essay "The Work of Art in the Age of Its Technological Reproducibility," to describe the way a particular aesthetic form registers the "shock" of history, something not fully assimilated to the structures and conventions that organize it. See Walter Benjamin, "Art in the Age of Mechanical Reproduction" in *Selected Writings Vol. 3*, trans. Edmund Jephcott, Howard Eiland, and others (Cambridge, MA: Harvard University Press, 2002), 119.

2 Kant suggests that the French Revolution may "succeed or miscarry" and be filled with all sorts of misery and atrocities, yet it nonetheless is an "event of our time which demonstrates Moral tendency in the human race." See Immanuel Kant, *Conflict of the Faculties*, trans. Mary J. Gregor (Lincoln: University of Nebraska Press, 1992), 153.

3 Gailus, Andreas "Language Unmoored: On Kleist's "The Betrothal in St. Domingue," *Germanic Review* 85, no. 1 (2010): 21.

4 For examples of the former tendency, see Sander Gilman, "The Aesthetics of Blackness in Heinrich Von Kleist's 'Die Verlobung in St. Domingo' *MLN* 90, no. 5 (1975): 661–72; Michael Perruadin, "Babekan's 'Brille,' and the Rejuvenation of Congo Hoango: a Reinterpretation of Kleist's story of the Haitian Revolution," *Oxford German Studies* 20, no. 1 (1991): 85–103; Ray Fleming "Race and the Difference it Makes in Kleist's 'Die Verlobung in St. Domingo,' *German Quarterly* 65, no. 3/4 (1992): 306–17; Hans Jakob Werlen, "Seduction and Betrayal: Race and Gender in Kleist's 'Die Verlobung in St. Domingo' *Monatshefte* 84, no. 4 (1992): 459–71; Susanne Zantorp, "Changing Color: Kleist's Die Verlobung in St. Domingo and the Discourse of Miscegenation," in *A Companion to the Works of Heirich von Kleist*, ed. Berndt Fischer (Camden House, 2003), 191–208; and more recently James Martin, "Reading Race in Kleist's 'Die Verlobung in St. Domingo,' *Monatshefte* 100, no. 1 (2008): 48–66. For examples of the latter tendency, see

Volker Kaiser, "Epistemological Breakdown and Passionate Eruptions: Kleist's 'Die Verlobung in St. Domingo,' *Studies in Romanticism* 42, no. 3 (2003): 341–67; and Joshua Gold, "Face Value: Kleist's 'Die Verlobung in St. Domingo,' *European Romantic Review* 21, no. 1 (2010): 77–93. One of the few exceptions to this disjunction is Andreas Gailus's excellent essay: Andreas Gailus, "Language Unmoored: On Kleist's "The Betrothal in St. Domingue," *Germanic Review* 85, no. 1 (2010): 20–43.

5   Gold, "Face Value," 82.

6   C. L. R. James's classical study, while situating the Haitian Revolution at the start of a long chain of postcolonial struggles, nevertheless makes a case for its status as a major world historical event. C. L. R. James, *The Black Jacobins* (New York: Vintage Books, 1989). More recently, Michel-Rolph Trouillot has argued that because of the way the Haitian Revolution disrupted ready-made categories of analysis, it "entered history with the peculiar characteristic of being unthinkable even as it happened"; see Michel-Rolph Trouillot, *Silencing The Past* (Boston: Beacon Press, 1995), 73. More recently, Peter Hallward, writing at the bicentenary of Haitian independence, suggests that "the achievement of Haitian independence reminds us that politics need not always proceed as 'the art of the possible.' Haitian independence brought to an end one of the most profoundly improbable sequences in all of world history." See Peter Hallward, "Haitian Inspiration: Notes on the Bicentenary of Haiti's Independence," *Radical Philosophy* 123: 3.

7   For what is still one of the best analyses to date of Kleist's relation to imperialism, see Ruth Angress, "Kleist's Treatment of Imperialism: *Die Hermannschlacht* and '*Die Verlobung in St. Domingo*,' *Monatshefte* 69, no. 1 (1977): 17–33. According to Angress, both works are critiques of imperialism. The obvious difference is that Kleist's depiction of German insurgency (in *Battle of Hermann*) is set in the first century, a far cry from the modern events (1803) depicted in *Betrothal*.

8   Daut, Marlene L., *Tropics of Haiti: Race and the literary History of the Haitian Revolution in the Atlantic World 1789–1865* (Liverpool: Liverpool University Press, 2015), 298.

9   See Heinrich von Kleist, *The Battle of Hermann*, trans. Rachel MagShamhráin (Wurzburg: Königshausen and Neumann, 2008).

10 The most obvious case in points would be *Michael Kohlhaas* and *Earthquake in Chili*. See Heinrich von Kleist, *Selected Writings*, trans. David Constantine (Indianapolis: Hackett, 1997), 211–80; 312–23 respectively. For the German see Heinrich von Kleist, *Sämtliche Werke und Briefe*, vol. 2 (München: Carl Hanser Verlag, 1993), 9–103; 144–59 respectively.

11 Perraudin argues that the law was instituted after Dessalines's victory in 1805, despite the fact that the story is set prior to Haiti's independence. See Perraudin, "Babekan's 'Brille,'" 88.

12 Carl Schmitt, examining the nature of the political as a space of necessary agonistics, makes the "friend/enemy" distinction constitutive of the political as such, since it "denotes the utmost degree of intensity of union or separation, of

an association or dissociation." See Carl Schmitt, *The Concept of the Political*, trans. George Schwab (Chicago: University of Chicago Press, 1996), 26.

13 I examine this notion of the "community of lovers" in Kleist's novella *Michael Kohlhaas* in "Impasse, Promise and Impossible Community: Blanchot's Community of Lovers and Kleist's *Michael Kohlhaas*," *Comparative Literature* 72, no. 2 (2020): 128–43.

14 Blanchot, Maurice, *The Unavowable Community*, trans. Pierre Joris (Barrytown: Station Hills Press, 1988), 50.

15 Blanchot, *Unavowable Community*, 48.

16 I engage with this background to Blanchot's argument in more detail in "Impasse, Promise and Impossible Community," 128–43.

17 Blanchot, *Unavowable Community*, 30.

18 Distinguishing between descriptive statements about the world and performative statements which constitute an act, J. L. Austin uses the term "felicity" to determine whether or not a verbal act has been carried out, or not. See J. L. Austin, *How to Do Things with Words* (Cambridge, MA: Harvard University Press, 1975).

19 In the English preface to his late critique of Blanchot, "The Disavowed Community," Jean-Luc Nancy argues that Blanchot's conception of the "community of lovers": "is the quintessential version of a founding of politics outside itself—in the heavens, in a spirit, or in a higher destination. It can involve any figure or non-figure as one likes—divine, mythical, of the people or of the 'neuter'—but it is necessarily an authority [*instance*] that must be qualified as nonpolitical, hyperpolitical, or metapolitical." Nancy, Jean Luc, *The Disavowed Community*, trans. Philip Armstrong (New York: Fordham University Press, 2016), x.

20 Schmitt, Carl, *Political Theology: Four Chapters on the Concept of Sovereignty*, trans. George Schwab (Chicago: University of Chicago Press, 1985), 5.

21 Kleist, *Selected Writings*, 325 and *Sämtliche Werke Vol 2*, 160.

22 For two very different positions regarding this question, see James Martin, "Reading Race" and Hans Jacob Werlen, "Seduction and Betrayal."

23 Gailus, "Language Unmoored," 29.

24 Kleist, *Selected Writings*, 324 and *Sämtliche Werke Vol 2*, 160.

25 Gailus, "Language Unmoored," 31.

26 Kleist, *Selected Writings*, 325 and *Sämtliche Werke Vol 2*, 161.

27 Kleist, *Selected Writings*, 325 and *Sämtliche Werke Vol 2*, 161–2.

28 Kleist, *Selected Writings*, 327 and *Sämtliche Werke Vol 2*, 163–4.

29 Kleist, *Selected Writings*, 327 and *Sämtliche Werke Vol 2*, 164.

30 Kleist, *Selected Writings*, 328 and *Sämtliche Werke Vol 2*, 165.

31 Kleist, *Selected Writings*, 328 and *Sämtliche Werke Vol 2*, 166.

32 Kleist, *Selected Writings*, 328 and *Sämtliche Werke Vol 2*, 165.

UNAVOWED COMMUNITY

33 Kleist, *Selected Writings*, 329 and *Sämtliche Werke Vol 2*, 167.

34 Kleist, *Selected Writings*, 330 and *Sämtliche Werke Vol 2*, 169.

35 Kleist, *Selected Writings*, 330–1 and *Sämtliche Werke Vol 2*, 169.

36 The mutual imbrication of what Benjamin calls "law-forming" and "law-preserving" violence is ubiquitous throughout his works. For an alternative reading of a "utopia of non-violence" in *Betrothal* see Anette Horn, "'Du hättest mir nicht misstrauen sollen!' Eine Utopie der Gewaltlosigkeit in Kleists 'Die Verlobung in St. Domingo," *Kleist-Jahrbuch*, 2013: 271–9.

37 Kleist, *Selected Writings*, 331 and *Sämtliche Werke Vol 2*, 170.

38 Kleist, *Selected Writings*, 331 and *Sämtliche Werke Vol 2*, 170.

39 Martin, "Reading Race," 53.

40 Kleist, *Selected Writings*, 332 and *Sämtliche Werke Vol 2*, 170–1.

41 Kleist, *Selected Writings*, 347 and *Sämtliche Werke Vol 2*, 191.

42 Gold, "Face Value," 84.

43 Gailus, "Language Unmoored," 36.

44 Gailus, "Language Unmoored," 40.

45 Gailus, "Language Unmoored," 33.

46 Kleist, *Selected Writings*, 333 and *Sämtliche Werke Vol 2*, 172.

47 Martin, "Reading Race," 53.

48 Martin, "Reading Race," 53.

49 Kleist, *Selected Writings*, 335 and *Sämtliche Werke Vol 2*, 175.

50 Kleist, *Selected Writings*, 335–6 and *Sämtliche Werke Vol 2*, 176.

51 Kleist, *Selected Writings*, 337 and *Sämtliche Werke Vol 2*, 177–8.

52 Kleist, *Selected Writings*, 340 and *Sämtliche Werke Vol 2*, 181.

53 Kleist, *Selected Writings*, 349 and *Sämtliche Werke Vol 2*, 193.

54 Kleist, *Selected Writings*, 350 and *Sämtliche Werke Vol 2*, 195.

55 Mariane is a well-known figure of the French republic, often depicted wearing a Phrygian cap and meant to embody the principles of the French republic.

56 Blanchot, *Unavowable Community*, 9.

57 Gailus, "Language Unmoored," 40.

6

"Despair Begins with Stupefaction": Unthinkable Agencies in Hugo's *Bug-Jargal*

Deborah Elise White

The Black Man is the one (or the thing) that one sees when one sees nothing, when one understands nothing, and, above all, when one wishes to understand nothing.

—ACHILLE MBEMBE, *CRITIQUE OF BLACK REASON*

Who or what does one see when one sees Bug-Jargal the eponymous Black hero of Hugo's 1826 novel?[1] Or should the question be: who or what does one see when one sees Pierrot, the slave whose melancholic, theatrical name, imposed by French colonists, seemingly erases "Bug-Jargal," his prior, African name? when one sees "Pierrot," whose name, unknown to those same French colonists, also shelters him from exposure *as* Bug-Jargal the leader of a revolution? And who, after all, is looking? Or, as readers of the novel might be tempted to reword the question: who is reading? Such questions are, in precise and telling ways, the very subject of Hugo's novel. With its paratextual apparatus, its narrative within a narrative, and its pseudo-historical footnotes *Bug-Jargal* repeatedly stages the scene of seeing and understanding nothing, reading and misreading.[2] At the center of its novelistic machinery is a narrator, Leopold d'Auverney, onetime heir to a Saint-Domingue plantation. His story looks back to a younger self who, on the eve of the August 1791 slave insurrection, understood nothing and never more so than when he saw Bug-Jargal (or should that be Pierrot?). Pausing his narrative at a critical moment, Leopold reflects on the uncomprehending malaise that informed his response to events at every turn—a malaise that the narration has by no means left behind: "For the man who has always been happy, despair begins with stupefaction" (*le désespoir commence par la stupeur*).[3] "Stupefaction," the very word "*stupeur*" and its cognates, echoes across the text at crucial moments of revelation. It thus repeatedly impels the narrative forward. Yet it also registers a blockage of that forward motion, for the moment of retrospection that might be expected to announce an insight concerning its own previous blindness never entirely arrives. The narrative remains stupefied, and the novel's implied readers are left to draw their own conclusions. One may well take comfort from seeing—or understanding— what Leopold does not. But one should be wary, too, of such comfort, for his stupefaction testifies to impasses of understanding that continue to deform the historical and literary reception of the Haitian Revolution.

Bug-Jargal thus speaks with almost uncanny prescience to Michel-Rolph Trouillot's well-known formulation in *Silencing the Past* that "the Haitian Revolution ... entered history with the peculiar characteristic of being unthinkable even as it happened."[4] Unthinkable here is not quite the same as unnarratable or, for that matter, unseeable: the Revolution was widely reported on and discussed in Europe and the Americas if not beyond. Drawing on Bourdieu, Trouillot defines the unthinkable, rather, as "that which one cannot conceive within the range of possible alternatives."[5] What the range of possible alternatives did not include was a revolution led by enslaved Blacks. The concepts brought to bear on events in Saint-Domingue were thus inadequate to the Revolution's radicalism. Trouillot's thesis has been both contested and refined since *Silencing the Past* appeared in 1995, but the unthinkability of the Haitian Revolution, its status as an inconceivable event "even as it happened," remains a revealing point of entry for reading *Bug-Jargal* with its decidedly unthinking and unseeing central narrator.

But what exactly is Leopold d'Auverney unable or unwilling to understand? Most critically, the narrative reveals his younger self's blindness to the very possibility of a Black slave's revolutionary or erotic agency, and when confronted with such agency beyond all doubt, an inability to interpret it outside scenarios of vengeance and rape.[6] Insofar as Leopold narrates— and bitterly regrets—his errors, he seems to have learned from them, but his recurrent stupor ultimately disturbs any possibility of a fully realized *Bildung*. Refracting Haiti's history through Leopold's eyes, *Bug-Jargal* is not so much a novel of education as a novel of stupefaction. As "*stupeur*" becomes despair, the suicidal urge that determines Leopold's behavior serves, at best, as a negative recognition of agencies that he experiences as if they were the undoing of his own. His stupefaction thus speaks, however unconsciously, to how the Euro-American world has, in Achille Mbembe's words, rendered "blackness and race ... twin figures of the delirium produced by modernity."[7] In describing and accounting for this delirium Mbembe puts forward the formulation with which I began: "the Black Man is the one (or the thing) that one sees when one sees nothing, when one understands nothing, and, above all, when one wishes to understand nothing." The gap between "the one" and "the thing," or the who and the what, opens the space of a "nothing" that is not so much negative as overdetermined: the inflection point of a (Euro-American, white) subject blind to its own implication in what it sees.

Some account of the novel's plot may help to clarify these claims. Leopold d'Auverney is the nephew and heir of a Saint-Domingue plantation owner, whose daughter Marie he is engaged to marry. Over time, he befriends Pierrot, a slave on the uncle's estate who is himself secretly in love with Marie. Pierrot had once attacked Leopold under cover of darkness, but shortly after that same nighttime assault saved Marie's life from a crocodile, an event that initiates their friendship. During the first night of the 1791 uprising Leopold sees Pierrot carry Marie away from Fort Galifet while signaling to him from across the battlefield. He assumes the worst of his onetime friend and returns home to find his uncle murdered and next to his uncle's body, the bloody clothes of another slave, Habibrah, a dwarf who had served as the uncle's much doted-on jester. Leopold, who had despised Habibrah for his servility and cruelty, concludes that the dwarf must have been murdered while selflessly defending his master. Later, having been captured by the rebel leader, Biassou, he observes a veiled and strangely familiar Obi (or priest) who is, like Habibrah, a dwarf and who wears the jester's former cap and bells, cementing his belief that Habibrah was murdered by the rebels.[8] Pierrot arrives at the camp to negotiate Leopold's freedom, but Biassou, playing on Leopold's newfound distrust of Pierrot, tricks him into promising that he will later return to captivity. To Leopold's surprise, Pierrot takes him to Marie, and he learns that Pierrot had rescued her from Fort Galifet and has been protecting her from any harm. He learns too, of Pierrot's history, as the son of an African King and now commander of the uprising known as Bug-Jargal—a figure already familar to Leopold by reputation as the uprising's most generous and merciful leader. Nonetheless, he feels obligated to keep his promise to return to Biassou's camp. When he does so, he faces execution at the hands of the mysterious Obi who reveals himself to be Habibrah, who is alive after all, and the murderer of Leopold's uncle. Bug-Jargal arrives to save Leopold one final time, but in consequence of his commitment to other prisoners being held hostage, Bug returns to the French camp ahead of Leopold and is executed by the French. Through the novel's frame narrative, set three years later, we learn that Marie has died in Saint-Domingue and that Leopold is serving as an

144 HAITI'S LITERARY LEGACIES

officer with the French revolutionary army in Europe. In conclusion, a final note to the novel informs readers of his death in battle—and of the arrival shortly thereafter of a representative from the National Convention with a warrant for his arrest for having told "a would be counter-revolutionary story."[9]

The novel's plot thus depends on Leopold repeatedly misjudging situations where the truth is more or less obvious. His misunderstandings follow a pattern that has an almost fetishistic quality: as if, in Octave Mannoni's well-known formulation, he might well say "je sais bien, mais quand-même."[10] Leopold *knows very well, but all the same* refuses to acknowledge anything that would interfere with the fantasies that undergird his status. Endowed, as he says, with "all the privileges of rank in a country where one's colour was enough to bestow it" he *sees* a Black man, or the slave Pierrot, in order *not* to see a chivalrous hero or a political revolutionary even when sign after sign or, for that matter, Pierrot himself, tells him otherwise.[11]

What is ultimately unthinkable is a Black political or erotic agency that can claim a legitimacy or an authority equivalent to Leopold's own. To return to the narrative's earliest scenes: Leopold claims that his impending marriage to Marie prevents him from taking an interest in the politics roiling Saint-Domingue in 1791. However, as he also recalls, colonial politics itself is caught in a web of misrecognitions:

> It's not that anyone at the time, even those quickest to sound the alarm, seriously expected a slave revolt—this class was too greatly despised for it to be feared; but between the whites and the free mulattoes alone there existed enough hatred for the volcano that had been bottled up so long to convulse the entire colony at the dreaded moment when it would rip open.[12]

While Leopold claims to be uninterested in politics, his romantic entanglements echo exactly this political error. When he realizes Marie has a secret admirer his first suspicion falls on a "*sang mêlé*" casting his romantic rivalry as a version of the political competition between "whites and free mulattoes" in which he supposedly has no interest. When his real rival confronts him, he simply refuses to understand what his senses clearly tell him. Marie's secret admirer attacks him by night, but lets him go on hearing Marie's cry of terror, saying " 'No! no! she would weep too much!' " Realizing that his attacker's strength and size rule out the "*sang mêlé*," Leopold ponders who he could be:[13]

> It seemed to me the individual with whom I'd been fighting had been naked from the waste up. Slaves were the only ones in the colony who

went around half-dressed like that. But it couldn't be a slave: feelings such as the one that had made him cast away the dagger did not strike me as the sort that a slave could possess and, besides, every bone in my body rejected the revolting supposition that I had a slave for a rival.[14]

He later hears his rival singing a Spanish romance whose lyrics identify their author as Black—"You are white, and I am black ..."—and as a slave who remembers "the land of my fathers, the land where I was free."[15] Nonetheless, it still remains outside what Trouillot calls the "range of possible alternatives" for Leopold d'Auverney to suppose he has "a slave for a rival." Shortly after, when he first encounters the Spanish-speaking slave Pierrot, who appears from nowhere to rescue Marie from a crocodile, he at least briefly considers whether Pierrot may be Marie's secret admirer only to dismiss the idea almost immediately: "Just because this slave had addressed a few words to me in Spanish, was that a reason to suppose he was the author of a romance in this language, something that necessarily bespoke a degree of mental culture which, as far as I was concerned, was altogether beyond the ken of negroes?"[16] Even his developing friendship with Pierrot does not cause him to revisit this judgment. Only when Leopold sees Pierrot seize Marie during the insurrection does he begin to understand that he does indeed have "a slave for a rival." But he still refuses to accept that it could be a genuine *rivalry*. What he (thinks he) sees is a kidnapping even though few readers can be in any doubt that Leopold is witnessing not a rape but a rescue. His inability to see anything other than a rapist when he sees a Black man with his bride testifies to phobias that are both the inevitable consequence and the phantasmatic support of "all the privileges of rank in a country where one's colour was enough to bestow it." So clearly does the fantasy image of the Black rapist and the white woman sustain Leopold's sense of his own privilege that he clings to it even though it eventually reduces him to feverish unconsciousness.

When he later learns that Pierrot had saved Marie and has been protecting her, Leopold is nonetheless overcome with joy and remorse—at least initially:

I fell at the slave's feet, incapable of saying a word, sobbing bitterly. He hurriedly lifted me up.

...

"Can I call you brother now?" He asked.

...

"I have regained my brother," I said to him. "I am no longer unhappy, but I am most certainly guilty."[17]

146 HAITI'S LITERARY LEGACIES

Shortly after, Pierrot tells Leopold his own story, which shows him to be the leader of his people in Saint-Domingue. It also reveals him to have been the actual subject of the horrors Leopold only imagined himself to have suffered—including the rape (and death) of his wife. But even having heard Pierrot's story and having witnessed the enormous respect accorded him by Biassou and his soldiers, Leopold still cannot or will not see Bug-Jargal. As the two men discuss recent events, he finally asks "Pierrot" in some puzzlement:

> "...what does this Bug-Jargal have to do with you?"
> He seemed astonished in turn, and answered solemnly:
> "I am Bug-Jargal."[18]

The "this" brings home the irony. It sets the public revolutionary actor apart from the private world of the two men's friendship and the brotherhood that bonds them. The revolutionary Bug-Jargal is more an object on the horizon of Leopold's consciousness than a potential subject of his intimacy—a *what* rather than a *who*. In French, Bug-Jargal's answer to the question that Leopold posed to "Pierrot" echoes the "this" (*ce*) back to Leopold as if to underline its estranging character: "Je suis ce Bug-Jargal";[19] "I am this Bug-Jargal." Bug-Jargal's "*Je suis*" or "I am" subsumes the "*ce*" to the subject, or the *who*, facing Leopold. But repeating back the "this," however ironically, draws attention to the distance not only between the two formulations but between the two men. Brotherhood cannot elide their asymmetrical positions within Saint-Domingue. The chasm between the "ce Bug-Jargal" and the "je suis ce Bug-Jargal" is just what Leopold, despite his remorse, never entirely grasps.

Late in the novel, after Bug-Jargal frees Leopold from Habibrah's attempt to execute him, the very form of Leopold's gratitude—his expression of brotherly love—betrays how little he still sees:

> I entreated him never to leave me again, to remain with me among the whites; I promised him a commission in the colonial army. He interrupted me with a brutal look:
>
> > "Brother, am I proposing that you should enlist among my own people?"
>
> I kept silent, knowing I was at fault.[20]

Leopold's guilty silence suggests that he may at least be beginning to think the divide that no friendship can overcome without a more substantial historical reckoning. At the same time, neither Leopold nor Bug-Jargal (nor Victor Hugo) seems able to conceive that Leopold might indeed join Bug's "people" even though, in the final stages of the Haitian Revolution, Polish troops, for example, had done just that. (Sent to Saint-Domingue to fight for the French, some concluded they were fighting on the wrong side and joined their opponents thus earning the right to become Haitian citizens in the new nation's constitution.[21])

Up to a point, then, Leopold d'Auverney does learn to think the political and erotic agency of a Black African slave and to recognize some of the ways in which he himself has been "at fault." From this perspective *Bug-Jargal is* a novel of education in which Leopold learns to overcome what he somewhat evasively identifies as "what people refer to as 'the prejudice of color.' "[22] As a narrator, he condemns his younger self or, at any rate, tells a story that clearly exposes his younger self to condemnation. But Leopold's education remains inhibited in ways yet to be explored, and his tale exposes a more radical disorientation than can be overcome by the generic plot reversals of romance and its melodramatic revelations. "Despair" as he says "begins in stupefaction"—"le désespoir commence par la stupeur."[23]

What characterizes stupefaction in Hugo's novel? And what are its implications for readers positioned to understand Leopold's story even when he does not? The word itself may not seem to require special comment as it belongs to a longer chain of melodramatic signifiers used to punctuate the novel's scenes of reversal and recognition. When Leopold hears Pierrot's story he is "frozen with horror;"[24] elsewhere he and other characters are "surprised," "astonished," and "awed," as well as "stupefied" by events. Yet "*stupeur*" with its cognates sets itself apart from this chain, not least because it serves as the crux of a short chapter in which Leopold interrupts his narrative to meditate directly on his state of mind during the insurrection. Following the trail of *stupeur* backwards and forwards from this short chapter takes the reader beyond the novel's melodramatic conventions or, rather, takes the reader further into the meaning of those conventions, for *stupeur* repeatedly marks the novel's most salient revelations of Black agency.

The word first appears quite early in the novel when Leopold sees the slave he still knows as Pierrot defend another slave against his uncle's injustice and cruelty: "The unexpected intervention ... his deed, his look, the commanding tone of his voice all left me stupefied" (*me frappèrent de stupeur*.)[25] A slave openly challenging his master and doing so for the sake of justice rather than revenge *stupefies*.[26] Elsewhere in the novel Bug-Jargal indeed appears motivated partly by vengeance; in this episode, the stake is clearly ethical and at least proto-political. For that very reason, it stops Leopold dead in his tracks. What does it mean, then, for him to be stupefied? According to *Littré, Stupeur* signifies astonishment and incomprehension but also paralysis and immobility. One is shocked to the point of numbness and even indifference. The first definition given is medical

148 HAITI'S LITERARY LEGACIES

and refers to a generalized state of torpor and loss of intellectual faculties *"accompagnée d'un air d'étonnement ou indifférence"* (accompanied by an attitude of astonishment or indifference).[27] The second, figurative definition emphasizes immobility created by a great surprise or fright. The passage from astonishment and fright to indifference and immobility suggests a crisis that bears upon agency. It is as if Leopold's encounter with the agency of a "class" he describes as "too greatly despised for it to be feared" (the captive Black population of Saint-Domingue) is experienced by him as if it were a direct assault on his *own* agency.

When he later meditates explicitly on his stupefied experience of the slave uprising—"despair begins in stupefaction"—he describes it as an experience of shocked immobilization, as if he had been struck by an electric eel.[28] To quote the passage at length:

> When extraordinary events, times of anguish and catastrophe, suddenly come hurling down into the midst of a happy and delightfully uniform life, those unexpected emotions, those blasts of fate rudely interrupt the slumber of a soul at rest ... And yet when misfortune arrives in this manner it does not seem like an awakening, but only a dream. For the man who has always been happy, despair begins with stupefaction. Unexpected adversity resembles the torpedo-fish: it strikes, but what it strikes it numbs, casting a sudden dire light before our eyes which is not the light of day. People, things, actions: they all pass before us, moving as if part of a dream, with something uncanny in their features ... If this violent condition of the soul persists it unravels the mind's equilibrium and turns into madness—[29]

The passage articulates everything the novel has to say about *stupeur*. Perhaps most importantly, the shock of the Revolution does not so much wake Leopold up from the slumbers of his youth as cast him into a deeper sleep; that which interrupts the "slumber of his soul" occurs not "like an awakening, but only a dream." Which is to say that it leaves him more than ever under the sway of fantasy. What should have been a moment of awakening turns into something he can only interpret as a nightmare. The passage from slumber to dream also inadvertently concedes that the once "happy" Saint-Domingue plantation heir had been living in a stupor all along, never more so than when seeing *nothing* that could disturb his happiness. *Stupeur* names the experience of shock that breaks in on his privileged life; by the same token, it turns out to be a good name for that privileged life.

In what to a Leopold d'Auverney might seem an unexpected irony, his stupor also seems to align him with Biassou's soldiers. Only shortly before interrupting his narrative to meditate on his own stupefaction, he had described their awed fascination with Biassou's veiled Obi (the disguised

Habibrah) as "express[ing] that sort of attentiveness that resembles stupefaction" (*qui ressemble à la stupeur*). But perhaps the indirect point is that their expression offers only a semblance of stupefaction; as Leopold sees them, they are not, in fact, stupefied but merely stupid. A few lines down the Obi himself says as much when he speaks mockingly to his audience of their "*stupidité naturelle*" in a way that they are presumed to be too stupid to notice.[30] In Leopold's mind, what one might call stupefy-ability turns out to be a signifier of whiteness. In this context, one may recall that one of Hugo's main sources for *Bug-Jargal*, Pamphile de Lacroix, describes the white inhabitants of Cap Français as "*frappé d'abord de stupeur*" by the onset of the 1791 insurrection—the same idiom Leopold uses to describe his reaction to seeing Pierrot challenge his uncle.[31]

Stupefaction marks yet another, still more crucial scene of revelation when the veiled Obi leads Leopold deep into the mountains to be executed. They enter a spectacular cavern where the Obi lifts the veil from his chest exposing the brand of his two former owners: "one of these names was Effingham and the other was that of my uncle, my own name, *d'Auverney*! I was struck dumb with surprise!" He is struck dumb, but he still does not *see* Habibrah. He cannot read his own name because (to return to Mbembe's formulation) at a fundamental, perhaps unconscious, level he "wishes to understand nothing." Only when Habibrah lifts the veil on his face does Leopold recognize him: "'Good God! I exclaimed, stupefied [*frappé de stupeur*]."[32]

Recognition is not exactly understanding, and he immediately taxes Habibrah with ingratitude to his former master. Habibrah's response, in turn, offers the novel's most powerful indictment of the plantation heir's obtuseness:

> Do you think just because I am a mulatto, a misshapen dwarf, that I am not a man? Ah! I've got a soul … I was passed on to your uncle as if I were a toy monkey. I was the servant of his pleasures, the plaything of his scorn. You say that he loved me, that I had a place in his heart. And so I did, somewhere between his real monkey and his parrot. But I carved out another place there with my dagger … You have laughed at me often enough, now you can shudder.[33]

For Leopold, Habibrah remains what he calls a "monster" even as the monstrosity whose signature appears branded on Habibrah's body—d'Auverney—escapes his understanding; when Bug-Jargal arrives to rescue him, he remains immobilized, stupefied in the face of the conflict between the two former slaves: "It seemed to me as if I were at the gates of hell awaiting the loss or salvation of my soul, bearing witness to a relentless struggle between my guardian angel and my evil genius."[34] The scene plays out as if it were the screened projection of his own psychic divisions onto

150 HAITI'S LITERARY LEGACIES

the idealized/vilified doublet of the two figures whose struggle allegorizes his (and the novel's) extreme ambivalence toward both slavery and revolution.

After Bug believes he has completed his rescue and temporarily departs, Habibrah makes one final attempt to execute Leopold by dragging him down into a chasm:

> An old tree leaned over [this] abyss, its topmost branches sprayed by the spume from the falls, its gnarled trunk piercing through the rock one or two feet below the edge. With both its top and bottom thus washed in the waters of the torrent, the tree—which jutted out over the chasm like a fleshless arm—was so stripped of foliage that its species was unrecognizable. It was an altogether singular phenomenon: the moisture soaking its roots was what kept it from dying, while the violence of the cataract kept tearing off its new limbs, forcing it to retain the same branches for all eternity.[35]

An image of torment that might have come from the *Inferno*, the tree is at once the genius loci of the cavern and an emblem of what is about to happen there.[36] As Habibrah tries to push Leopold into the chasm, he falls into it himself and his robes catch on the tree so precariously perched over the abyss. He pleads for Leopold's aid, but when Leopold reaches down to help him, Habibrah, "with a diabolical laugh" attempts to drag Leopold into the abyss with him: "'This is my consolation, my death is an act of vengeance;'" Leopold temporarily saves himself by holding onto the trunk of the same tree and is ultimately saved by Bug-Jargal's dog Rask who pulls him away from Habibrah's grasp: "The miserable dwarf was engulphed by the spume of the dark falls. As he fell, he hurled a curse at me [... which] sank back down with him into the abyss."[37] The falling figure finds its ghostly after image in a poem Hugo wrote over a decade later entitled "After a Reading of Dante": "plus bas encore tout au fond du gouffre / Le masque grimaçant de la haine qui souffre" (at the very bottom of the abyss / The grimacing mask of suffering hate).[38]

The image of the tree itself evokes Dante's *Inferno* in more direct ways. To return to the passage: "the moisture soaking [the tree's] roots was what kept it from dying, while the violence of the cataract kept tearing off its new limbs, forcing it to retain the same branches for all eternity." A tree that never dies even as its limbs are violently torn from it "for all eternity" recalls the wood of the suicides in Dante's poem, where the souls of the damned are bound in trees whose limbs are eternally and violently torn off by the harpies: "no green leaves in that forest, only black; / No branches straight and smooth, but knotted, gnarled;" as Dante departs the wood, he sees the plane "where distended flakes / of fire shower down" much as Leopold describes the scenes of burning cane fields earlier in the novel.[39] The tree is thus an image of hellish fixation or, rather, in the context of *Bug Jargal*, a figure of *stupefaction*. Its sterile circuit of life-in-death and death-in-life figures both Leopold's self-destructive stupefaction and Habibrah's self-destructive vengefulness as well as the sterile circuit that binds the two together.

The cavern of Habibrah's death is indeed a cavern of suicides: Habibrah chooses death in the hope of bringing Leopold down with him, rather than life at Leopold's hands. In the frame narrative, the French officers listening to the story are skeptical on just this point which serves to underline it: "'How believable is it that he'd be ready to drown himself just so he could drown his enemy;'" Leopold portrays himself, too, as a suicide when he first enters the cavern with Biassou's men: he walks along "the edge of this abyss into which I—of my own free will, as it were— was going to hurl myself."[40] The tree living and yet not living, dying and yet not dying, evokes Dante's forest of suicides because it is the site and the emblem of suicidal struggle in the novel. Even beyond the cavern, as Leopold lives on in stupefied despair, he can imagine no other agency for himself than a suicidal one. By the time of the frame narrative, when he tells his story: "d'Auverney, among all the chance circumstances of war, desired only death."[41]

Addressing the Anglo-American context, Deanna Koretsky has argued that Romantic writers "became interested in stories of suicide because they resonated with political discourses of sovereignty," and Habibrah's suicidal gesture speaks to her argument, as does Bug-Jargal's self-sacrificing return to the French camp where he knows he will be executed in place of his men.[42] Leopold, however, dies in suicidal despair because he experiences his own sovereignty as impossible in the face of theirs. His problem is not simply that he has lost his status as heir to a wealthy estate—or that France has lost Saint-Domingue—but that he (imagines that he) has been wounded in his very being. In one sense, he is correct: the Haitian Revolution overturns everything that founds his subjectivity within the social and political world of the novel.

In the frame narrative, Leopold has to be brow-beaten into telling his story, and is otherwise described as taciturn and melancholic, with little connection to others except two companions who have come with him from Saint-Domingue, his sergeant Thaddeus and Bug-Jargal's dog Rask. His looks express "indifference" to everything about him, recalling the effects of *stupeur* cited in the definitions given above; his indifference is thus the after-effect of shock or trauma—in other words, it is anything but indifferent: "Underneath his glacial indifference, you could see the incurable wound inside him and the tremors it provoked."[43] Nor does the telling of his tale prove cathartic except in the most ironic of ways. The day after telling it, he is killed in battle alongside both Thaddeus and Rask.[44]

Is it entirely fair to conclude that Leopold knows no awakening from the slumbers of his youth? Is he not perhaps merely nostalgic rather than stupefied, melancholy rather than shocked? I would argue that even as one can trace a (post) colonial melancholy in his narrative, something more than nostalgia invests its language from the beginning:

> Surrounded almost from birth with all the gratifications of wealth, with all the privileges of rank in a country where one's colour was enough to confer it; passing my days next to the being who possessed all of my love; seeing this love looked upon favorably by our relatives, the only ones who could have blocked it; ... Surly that is reason enough to give me the right to say [*le droit de dire*] that few men have spent their early years more happily than I?[45]

Certainly, the transposition of revolutionary right (or *droit*) into the right of the former colonist to mourn lost happiness expresses the nostalgia of the postcolonial exile even as it points toward an inchoate and reactionary politics. However, what appears more than nostalgic in this passage is Leopold's reference to his relatives as the only ones who could have blocked his marriage to Marie, for the phrasing implies that he still, years after the fact, sees them alone as having had that power. Yet the entire burden of the story is that his wedding night was interrupted by the opening salvos of the *Revolution*. (Moreover, that interruption had been abetted by his own refusal to contemplate its possibility: when Pierrot warns him to marry and leave with his bride for Cap Français before August 22, Leopold ignores him.) One might argue that Leopold is here merely ventriloquizing his earlier illusions, not reiterating them, but the grammatical ambiguity tells its own tale. The very words that might sound like an acknowledgment of past error import that error into the present moment. In other words, through Leopold d'Auverney, the novel features a narrative in which blindness gives way to insight *and*, simultaneously, insight gives way to disavowal.[46]

Even when Leopold is restored to Marie and learns that she is still his virgin bride, he remains apparently indifferent to the happy ending that Bug-Jargal has made possible. He insists on abandoning her in order to keep his promise to return to Biassou—a promise made when he was ignorant of the truth. Though Marie is not dead to him, as he had thought, by virtue of having been raped, one may wonder whether she is still dead to him by virtue of having been rescued by a Black revolutionary. As the gift of Bug-Jargal, rather than Leopold's Uncle, she no longer symbolizes what she once symbolized. Bug-Jargal's rescue of Marie thus impacts Leopold *as if* it were a more radical blow to his sense of self and plans for the future than her rape would have been.[47] Leopold's return to Biassou and, more generally, his desire to die effectively remain bound up with the racist imaginary that defines him. Speaking to the pathologies that underwrite such imaginaries, Frank Wilderson has written about the psychic and social consolidation of non-Black subjects as dependent upon an externalization of "Blackness that is *without*": "Categories of non-Black must establish their boundaries for inclusion in a group (humanity) by having a recognizable self *within*. There must also, consequently, be an outside to each group, and, as with the concept of humanity, it is Blackness that is *without*; it is Blackness that is the dark matter surrounding and holding together the categories of non-Black."[48] Pierrot/Bug Jargal's Blackness grants Leopold his "within," which is to say his agency as a self-sovereign subject, his so-called humanity, only as long as he is able to overlook the agency, sovereignty, and humanity of "this Bug Jargal." When he cannot, he returns willingly to Biassou and, as he believes, death.

To remark that Leopold is stupefied to the very end is quite different from saying that the novel, *Bug-Jargal*, is—though an exhaustive reading would show (as indeed a number of readings *have* shown) that it does not entirely escape a certain *stupeur* not to say a certain stupidity. But insofar as *Bug-Jargal* explicitly stages the colonial wish to "understand nothing," it promises to see past that wish, to think Trouillot's unthinkability, and to invite the critical reader (or teacher) to fill in the blanks of Leopold's racist narrative with an anti-racist critique. However, at the same time, one cannot help but notice that this conclusion runs the risk of a certain complacency. It may even miss the radicalism of Haiti's revolutionary achievement. One needs, therefore, to think beyond it. What I'm referring to as critical complacency can take many forms and I will touch on just a few of them. The first of course is that the novel's Bug-Jargal—its chivalric yet revolutionary hero—remains much more of a literary topos than a national leader. That is, he is a figure out of the same Spanish romances that he sings throughout the novel and a descendant of Aphra Behn's *Oroonoko* much more than he is a refraction of Louverture or Dessalines. The reader positioned to see through Leopold's blindness is still left to ponder a relatively retrograde figure of political agency—one who regularly sacrifices the interests of the Revolution to Leopold's safety and whose motives outside the scene in which he challenges Leopold's uncle are characterized in a largely depoliticized language of vengeance and personal loyalty. In *Bug-Jargal*, the villainous Biassou carries the weight of allusion to Toussaint Louverture, though ironically, in the slave name Pierrot, the novel smuggles in an allusion to Dessalines's heroic resistance to the French at the fortress of Crête-à-Pierrot.[49]

The novel's frame narrative raises still more interesting ways of addressing critical complacency, for it concludes with the explicit appearance of a critical reader—the representative of the Convention who arrives to arrest Leopold d'Auverney for telling "a would-be counter-revolutionary story tending to ridicule the principles of equality and liberty."[50] The Convention offers its own conclusion to his tale, speaking a language that in its supposed sympathy for the Saint-Domingue uprising reveals itself to be as willfully determined to understand nothing as Leopold's. The novel presumably intends to satirize the Jacobin position. For one thing, the young Hugo's royalist politics place him clearly on the side of monarchs throughout the novel; even Toussaint Louverture gets a rare nod in the novel's notes for being possibly descended from "royal African stock."[51] But the satire of Jacobinism has the supplemental effect of showing the stupefied character of any revolutionary universalism that remains complacently Eurocentric in its assumptions. The convention thus declares Leopold guilty "of having made use of expressions condemned by all good sansculottes when characterizing various memorable events, notably the enfranchisement of the ci-devant 'blacks' of Saint-Domingue."[52] These words draw out the universalizing claim of the French Revolutionary project and its limits. For the Jacobins, the "sansculottes" remain the privileged bearers of a (supposedly) universalized agency even as the Black slaves are subsumed to that agency. With the words "*ci-devant* blacks" the Jacobins appear to abolish the singularity of Black revolution as surely as they claim to have abolished aristocracy. Subsuming Black history to universal history, as it were, prematurely, the Jacobin representative misunderstands the singularity and specificity of what the Black slaves of Saint-Domingue have accomplished *even* within the highly inadequate terms of Hugo's novel. The Jacobin bill of indictment speaks for a system that can claim "enfranchisement" as its own accomplishment—the Convention voted to end slavery in all French colonies—only by erasing the self-enfranchisement of the onetime slaves of Saint-Domingue. The episode thus raises the question of whether Hugo's implied white/French readers (and their descendants) may not awaken from Leopold-like illusions only to reiterate their own dreams of a universalism that has repeatedly proven to be something other than it claims. Bug-Jargal's agency as a lover and as a revolutionary cannot be understood as merely the fraternal equivalent of Leopold's. The revolutionary energies he represents (however inadequately in Hugo's novel) ultimately challenge the very concept of agency or, indeed, of revolution that is still part of the Jacobin legacy.[53]

Nor should one take for granted the corrective completion of Leopold's education in the contemporary United States classroom. Teaching inevitably comes up against its own history and the unthinkability of the very things one assumes have been learned. The first time I taught *Bug Jargal,* the second session devoted to it fell on the day immediately following the 2016 election of Donald Trump. Without discussing the election directly, the class pondered the significance of Leopold's stupefaction. The students came from a variety of educational, ethnic, racial, and social backgrounds, and they were all experiencing their own version of *stupeur* at the election results. Their stupefaction was thus very different in context and motive from Leopold's even as it shared his inability to make sense of large-scale events that were nonetheless shaping their lives in incalculable ways. At the same time, however *differently* positioned in relation to the history of colonialism and slavery the students were, all of them appeared to register that we, in that room, remained the inheritors of the same colonial stupefaction critiqued in Hugo's novel and in our larger academic setting. To put that classroom experience aside and resume the larger argument: the universalist pretense of living in a world of "ci-devant blacks" as the Convention claims to do finds an echo in the more recent Obama-era pretense of living in a world of ci-devant racism—the post-racial fantasy that ushered in, precisely, the racist regime of Donald Trump.

Trouillot's dictum on the unthinkability of the Haitian Revolution has proven resilient because it does not merely index a mistake to be corrected but a fundamental way of being in the world that the Haitian Revolution disrupted. It recognizes the radicalism of Haiti's achievement. The stupefied Leopold d'Auverney reveals many things inadvertently, but his stupefaction itself may instantiate a truth of sorts worth pondering. On the one hand, as he looks over the mass of Biassou's men and sees what to him is merely a chaos of slogans from across the political spectrum he makes mistakes that critics can and should correct:

> Fluttering above all these heads were flags of every color, displaying every slogan imaginable: white ones, red ones, tricoloured ones, flags with the fleur-de-lis or topped with the bonnet of liberty and bearing such inscriptions as "Death to priests and to aristocrats!"... "Long live religion!"... "Liberty!"... "Equality!"... "Long live the king!" This striking confusion was indicative of the fact that all these rebel forces were nothing more than an agglomeration of means without end [*moyens sans but*]: it was an army whose aims were just as disordered as its men.[54]

Where a stupefied Leopold d'Auverney sees disorder, one may instead trace a complex of overdetermined forces, revolutionary and royalist, that went into the insurrection, and one may also fill in, for example, from African history and politics much that the scene leaves out. On the other hand, is "disorder" the insult Leopold imagines and that criticism must essay to correct? Perhaps the disordering of European orders of meanings is exactly what is at stake in this *bricolage* of political citations.[55] The French revolution's own orders of liberty, equality, and fraternity belong to what is being disordered as is, at the end of the novel, the convention's sansculottist ideology. In other words, one may read Leopold's stupefied words against the grain, not so much by reading them *critically* as by taking them at their word. To give the revolution an end or an aim is inevitably to hierarchize and order its energies. As a means without end, revolution, any revolution worthy of the name, is—for good and ill—a disordering force. Biassou's men cut across the teleological horizon of European history and, *a fortiori*, of universal history by suspending meanings inherited from the past *and* meanings projected toward the future.

Here, as elsewhere in the novel, to read Leopold's words critically is to recognize that he remains incapable of seeing or thinking Black agency and thus incapable of understanding the ends the uprising has set for itself and to which it has appropriated European slogans. However, reading his words in the same fragmented way that he reads the slogans about him and taking them, as it were, literally—at their word—exposes the revolution's radical challenge to all teleological structures. By suspending European teleologies, the Haitian Revolution opens the way to suspending teleology altogether and thus to suspending those teleologically structured historicisms that imply an *end* or an *aim* to history. At the very least, the revolution's accumulation of means without end becomes an index of its resistance to assimilation into even the most apparently benign of progressive historical fantasies.

The phrase itself ("means without end") inevitably recalls Benjamin's enigmatic invocation of a divine violence that suspends repetitive cycles of violence that found law on the one hand and preserve it on the other.[56] For Benjamin, the revolutionary act that founds a state is ultimately subsumed to a state apparatus that eventually loses contact with its revolutionary origins, thereby setting the cycle in motion once more. Divine violence interrupts that cycle by refusing ends altogether: it is what Benjamin calls a pure means. Insofar as revolution can ever be a pure means, it broaches a freedom that may include, but is always something more than, the constitutional rights of the man or citizen enshrined by the French Revolution, or any rights granted and guaranteed by a state. Neither the state nor a rights-bearing subject is its end, for it has no end, not even a universalized and self-sovereign humanity.[57] Such a fragmentation and dispersal of revolutionary ends defies lawful containment much as it defies Leopold d'Auverney's narrativizing consciousness. But just as no one can live for very long in a stupor, no revolution, however radical, can sustain itself without eventually founding a new order. The Haitians did so in 1804 when they founded a sovereign state "by ourselves and for ourselves."[58] That order, in and of itself, marks a radical departure in global history with which the world has yet to come to grips. But as August 22, 1791, erupts across Hugo's troubling and contradictory novel, one may also catch a glimpse of all that is not contingently but *constitutively* incomplete in the project of freedom that the Haitian Revolution once announced—and announces still—to an unthinking world.

Notes

1 A shorter version of this essay was delivered as part of a panel on Romanticism and the Haitian Revolution organized by Kir Kuiken and myself for the 2017 conference of the North American Society for the Study of Romanticism, and a revised version was delivered at the 2019

International Conference on Romanticism. The epigraph comes from Achille Mmembe, *Critique of Black Reason* and is discussed directly later in the essay (Durham: Duke University Press, 2017), 2. I would like to thank Kir Kuiken and Elissa Marder for their advice and comments on the manuscript; its mistakes and weaknesses are my own.

2 Many readings of the novel include attention to unstable, creolized, or opaque systems of signification including Chris Bongie, *Islands and Exiles: The Creole Identities of Post/Colonial Literature* (Stanford: Stanford University Press, 1998), esp. 242–7; Kathrine Bonin, "Signs of Origin: Victor-Hugo's *Bug-Jargal*," *Nineteenth-Century French Studies* 36, nos. 3 and 4 (Spring–Summer, 2008): 193–204; Susan Gilman, "Victor Hugo's *Bug-Jargal*, Translationally," *J19: The Journal of Nineteenth-Century Americanists* 3, no. 4 (Fall 2015): 376–84; Heather Turo, "'Bug-Jargal' and Victor Hugo's Linguistic Commentary on Haitian Creole," *Journal of the Midwest Modern Language Association* 43, no. 2 (Fall 2010): 169–85; and Jennifer Yee, *Exotic Subversions in Nineteenth-Century French Fiction* (Abingdon: Legenda, 2007), esp. 47–57.

3 Victor Hugo, *Bug-Jargal*, ed. and trans. Chris Bongie (Peterborough, Ontario: Broadview Press, 2004), 154; for the French text: Victor Hugo, *Oeuvres Complètes: Roman I*, ed. Jacques Seebacher (Paris: Robert Laffont, 1985), 358.

4 Michel-Rolph Trouillot, *Silencing the Past: Power and the Production of History* (Boston: Beacon Press, 1995), 73. Citing Trouillot, Jared Hickman's magisterial *Black Prometheus: Race and Radicalism in the Age of Atlantic Slavery* (Oxford: Oxford University Press, 2017) situates *Bug Jargal* within a cluster of transatlantic novels "in which the unthinkability of slave revolt is reflected and reflected upon" (305, 306). My reading overlaps at crucial points with his while my conclusion aims to underline how the novel's implied readers risk remaining inscribed within the very structures they critique. On Leopold's self-involved naivete see, too, Kathryn Grossman, *The Early Novels of Victor Hugo: Towards a Poetics of Harmony* (Paris: Droz, 1986), 59–110 and Dominique Julien, "Bug-Jargal: la Révolution et ses Doubles," *Marges* no. 139 (Septembre 2005): 78–92, esp. 81–2.

5 Trouillot, *Silencing*, 82. For an extended discussion of Trouillot's thesis and its reception, see Kuiken and White's introduction to this volume.

6 On the "Black Avenger" as a trope through which Black political agency is contained/delimited (and on the role of rape in that trope), see Grégory Pierrot, *The Black Avenger in Atlantic Culture* (Athens: University of Georgia Press, 2019). Pierrot and others have addressed the popular portrayal of Toussaint Louverture as the Black avenger supposedly predicted in the third edition of Abbé Raynal's *Histoire des Deux Indes*. See, for additional examples, Srinivas Aravamudan, *Tropicopolitans: Colonialism and Agency, 1688–1804* (Durham: Duke University Press, 1999), 199–325, Marlene Daut, *Tropics of Haiti: Race and the Literary History of the Haitian Revolution in the Atlantic World 1789–1865* (Liverpool: Liverpool University Press, 2015), 49–55, and Theresa Kelley's essay in this volume.

7 Mbembe, *Critique of Black Reason,* 2.

8   The novel's portrait of Biassou and other historical figures has numerous gross distortions. Additionally, the novel represents Biassou (as it does the fictional character Habibrah) as a "mixed" racial figure, although the historical record indicates otherwise. On the novel's scapegoating of its mixed race characters, as well as some of the complexities and contradictions involved in that scapegoating, see Bongie, *Islands and Exiles*, 231–61 as well as his more recent essay, "Victor Hugo and the Melancholy Novel: Reading the Haitian Revolution in *Bug-Jargal*," *French Studies* 72, no. 2: 176–93. See, too, Bongie's preface to Hugo, *Bug-Jargal*. Cf. Marlene Daut's argument addressing how "anxieties about the righteousness of the Haitian Revolution most readily surface in the figure of the 'monstrous hybrid,' who was ambivalently portrayed as at once capable of the most outrageous crimes and the most daring displays of humanity, the most heinous justifications of parricidal revenge and the most moving rhetoric of revolution" in *Tropics of Haiti*, 158. On the vilification of mixed race characters in the novel see, too, Gilman, "Victor Hugo's *Bug-Jargal,* Translationally."

9   Hugo, *Bug-Jargal*, 198.

10   Octave Mannoni, "*Je sais bien, mais quand-même…*" *Clefs pour l'imaginaire ou l'autre scène* (Paris: Editions du Seuil, 1969), 9–33.

11   Hugo, *Bug-Jargal*, 69.

12   Hugo, *Bug-Jargal*, 71.

13   Hugo, *Bug-Jargal*, 72. Cf. Hickman, *Black Prometheus*, 306: "The rest of this story is strung on the repetition of this initial scene of *mis*recognition, this nondialectic of master and slave."

14   Hugo, *Bug-Jargal*, 73.

15   Hugo, *Bug-Jargal*, 75 and 76.

16   Hugo, *Bug-Jargal*, 80.

17   Hugo, *Bug-Jargal*, 170.

18   Hugo, *Bug-Jargal*, 170.

19   Hugo, *Roman I*, 373.

20   Hugo, *Bug-Jargal*, 192.

21   Cf. Colin Dayan, *Haiti, History, and the Gods* (Berkeley: University of California Press, 1995), 24: "For Dessalines, certain whites could be naturalized as Haitians: for example … those Germans and Poles who deserted Leclerc's army during 1802–1803 in order to fight with the indigènes (article 13)."

22   Hugo, *Bug-Jargal*, 7.

23   Hugo, *Bug-Jargal*, 154; *Roman I*, 358.

24   Hugo, *Bug-Jargal*, 179.

25   Hugo, *Bug-Jargal*, 82; *Roman I*, 298. I have modified Bongie's English translation of the French as "left me dumbfounded" as it obscures the continuity of references to stupor/stupefaction in the novel.

26 On the figure of the Black avenger see Pierrot, *The Black Avenger*. On the figure of Mullato/a vengeance in accounts of the Haitian Revolution see Daut *Tropics of Haiti*.

27 É. Littré, *Dictionnaire de la Langue Française*: www.littré.org.

28 Leopold's allusion to the "*torpille*" or torpedo fish recalls the "numb eel" in Aphra Behn's *Oroonoko*. However, Laplace's eighteenth-century French translation of *Oroonoko* appears to leave out this episode and Hugo is unlikely to have read the novel in English.

29 Hugo, *Bug-Jargal*, 154–5.

30 Hugo, *Bug-Jargal*, 128; *Roman I*, 336.

31 Pamphile de Lacroix *Mémoires pour Servir à l'histoire de la Révolution de San Domingue* (Paris: Chez Pillet Aîné, 1819), vol. I, 90. Bongie includes this passage from Lacroix in his edition of Hugo's *Bug-Jargal* translating the phrase as "in a state of shock" (307). In the same passage, Lacroix recalls Mirabeau's well-known saying that the colonists of Saint-Domingue were sleeping at the foot of Mount Vesuvius and adds that "the first blasts of the Volcano did not awaken them. In their spellbound eyes, the blacks were simply not creatures of any consequence" (307).

32 Hugo, *Bug-Jargal*, 182 (translation modified); *Roman I*, 381.

33 Hugo, *Bug-Jargal*, 183. Excerpts do not do the speech justice. On some of the textual sources of Habibrah's eloquence, see Daut, *Tropics of Haiti,* 168–70 and 180.

34 Hugo, *Bug-Jargal*, 184, 186.

35 Hugo, *Bug-Jargal*, 181.

36 Seebacher refers to the tree's symbolic character without further elaboration. See his notes in Hugo, *Roman I*, 923. Dante is an intertext here and elsewhere in the novel: the *Inferno* haunts its descriptions of burning cane fields as it does Leopold's obsession with the demonic character of the revolution on the one hand and Biassou's references to the demonic character of the white colonials on the other. Biassou is also the master creator of Dantesque punishments that fit his prisoners' crimes by in some way re-enacting or reversing them. See, for example, 134–40. On Dante in Hugo's oeuvre see Michael Pittwood, *Dante and the French Romantics* (Paris: Droz, 1985). Pittwood does not discuss *Bug-Jargal*, but does address Dante's importance to the aesthetic of the grotesque announced in the 1827 "Préface à Cromwell."

37 Hugo, *Bug-Jargal*, 189–90.

38 The poem appears in *Les Voix Intérieurs* (1837). See Hugo, *Oeuvres Complètes: Poésie I*, ed. Claude Gély, 887. My translation.

39 From Allen Mandlebaum's translation of *The Divine Comedy of Dante Alighieri: Inferno* (New York: Bantam Books, 1982); Canto XIII line 4 and Canto XIV lines 28–9. The episode also includes violent dogs tearing at flesh which, in turn, calls to mind the horrors of Rochambeau's final campaign in Saint-Domingue.

40 Hugo, *Bug-Jargal*, 193 and 182. On the pervasiveness of suicide in Hugo's major writings, see J. A. Hiddleston, "Suicide in the Novels of Victor Hugo" in *Victor Hugo, Romancier de L'abîme: New Studies*, ed. J. A. Hiddleston (Oxford: Legenda, 2002), 196–212.

41 Hugo, *Bug-Jargal*, 64.

42 Deanna Koretsky, "Boundaries between Things Misnamed: Social Death and Radical (Non-)Existence in Frederick Douglass and Lord Byron," *European Romantic Review* 29, no. 4 (2018): 473–84: https://www-tandfonline-com. proxy.library.emory.edu/doi/full/10.1080/10509585.2018.1487381:

43 Hugo, *Bug-Jargal*, 62 and 63.

44 On the novel's relation to the "post-colonial melancholy" that informs the writings of onetime Saint-Domingue colonists that were among Hugo's sources, see Bongie, "Victor Hugo and the Melancholy Novel." On the affective role played by Rask in connecting otherwise divided characters in the novel see the paper by Brigitte Fielder, "Race and Affective Kinship in Victor Hugo's Bug-Jargal," YouTube video, 13:11, February 2, 2021, https://www. youtube.com/watch?v=ncdBj1giKOw. The paper was originally delivered at the Center for Science, Technology, Medicine, and Society at the University of California, Berkeley.

45 Hugo, *Bug-Jargal*, 82; *Roman I*, 298.

46 Sibylle Fischer offers a powerful account of different kinds of disavowal in relation to the Haitian Revolution in *Modernity Disavowed: Haiti and the Cultures of Slavery in the Age of Revolution* (Durham: Duke University Press, 2004). Citing Freud, her introduction clarifies that disavowal is always intertwined with recognition: "it is productive in that it brings forth further stories, screens, and fantasies that hide from view what must not be seen" (38).

47 Unlike an earlier scene in which "Pierrot" rescues Marie from a crocodile, when Bug-Jargal rescues her the second time, he does so in his character as a revolutionary political and military figure. Hence the greater threat to Leopold's sense of self. For a different account of Leopold's ambivalence toward his own wedding night, see George Piroué, "Les Deux Bug-Jargal," in Volume I of Victor Hugo, *Oeuvres Complètes*, ed. Jean Massin (Paris: Club Français du Livre, 1967–1971), 356–7.

48 Frank Wilderson et al. *Afropessimism: An Introduction* (Racked and Dispatched 2017), 9. Cf. the interview included in the same volume in which he says that "violence against the slave sustains a kind of psychic stability for all who are not slaves" (19). The latter category includes those who, like Leopold, do not recognize their own violence.

49 For examples of how Biassou's words and actions recall anecdotes associated with Louverture, see Bongie's notes throughout his edition of the novel. On Crête-à-Pierrot see, for example, Dubois *Avengers*, 271–4.

50 Hugo, *Bug-Jargal*, 198.

51 Hugo, *Bug-Jargal*, 149.

52 Hugo, *Bug-Jargal*, 198–9.

"DESPAIR BEGINS WITH STUPEFACTION" 161

53 Even allowing that Hugo's brand of anti-Jacobinism is reactionary, the import of the criticism still holds. Perhaps somewhat paradoxically, some of the most innovative and important work on the Haitian Revolution focuses on its implications for "universal" history and politics, and thus finds itself having to grapple repeatedly with the troubled history of universalism. See, for example, Susan Buck-Morss, *Haiti, Hegel, and Universal History* (Pittsburgh: University of Pittsburgh Press, 2009) and Nick Nesbitt, *Universal Emancipation: The Haitian Revolution and the Radical Enlightenment* (Charlottesville: University of Virginia Press, 2008). Cf. David Scott on how Haiti gets invoked in relation to the universal in "The Theory of Haiti: *The Black Jacobins* and the Poetics of Universal History," in *The Black Jacobins Reader*, ed. Charles Forsdick and Christian Høgsberg (Durham: Duke University Press, 2007), 115–38.

54 Hugo, *Bug-Jargal*, 150 (translation modified); *Roman I*, 355. The unbracketed ellipses appear in Hugo's text.

55 Cf. Jennifer Yee's discussion of this passage and its "carnavalesque derision" in *Exotic Subversions*, 56–7.

56 Walter Benjamin, "Critique of Violence," in *Selected Writings: Volume I 1913–1926*, ed. Marcus Bullock and Michael W. Jennings (New York: Schocken Books, 1986), 236–52. Alluding to Benjamin, Giorgio Agamben uses the phrase for the title of a collection of short political essays: *Means Without End: Notes on Politics*, trans. Vincenzo Binetti and Cesare Casarino (Minneapolis: University of Minnesota Press, 2000).

57 Which may be one way to understand the prominence of Rask in the story, a prominence which I do not have space to discuss.

58 From the Haitian Declaration of Independence as translated in Laurent Dubois and John D. Garrigus, *Slave Revolution in the Caribbean 1789–1804: A Brief History with Documents*, 2nd ed. (Boston: Bedford/St. Martins 2017/2006), 189.

7

Revolutionary Resonances in Frances Watkins Harper's "Triumph of Freedom"

Brigitte Fielder

Frances Ellen Watkins Harper's "The Triumph of Freedom—A Dream" is a fantastical imagining of slavery's defeat.[1] The story was published in 1860, in the *Anglo-African Magazine*, a monthly periodical founded and edited by the Black journalist and activist Thomas Hamilton.[2] The periodical included short and long serialized fiction, poetry, and essays by some of the era's most prominent Black intellectuals, including Martin Delany, Sarah Mapps Douglass, James T. Holly, James McCune Smith, William J. Wilson, and Frances Watkins Harper. Set in no specific time or place, "The Triumph of Freedom" does not explicitly reference and is not about Haiti, but it is a narrative of violent revolution that requires Haiti for its contextualization. The specter of the Haitian Revolution looms over this text, as it does other mid-nineteenth-century African American print contexts. This key event in what Crystal Temple refers to as a diasporic Black cultural mythology has prompted, as scholars including Jeremy Popkin and Marlene Daut have shown, a plethora of literature. Generally understood to be an allegory inspired at least in part by John Brown's raid on Harper's Ferry, "The Triumph of Freedom" extends the scope of these events to a longer revolutionary abolitionism that is ultimately successful. The Haitian Revolution, and its circulation in the Black press, is key to understanding Harper's revisionary, futuristic "Dream" of success.

Harper's story is better understood with the Haitian Revolution in mind. Even though this story is not about the Revolution, in order to understand Harper's mythic and fantastical text, we must take into account the Revolution's resonance in African American print culture more broadly. Reading Harper's fiction alongside the genre of revolutionary texts that would be sprinkled throughout the Black press over the first half of the century, we gain a better sense of the generic context for the piece. That is to say, by taking the Haitian Revolution into account as a genre running through the background of mid-century discourses of Black abolitionism, we come to understand what "kind" of text Harper's unusual piece is: it is part of a larger genre of revolutionary antislavery writing that was fairly dominated by stories of the Haitian Revolution.

This essay will discuss Harper's early story as resonant with Black histories of the Haitian Revolution in the early African American press, despite the fact that her story makes no overt reference to Haiti. I argue here that the Revolution's historical resonance for early African American history—including the historical narrative produced within the pages of the *Anglo-African Magazine*—is a necessary context for reading Watkins Harper's early contributions to African American newspapers. I read this and Harper's other "revolutionary" mid-century writing against the *Weekly Anglo-African*'s backdrop of Haitian hagiography, showing how Harper's story evokes the Haitian Revolution even without naming it. Moreover, because Haiti's abolitionist success is stipulated in the pages of the *Anglo-African Magazine*, she does not need to do so. Rather than revisiting the familiar genre that would retell an already well-known story of the Haitian Revolution, Harper's short fiction straddles this event, reaching into both earlier and later moments for thinking Black abolitionist revolution. This is not, however a simple omission, as Haiti is necessarily nested within the genealogy of Black revolution that Harper suggests. Reading Harper's revolutionary writing within this longer historical arc of Black emancipation, Haiti rests at the center, even when unspoken.

Derrick Spires has discussed Harper's theorization of citizenship amid a struggle toward emancipation in which "violent conflict seemed not only imminent but also necessary."[3] I argue here that literatures of the Haitian Revolution are one of the "multiple directions" toward which Harper's story "proliferates" its abolitionist discourses.[4] It is not just the failed John Brown raid on Harper's Ferry, but the longer histories of Black revolution that resonate in Harper's dreamscape. Hers is a hopeful abolitionist anticipation that is not only imagined but also grounded in historical knowledge. Wrapped in the *Anglo-African Magazine*'s broader discourse that includes Haitian Revolutionary history, the "Dream" that Watkins Harper produces is not a starry-eyed utopian fantasy. Rather, it is grounded in Black history and in the political reality of Haiti as a Black nation that has successfully wrested itself from an enslaver nation.

Reading this story within this context of the Haitian Revolution's nearly mythological resonance allows us to understand Harper's "Dream" story as neither simply an allegory of the violence building in the United States, nor a hopeful prediction of future American abolition, but as informed by a drastic historical precedent for the overthrow of an enslaver nation. Taking Harper's story alongside the historical fact of Haiti's successful Revolution allows us to understand her allegorical "Dream" as not only hopefully predictive, but as historically possible. Reading thus against the grain of the fantastical, I interpret Harper's "Dream" as understanding the fact of Black emancipation and Black revolutionary success as a historical fact, rather than as a projected possibility.

An Abolitionist Dream

Watkins Harper's short story is one of her earliest known pieces of fiction.[5] While Harper has more often been associated with themes of domesticity and respectability, scholars of nineteenth-century African American women writers, including Frances Smith Foster, Carla Peterson, and P. Gabrielle Foreman, have long recognized more radical gestures in her work. "The Triumph of Freedom" is a vastly different story than the first that Harper published in the *Anglo-African Magazine*: "The Two Offers," a proto-feminist story about one young woman who marries only to be disappointed and another who finds fulfillment, instead, in other relationships and in working in her community.[6] This first story fits well with Harper's other realist short fiction, which (as in the "Fancy Sketches" series which also appeared in the *Anglo-African Magazine*), presented domestic scenes as a site for women's political conversation.

Much like the Haitian Revolution, Harper's story does not describe a simple violent uprising, but a response to an already bloody reality. "The Triumph of Freedom—A Dream" differs from Harper's realist fiction most obviously in its fantastical imagery and use of allegory. The dream begins on a "beautiful day in spring" when a "startling shriek" suddenly rouses the unnamed speaker from their "dreamy, delicious languor."[7] The speaker comes to consciousness to meet a spirit on whose face is "a look of unmistakeable sadness." Following her, they are then introduced to "the goddess of this place," who sits upon a bejeweled throne and wears a robe of white. But the speaker notices that her robe "was not pure white" for "upon its hem and amid its seams and folds were great spots of blood." The priests who worship this goddess perform a rite in which they attempt to cover over these bloodstains with various "texts and passages." They praise the goddess as "the handmaid of Christianity" and her mission as "heaven-appointed and divine." A "young man" contradicts this claim, stating simply "it is false," and he is immediately derided as a "fanatic, madman, traitor, and infidel." The dissenter is imprisoned but this does not stop others from coming to him to "learn his meaning." He then shows them the throne and altar of the goddess, in which the speaker sees "a number of little hearts all filed together and quivering": "the hearts of a hundred thousand new-born babes."[8]

Exploring the layers beneath the throne, the guide shows the speaker similar horrors: piles and piles of human hearts, the first, "rocking to and fro, as if smitten with a great agony ... the hearts of desolate slave mothers, robbed of their little ones"; next the "poor, bruised, and seared ... hearts out of which the manhood has been crushed" and "young, fresh hearts, from which the blood was constantly streaming ... the hearts of young girls, sold from the warm clasp of their mothers' arms to the brutal clutches of a libertine or a profligate—from the temples of Christ to the altars of shame"; and last, "a row of withered hearts, from which the blood still dropped ... hearts in which the manhood has never been developed." The "young man" gestures at these and speaks, "his lips trembling with the burden of a heaven-sent message." Readers do not hear what he says, but the crowd variously listens to him earnestly or mocks him, setting "a price on his head." At any rate, "he had awakened the spirit of Agitation." The goddess cries to her worshipers to be hidden "beneath your constitutions and laws—shield me beneath your parchments and opinions" or "beneath the shadows of your pulpits, throw around me the robes of your religion; spread over me your altar clothes, and dye my lips with sacramental blood."[9]

Our speaker then sees "an aged man" who rises up with "a solemn radiance" in his eye and "a lofty purpose" upon his brow. Looking at the goddess, "he laid his aged hands upon her blood-cemented throne, and it shook and trembled to its base." Rising against him to fight, the speaker then sees "bristling with bayonets, a blood-stained ruffian, named the General Government." The old man is caught, fettered, and taken first to prison and then to the scaffold. The plot here turns: "Her minions drained the blood from his veins, and they thought they had conquered him, but it was a delusion. From the prison came forth a cry of victory; from the gallows a shout of triumph over that power whose ethics are robbery of the weak and oppression of the feeble; the trophies of whose chivalry are a plundered cradle and a scourged and bleeding woman." The metaphor of blood too shifts from evidence of pain and suffering to take on a revolutionary purpose. From this murdered man drips drops of blood that bring about renewal: "It seems as if the blood had been instilled into the veins of freemen and given them fresh vigor to battle ... His blood was a new baptism of Liberty." Freedom, herself, rises up, "like a glorified angel [she] smiled over the glorious jubilee and stood triumphant on the very spot where the terrible goddess had reigned for centuries." Freedom's reign seems complete and permanent. "Truth and Justice crown her radiant brow ... Peace, like dew, descended where Slavery had spread ruin and desolation ... the guilty goddess ... ashamed of her meanness and guilt, skulked from the habitations of men, and ceased to curse the land with her presence." The story ends, however, with an explanation of the price of this peace, reminding us that "the first stepping-stones of Freedom to power, were the lifeless bodies of the old man and his brave companions."[10]

The gory details of the story anticipate the bloodshed of the Civil War, and it is no surprise that African Americans in 1860 might imagine the end of slavery in the United States emerging only from a violent overthrowing of enslaver power. Scholars including Carla Peterson, Derrick Spires, and Michael Stancliff have discussed how Watkins Harper here recalls John Brown's raid on Harpers Ferry and his subsequent execution by the state.[11] "The Triumph of Freedom" repeats some of the language Harper used in letters to both Brown and his wife, Mary, sent in November of 1859. But even in the specificity of allegorizing local events, Harper's story stipulates the possibility of abolitionist revolutionary success. The Haitian Revolution, though unmentioned in Harper's story, is a necessary source of this possibility. Michael Stancliff calls "Triumph of Freedom" "a republican allegory of the abolitionist moment within Jacksonian culture," writing that the story "serves as a brief history of abolitionist rhetoric, a figuration of its providential import and its place in the progress of the republic."[12] One can read in this allegory an allusion to John Brown's raid and subsequent martyrdom for the abolitionist cause, as "They forced him into prison, but they had no chains strong enough to bind his freeborn spirit."[13] Merging historical themes with those of progress, Harper's "Dream" story reads not only as allegory of past occurrences, but also as predictive of a pattern.

Inasmuch as Harper allegorizes John Brown's raid and execution, she also projects the effects of his attempt into a future she cannot yet foresee. Harper's prediction is not simply hopeful. Any mid-nineteenth century hope for antislavery revolution would have been informed by the Haitian Revolution's success. To understand Harper's and other African American writers' antebellum revolutionary writing, we must understand slave rebellion in light of its revolutionary success, rather than just in terms of its curtailment.

Haiti as a Revolutionary Genre

African Americans largely regarded the Haitian Revolution as a triumph for abolition having implications for the larger Black diaspora. Black people successfully overthrew the enslaver power and established a Black-led nation where there was once an enslaver colony. Despite what Michel-Rolph Trouillot and other historians have characterized as an underappreciation of the Haitian Revolution's importance in mainstream white history, scholars including Colin Dayan, Susan Buck-Morss, Elizabeth Maddock Dillon, and

Michael Drexler have emphasized its importance. As Marlene Daut writes, "when it comes to the eighteenth and nineteenth centuries there is almost too much written material on the Haitian Revolution."[14] African Americans, in particular, have long understood its significance.

Unsurprisingly, the story of Haiti's abolitionist triumph quickly became a mainstay of early African American history. Gabriele Pisarz-Ramirez describes how "Saint-Domingue had become a trope of resistance already in the late eighteenth century."[15] Prince Hall, for example, used Haiti as a point of hope for Black people in the United States even before the close of the legal transatlantic slave trade. In a 1797 speech to a Boston Freemasons African Lodge, he offered the comfort of this reminder: "My brethren, let us remember what a dark day it was with our African brethren six years ago, in the French West Indies."[16] In 1832 Maria Stewart noted this disparity in acknowledgment, writing that "the Haytians [*sic*], though they have not been acknowledged as a nation, yet their firmness of character and independence of spirit have been greatly admired, and high applauded."[17]

African American newspapers maintained attention on the contemporary Haitian nation while repeating—at times to the point of mythologization—histories of the Haitian Revolution. Scholars from C. L. R. James to Marlene Daut have recognized what Maurice Jackson describes as the Haitian Revolution's "profound influence on the development of African American history, culture, and political thought" from the late eighteenth century forward.[18] Colleen O'Brien shows how images of the Haitian Revolution "permeate the imaginative and political discourses" of the era of reform between 1835 and 1870.[19] Haiti's revolutionary resonance becomes clearest perhaps in the literary contexts of the Black press, and the Black abolitionist discourse in which Harper takes part.

Early African American newspapers such as *Freedom's Journal* and the *Colored American* celebrated Haiti. Charlton Yingling calls this celebration "a racial formation project that centered the racially redemptive power of Haiti as its incontrovertible evidence, countering hegemonic aspersions against blacks' intelligence, solvency, social responsibility, and ethics."[20] Histories of the Revolution and its leaders were accompanied by contemporary news about Haiti in the Black press, including debates about African American emigration to Haiti. While emigrationists were often pessimistic about the possibilities for Black emancipation and citizenship in the United States, anti-emigrationists built arguments around the principle (even if not the probability) that African American people ought to enjoy racial equality in the country of their birth.

In the *Anglo-African Magazine*, Haiti appeared in similar ways. The conclusion to J. Theodore Holly's seven-part "Thoughts on Hayti" was published in the January 1860 issue of the *Anglo-African Magazine* alongside "The Triumph of Freedom." In an 1857 pamphlet Holly had called the Revolution "one of the noblest, grandest, and most justifiable outbursts against tyrannical oppression that is recorded on the pages of the world's history."[21] In the *Anglo-African Magazine*, although Holly critiques early leaders such as Jean Jacques Dessalines and Henri Christophe, he recounts a general narrative of national progress from emancipation to "the golden dawn of Haytian prosperity," praising Haiti's newly elected president, General Fabre-Nicolas Geffard.[22] He concludes his thoughts by connecting this history of Haiti to the larger Black diaspora and the project of African American emigration, "with every prospect of ultimate success in the regeneration of that people, and the promotion of the cause of the descendants of Africa throughout the world."[23]

Haitian Revolutionary history and hagiography resonated alongside and sometimes counter to both praise and critique of contemporary Haiti. Across a spectrum of varying relationships to, and political beliefs about, the nation of Haiti in the mid-century, African American people acknowledged the Revolution's significance. Even African American writers with disparate ideas about matters of foreign policy and African American emigration, or the Haitian government and economy, nevertheless shared a consensus regarding the necessity of global abolition, which in turn solidified the importance of the Haitian Revolution for Black history. Whatever their thoughts on contemporary Haitian political leaders or emigration, they would have been familiar with a mythologized story of the revolution. Regardless of what one thought about the contemporary state of the Haitian nation and its relationship to African American people, its existence as a Black-led nation evidenced the possibility of revolutionary abolition.

Stories of the Haitian Revolution thus constituted a recognizable literary genre, with a shared general plot and racialized variances in interpretation. They also served as an ur-text for imagining Black people's violent overthrow of their enslavers. For white people who saw Black emancipation as a threat, this genre took the form of a horror story. At one end of the spectrum, this story described violence against white people while refusing to acknowledge the violence of slavery itself.[24] Both the history and mythology surrounding the Revolution's success loomed behind white anxieties about slave insurrections. The prospect of Black revolutionary abolition contributed to British emancipation as well as to attempts to preserve slavery in the United States by limiting the gathering of, and communication among, enslaved Black people.

But for Black people and others who regarded the Revolution as a positive step toward global Black emancipation, the literary mythologization of this history constituted a genre of its own. Recognizing Black people's humanity and inherent right to freedom, this genre understood the Revolution as necessary violence, a form of self-defense against violent abusers who would not otherwise yield their hold on power. The framing of the Haitian Revolution *as revolution* was itself an evaluative assessment that painted these events alongside other world revolutions. It regarded revolution as both necessary and ethical, coding the relationship between colonizer and colonized as one of unjust power, and violent uprising as a corrective. To recognize Black Revolution as such was to acknowledge racial injustice and to approve of a "just" war in the interest of freedom. African American newspapers took up the Haitian Revolution for an audience that did not need to be convinced of Black humanity, the need for freedom, or the probability that this freedom might only be collectively achieved through violence.

To put it plainly, the Haitian Revolution constituted a literary genre of its own in the African American press. This genre comprised histories of the revolution and biographies of its key figures retold and reprinted since the publication of the first known African American newspaper, *Freedom's Journal* in 1827, through the rest of the century, and into the next. In its repetition, the genre became prominent enough that it must have been familiar to readers of the Black press. The continual fictionalization of the Haitian Revolution contributed to its mythologization. Rather than creating what Michel-Rolph Trouillot has called a "weird" "fiction of Haitian exceptionalism," the Revolution was—particularly for Black Americans— not "unthinkable" but quite thinkable, the stuff of dreams.[25] Amid white fears about revolts, Edlie Wong writes that "many black Americans welcomed these same events as a powerful portent of black political progress and possibility in the Atlantic."[26] Moreover, this Haitian Revolutionary story tied this history to a longer arc of Black emancipation.

Understanding the Haitian Revolution as just one point in a longer timeline of Black diasporic history allowed African Americans to rehearse the literature of emancipation. In what Daut calls the *"transatlantic print culture of the Haitian Revolution,"* the African American press presented this genre less as a "mulatto/a vengeance narrative" (as it appeared in literature by white writers like Victor Hugo and Leonora Sansay) than as a narrative of Black diasporic revolution.[27] Discourses about the Haitian Revolution helped African American people extend discussions about Black diasporic identity from a shared genealogical relationship to Africa to a quest for Black futures beyond enslavement and other forms of racist oppression.

As Daut and others have shown, the Haitian Revolution resonates throughout African American fiction. In Frank Webb's 1857 novel *The Garies and their Friends*, the Black Philadelphia businessman Mr. Walters has a portrait of "Toussaint L'Ouverture" in his home.[28] Noting this, Eric Gardner writes that this gesture to Haiti indicates that Webb "was well-educated— not only in Anglo-centric history, but also in a Pan-Africanist sense of Black history."[29] William J. Wilson's "Afric-American Picture Gallery" (published in the *Anglo-African Magazine* in February of 1859) walked its readers through an imagined gallery of Black art, which included a description of a sculpture of "Toussaint L'Ouverture in his home."[30] These imagined memorializations of the revolutionary hero give a sense of the subtle resonance of the revolution in Black fiction of the mid-century, but other texts treated the revolution even more directly.

The *Anglo-African Magazine* included the beginning chapters of Martin Delany's novel, *Blake, or the Huts of America*, which was serialized in 1859. Although *Blake* is not about the Haitian Revolution, Jean Lee Cole situates Delany's novel in a longer history of Black periodical fiction that begins with "Theresa—A Haytian Tale," published anonymously in *Freedom's Journal* in 1828. Both of these "fanciful" revolutionary stories, she writes, "test the boundaries of believable storytelling."[31] But it is not Black revolution that is unbelievable. As Cole writes, "the authors of these works were able to imagine possibilities—what *could* happen, what *might* be possible."[32] To understand this imagining one must shift focus from exceptional examples to everyday heroes who, through various types of work, render revolution possible. For Harper, the question of what *could* happen does not depend upon individual revolutionary heroes, but how the revolutionary resonates in the everyday. This everyday resonance is also a question of scale and scope; it asks how revolutionary events and histories inspire longer historical arcs.

"Our Greatest Want": Revolutionary Collectivity

Harper's acknowledgement, but only tangential address, of Haiti in her other writing amounts not simply to an omission of, or disinterest in, the Haitian Revolution, but suggests the non-necessity of recounting this history herself. In the context of the mid-century Black press, "The Triumph of Freedom" appears within this larger print history of celebrating the Haitian Revolution and its Black military and political heroes—and especially Toussaint Louverture—for a larger Black diasporic history. Harper would have been well aware of this history.

Moreover, Haiti is not entirely absent from Watkins Harper's other writing. Colleen O'Brien reads Harper's first novel *Minnie's Sacrifice*, serialized in the *Christian Recorder* in 1869, as inspired by the Revolution and the subsequent recognition of the Haitian nation, connecting African American economic uplift writing to Haitian success. Reading Haiti as an influential literary genre, she writes also that both interracial sex and interracial violence become "essential gothic tropes that characterized the effect of the Haitian Revolution on race and gender relations" in transatlantic literature more generally, including in the writing of African American women such as Julia C. Collins and Frances Harper.[33] In her reading of *Minnie's Sacrifice*, Carla Peterson writes that "In Harper's literary imagination, Southern slaveholding culture has its origins in the foreign Creole culture of pre-revolutionary Haiti and is characterized by ostentatious displays of wealth and moral self-indulgence. As such, it stands in negative contrast both to the many accounts of the independent black Republic of Haiti published in the *Recorder* and to Harper's vision of the North as a site of industrious free labor."[34] Still, Harper's imagination of pre-Revolutionary Haiti was juxtaposed with her historical fictionalizations of the US antebellum South. Harper thereby drew connections across the Black diaspora that readers encountered alongside interpretations of contemporary Haitian progress or success, contrasting these with African American post-emancipation futures and particularly the failure of Reconstruction to enact racial equality.

The genre of Haitian Revolutionary literary history that is inscribed in the early African American press is both local and global. The Haitian Revolution resonated into the larger Black diaspora in which slavery would continue late into the nineteenth century. The celebration of Black revolutionary heroes is prominent in many of the Black publications in which Harper published (including the *Anglo-African Magazine*, its counterpart the *Weekly Anglo-African* and successor the *Pine and Palm*, and the official newspaper of the African Methodist Episcopal Church, the *Christian Recorder*) and therefore told a history that had clear implications for Black people in the United States. Black writers not only addressed possibilities for emancipation in the United States but sought to connect African American people to broader histories and futures of Black emancipation. This was not simply a comparative reading of Haiti and the United States; both of these were situated in the broader landscape of the Black Atlantic.

While Harper's revolutionary writing was built upon this broader context for Black revolutionary history, necessity, and possibility, in her short fiction Harper ultimately sidesteps focus on Haiti and its prominent heroes in favor of promoting different revolutionary models. In her fourth installment of the serialization, "Zombi, or Fancy Sketches," Watkins Harper depicts an earlier revolutionary leader. "Fancy Sketches" was serialized in the *Anglo-African Magazine* under the pseudonym "Jane Rustic" and the introduction of the Zombi story into the narrative is just one example of Harper's tendency to bring domestic affairs in the national sense to bear upon domestic affairs of the parlor. Harper introduces this story specifically as a piece of global Black history that her characters want to share with their children.

Harper situates her story within a landscape in which Haiti's history and heroes are known. In the previous January 1860 installment of "Fancy Sketches," Mr. Ballard names Black leaders to whom one might look as examples of courage and leadership and imagines gathering his children to tell them "stories of Margaret Garner, of Aunt Sally, of Toussaint L'Ouverture, of Denmark Vesey, of Nathaniel Turner, of Zombi and others."[35] Peterson notes that "of all the heroes Mr. Ballard enumerates ...Watkins demanded that he tell the history of the last named. She undoubtedly assumed that her readers would be familiar with the first three men named and so sought to give prominence to a much less well-known figure of the African diaspora."[36]

REVOLUTIONARY RESONANCES

Harper's own reference to the Haitian Revolution figures, then, in terms of mythic history that aligns with the genre of revolutionary writing she recalls, which traces the revolutionary heroes of Black history.

In the tale within the February 1860 sketch, "Zombi, and the Negro Kingdom," Harper tells the story of the quilombo/maroon community of Palmeres in seventeenth-century colonial Brazil. As Dutch and Portuguese colonizers vie for control, Harper explains, Black people arm themselves. We read that "instead of laying aside the instruments of war for the badges of slavery, and tamely submitting their necks to the yolk of oppression, they set up a kingdom for themselves."[37] Harper then gives a brief history describing how the maroon community was formed and established itself:

> They found a place of refuge ... and in course of time a number of fugitive negroes resorted to them, and their numbers soon became formidable ... They established equal laws among themselves ... they established equal rights among themselves ... They formed a government under an elector named Zombi ...Two decades passed over their heads, and this new kingdom had increased to more than twenty thousand inhabitants.[38]

Finally, in 1694, the Portuguese government assailed the settlement and, though with difficulty, "The sadly fated place was stormed and taken." Watkins Harper ends her story with the final act of her hero:

> Zombi and his chief adherents resolved not to be taken alive; death in one of its terrible forms was before them; but they rushed to it in preference to captivity. Over the high and rocky precipices of the fort they leaped, and were dashed to death. Instead of dragging to death's shadowy portals slavery's heavy, galling chain, they met a sudden and fearful death; the rest of the captured inhabitants were sold as slaves—and thus ended the first, though possibly not the last, negro kingdom on this continent.[39]

To readers unfamiliar with this story, this ending may be surprisingly un-triumphant. But for antebellum readers of the Black press or of antislavery literature, the idea that death may be preferable to slavery was familiar (hence the inclusion of Margaret Garner among Harper's heroes). Harper presents this story not for its depiction of a successful revolution, but for the struggle against slavery itself. Considered alongside the history of some other heroes she mentions—Garner, Vessey, or Turner—Zombi's death might be understood not as final, but as part of a longer revolutionary history that Harper seems to hold would tend toward justice.

The retelling of the history revisits a topic Watkins Harper had addressed previously, in her 1857 poem, "Death of Zombi, the Chief of a Negro Kingdom in Latin America." Like her later *mise-en-abyme* retelling of this story, the poem, as Monique-Adelle Callahan writes, "translates Zombi from a symbol of African resistance in Brazil to a figure for the transnational phenomenon of black resistance in the Americas as a whole."[40] Straddling the Haitian Revolution, Harper illustrates a longer arc of Black resistance to slavery. Discussing this story, Carla Peterson regards Harper's choice of focus as deliberate, writing that "Watkins chose to focus not on Haiti, whose revolutionary history had provided such a beacon of hope to U.S. blacks throughout the nineteenth century, but on the much less well-known maroon community of Palmares and its leader, Zumbi."[41] Seen in this light, this focus was not a denial of Haiti's importance to nineteenth-century African American discourses on emancipation and revolution, but a result of Haiti's prominence in that discourse. Derrick Spires surmises that Harper may have chosen the Palmares story in part because it did not necessitate wading into debates about contemporary Haiti as a place for African American emigration. Whatever ideas Harper had about the state of the Haitian nation in the mid-century or the question of African American emigration, she found hope for the future in global revolution, which extended beyond any individual failure or success. This becomes clear as we focus on the resistance within, rather than the conclusion of, "Zombi, and the Negro Kingdom." Even Toussaint Louverture died in a French prison in 1803, not as a triumphant leader of a successful Black nation. By considering the longer arc of these revolutionary stories, the whole becomes more than the sum of its parts.

Harper's story thus functioned not simply in lieu of her presenting another retelling of the Haitian Revolution, but as part of the longer arc of Black Revolutionary history that included Palmeres, Haiti, and the future she foresaw for Black emancipation in the United States. As Harper contributed yet another piece to this Black revolutionary timeline, she implicitly signaled Haiti's importance for the Black diaspora. While important, however, she refrains from regarding Haiti as exceptional. By tracing a longer revolutionary history that both predates the Haitian Revolution and extends itself to an unknowable future, Harper deemphasizes the specificity of these events in favor of highlighting the larger phenomenon of which they are representative.

This lack of specificity is central to Harper's allegory. By leaving John Brown's name unstated in "Triumph of Freedom," Harper writes not only the story of a single event or series of events but maps a kind of genre for understanding them. Though inspired by Brown's raid, Harper views these events according to a type that she finds both familiar and predictive. Like the particular genre with which we might associate writing about Haiti in the early nineteenth-century Black press, Harper's allegory is a particular kind of story about slavery, revolution, and ultimately justice. The comfort of genre is that it provides a map of sorts for the reader's comprehension. Not entirely predictable, genre nevertheless allows readers to make assumptions about how a story will play out. If Brown's raid and Harper's allegory are the same kind of story as the Haitian Revolution, readers yearning for racial justice are asked to read this genre hopefully. Read against Haiti's history, Watkins Harper's story becomes that much more hopeful in its possibility.

The omission of particulars in "Triumph of Freedom" also shifts focus from individual leaders like Brown (or Louverture or other male revolutionary heroes) and instead emphasizes a revolution of the masses, painting a picture of revolution that would require not only exceptional figures but ordinary people. This point is essential for understanding the hope with which Watkins Harper leaves us at the end of "The Triumph of Freedom—A Dream." While these various revolutionary heroes may provide inspiration, they are not the sum of these movements. Derrick Spires discusses the "pedagogies of revolutionary citizenship" in Harper's *Anglo-African Magazine* fiction, suggesting the importance of ordinary people's contributions and contexts for revolutionary lineages.[42] Harper traces a long revolutionary history in her theorization of citizenship, as Spires shows in his discussion of "The Triumph of Freedom" and "Fancy Sketches." The connections between these *Anglo-African Magazine* pieces show, also, Harper's broad scope for revolutionary action.

Harper's revolution will not be tokenized. The most powerful revolutionary actions she describes are not the exceptional events of pointed violence, but the everyday actions that help to comprise a much longer historical arc. The violence of revolution is therefore inseparable from the everyday actions of everyday activists. Harper associates the revolution with familiar images of bloody martyrdom in her short essay, "Our Greatest Want," published in the *Anglo-African Magazine* in 1859. Here Harper connects US slavery to emancipation in both the British and French empires. On the latter, she writes that

> visions of dominion, proud dreams of conquest fill the soul of Napoleon Bonaparte, and he infuses them into the mind of France, and the peace of Europe is invaded. His bloodstained armies dazzled and misled, follow him through carnage and blood, to shake earth's proudest kingdoms to their base, and the march of a true progression is stayed by a river of blood.[43]

Here we see the Haitian Revolution positioned against the "proudest kingdoms" of colonizer, enslaver nations. But the "march of a true progression" is not the work of any single figure and extends beyond revolutionary violence.

Ultimately, the Black community's "greatest want," as Harper describes it, is not for a Moses or a John Brown or a Toussaint Louverture, but for the collective work of ordinary people. She argues, "We need men and women whose hearts are the homes of a high and lofty enthusiasm, and a noble devotion to the cause of emancipation, who are ready and willing to lay time, talent and money on the altar of universal freedom."[44] Harper's dream for the reign of post-emancipation "Truth," "Justice," and "Peace" would not—as Harper well knew—result from white saviordom (or even white martyrdom).[45] Neither would it arise from Black saviordom or martyrdom, but only from collective, continued effort.

A Dream of Emancipatory Black Futures

Thinking beyond individual heroes, Black activists have often recognized the power of collective action. Even as he lauded Toussaint Louverture as "one of the most remarkable men of a period rich in remarkable men" C. L. R. James noted, "Yet Toussaint did not make the revolution. It was the revolution that made Toussaint. And even that is not the whole truth."[46] In her own revolutionary allegory, Harper too resists even the valorization of a singular figure in John Brown, whom she represents as a martyr to the antislavery cause, but not as its only significant revolutionary. While the "old man" of Harper's allegory seems most clearly tied to John Brown, the "young man" with whom she opens her story is more of a mystery. Derrick Spires suggests a number of possibilities, from David Walker to Elijah Lovejoy as historical inspirations for this "young man."[47] There were also young men at Brown's Harper's Ferry raid, some of whom were also executed for their participation. Shields Green, a formerly enslaved man who was hanged two weeks after Brown, was twenty-two or twenty-three at the time of his death. Young free-born Black men were also executed for their participation in the raid. Lewis Sheridon Leary was 24 years old and John Anthony Copeland, Jr. was 24 or 25. The white abolitionist Aaron Dwight Stephens was 28 at the time of the raid and 29 at the time of his execution.[48]

Osborne Perry Anderson, the only Black man to survive the raid, was also 29 years old in 1859. Anderson escaped execution with the help of the Underground Railroad and moved to Ontario, Canada, where he had lived previously, and worked for the *Provincial Freeman*. He published his account of the raid in an 1861 pamphlet, *A Voice from Harper's Ferry*. Anderson's revolutionary history is worth mentioning because it is similar to Harper's. In his opening chapter, he argues for "an unbroken chain of sentiment and purpose from Moses of the Jews to John Brown of America," making familiar connections between Old Testament and African American slavery and comparing European revolutions and slave insurrections "from Kossuth, and the liberators of France and Italy, to the untutored Gabriel, and the Denmark Veseys, Nat Turners and Madison Washingtons of the Southern American States."[49] As with Harper's litany of revolutionary figures, Anderson further connects antislavery sentiment throughout the Black diaspora. This includes Haiti, as he writes that "The shaping and expressing of a thought for freedom takes the same consistence with the colored American—whether he be an independent citizen of the Haytian nation, a proscribed but humble nominally free colored man, a patient, toiling, but hopeful slave—as with the proudest or noblest representative of European or American civilization and Christianity."[50] Reading Watkins Harper's allegory about John Brown within an African American literary genre that includes Haitian Revolutionary history and mythologization, we also understand the connections she makes between individual African American people and a larger Black diaspora, as well as to future generations.

To read Harper's story as a "Dream" is not only to understand her hopeful anticipation of abolition in the United States, but also to understand a gesture toward both what the Haitian Revolution had accomplished and, especially, toward what it might still inspire. Contextualizing Harper's fantasy alongside historical accounts of Haitian independence provides a hint of realism, suggesting that the Triumph of Freedom she imagines is not out of reach, but is in fact a realizable future. Similarly to how Jean Lee Cole describes the author of "Theresa" as allowing the Haitian Revolution to "transcend, if incompletely, the historical moment [and] … approach… the level of myth," Harper's revolutionary dream is transcendent of her historical context.[51] It points, rather, to possibilities that may even be outside its temporal scope.

Along similar lines, John Ernest calls it "no surprise that so many black abolitionists viewed the Civil War as the second American Revolution."[52] African American writers also created associations between slave rebellion and the Civil War, though Jennifer James notes that such associations obscure the fact that civil war and slave revolts were decidedly different types of events.[53] Before the war, however, it was not yet clear what form the inevitable coming violence would take. Neither was it clear what the scope of that violence's effects would be. With the Haitian Revolution, historians and political commentators would also consider the potential scope of its afterlives. C. L. R. James wrote, in his 1963 preface to *The Black Jacobins*, that the concluding pages of his Appendix "From Toussaint L'Ouverture to Fidel Castro" "were intended to stimulate the coming emancipation of Africa."[54] Noting that "Writers on the West Indies always relate them to their approximation to Britain, France, Spain, and America … never in relation to their own history" James attempts to correct a misalignment of writing on Haiti.[55] Taken in the larger genre of Black writing on the revolution from the eighteenth century forward, however, we can understand James's definitive work as fitting within a long arc of interpreting the Revolution through histories of global Black emancipation. Like James's extension of this narrative toward African decolonialization, nineteenth-century African American writers on Haiti read the events of late-eighteenth-century Saint-Domingue not only as exceptional but as having the power to resonate throughout the Black Atlantic world.

That resonance echoed for this foundational writer of Black history much as it did for those who reproduced accounts and reverberations of the Revolution in the early African American press. As the Haitian Revolution approached the level of myth, Harper in "Triumph of Freedom" writes antislavery revolution more generally as mythic. Reading Harper's story as allegory, there is an impulse to understand her framing as utopian. But Harper's dreamscape is not a non-place. Her dream is not only a wish or even a hope, but an act of faith informed not only by understandings of history and theodicy, but also by the collective will of people whose struggle will not end with a single battle. Harper's "Dream" traces the relationship between history and myth, allegory and futurity. Saidiya Hartman discusses the implications of this kind of speculative dreaming for post-slavery imagining. In "Venus in Two Acts," Hartman writes, she attempts "to imagine a *free state*, not as the time before captivity or slavery, but rather as the anticipated future of this writing."[56] Harper too imagines this free state as an anticipated future for her writing.

That free state is not simply a return to a time before captivity or an alignment with past revolutions, but a revolutionary future, a propelled movement forward. However we characterize Harper's revolutionary dream, we can understand it as pointing toward a moment of Black emancipation that does not orient us to any one specific historical context, but gestures toward broader historical and geographic implications yet to be realized. In truth, neither John Brown's raid nor the US Civil War brought the change many had hoped for. The latter failed to bring more revolutionary changes for African Americans, the oppression of whom shifted to other forms following emancipation. It would be a mistake to say that this fact came as a surprise to Harper. Even in 1859 she must have expected US emancipation to require a longer, sustained movement toward racial equality.

The perpetually unfinished nature of revolution becomes evident in the framing of Harper's Zombi retelling. Harper juxtaposes Black heroes and history with Black domestic spaces, situating this story within a contemporary discussion of politics and work. As the story closes, Miranda is tearful and comments on its sadness, adding also "how much these things stir my soul against the wrongs which our people have endured age after age. But I feel that we are living in the beginning of the end, and that a better day is about to dawn on the fortunes of our race; and in the future that is before us I want to be an active worker, and not an idle spectator."[57] Harper did not relegate revolution only to the historical or fantastical. Nor did she imagine revolution only in exceptional moments, as with Harper's Ferry. She imagined it, instead, in the continued and continuing everyday work of those people who found inspiration in stories of the revolutionary.

* * *

Harper continued to find revolutionary potential even in failed events, and ones much less grandiose than Brown's attempt. In "An Appeal for the Philadelphia Rescuers," a letter to the editor published in the *Weekly Anglo-African* in June of 1860, Harper responded to the failed attempt to free Moses Horner, a self-emancipated fugitive, from a Philadelphia jail. The event ended with the jailing of ten of the attempted rescuers and the return of Horner to slavery in Virginia. Harper's letter asks the *Weekly Anglo-African's* editor, Thomas Hamilton, why she has found no response to these events from the newspaper. She asks, "Shall these men throw themselves across the track of the general government and be crushed by the mo[n]strous Juggernaut of organized villainy, the Fugitive Slave Law, and we sit silent, with our hands folded, in selfish inactivity?"[58] Watkins Harper goes on to argue that "It is not enough to express our sympathy by words; we should be ready to crystalize it into actions."[59] What Harper calls for are financial contributions to support their trial expenses, noting the insufficiency of her own small contribution, arguing that it ought to be supported with gratitude by a community who supports the abolitionist cause.

Harper anticipates a critique of the failed rescuers' attempt, but she rejects the idea that their attempt was futile. "Do not stop to cavil and find fault by saying they were rash and imprudent, and engaged in a hopeless contest. Their ears were quicker than ours; they heard the death-knell of freedom sound in the ears of a doomed and fated brother, and to them they were clarion sounds, rousing their souls to deeds of noble daring—trumpet tones, inciting them to brave and lofty actions"[60] The rescuers' attempt was not simply a futile one; there had been some similar, though successful, rescues. On October 1, 1851, a group of local abolitionists freed William "Jerry" Henry, who had been arrested under the Fugitive Slave Law, from a jail in Syracuse, NY, ultimately helping him to escape to Canada. A crowd that Gerrit Smith later claimed numbered as many as twenty-five hundred people (many of whom were attendees of the abolitionist Liberty Party's state convention in Syracuse), stormed the Police Justice offices during what became known as the "Jerry Rescue." This rescue would be commemorated annually in the years that followed.

But far more than the question of the Philadelphia rescuers' probability of success, Harper seems most invested in the attempt itself and what work her reporting on this attempt might inspire. The "fearful death" of Zombi and his followers inspires those who hear this story in the Fancy Sketches to action and to inspire others. The "lifeless bodies of the old man and his brave companions" allow others to step toward freedom in her allegory of triumph. And Haitian Revolutionary history, told and retold in the pages of African American newspapers, framed the antislavery efforts of people who chose to assume rather than doubt the possibility of Black emancipation. Viewed in this context for revolutionary imaginings, Harper's fantastical allegory imbues meanings both historical and anticipatory, reverberating a Dream that gathers the Haitian Revolution up in its hopeful trajectories.

Notes

1 I owe thanks to Derrick Spires for helpful conversation about Harper's Anglo-African fiction and the resonances of the Haitian Revolution in the early African American press. Thanks also to Jonathan Senchyne for his careful reading and comments as I revised this piece.

2 The *Anglo-African Magazine* was published from January 1859 to March 1860. In July 1859 Hamilton also created a weekly counterpart to the magazine, the *Weekly Anglo-African*. Despite the plethora of prominent African American writers whose work appeared in these periodicals, like most nineteenth-century newspapers, the longevity of Hamilton's endeavors was determined by financial difficulties. Hamilton's poor health compounded with these, causing him to end publication of the *Anglo-African Magazine* at the beginning of its second year. The *Weekly Anglo-African* ran until 1861, at which point Hamilton sold this newspaper to the Scottish-American publisher, abolitionist, and promoter of Black emigration to Haiti, James Redpath. In May of 1861, the *Weekly Anglo-African* was then rebranded as *The Pine and Palm* and the newspaper was financed by the Haitian government. *The Pine and Palm* continued to publish prominent African American authors (including Frances Watkins Harper) until its publication ended in September 1862, as Redpath also stepped down as Commissioner for Haitian Emigration from the United States and Canada, a position he had held since 1860. On the transition from the *Weekly Anglo-African* to the *Pine and Palm*, including the importance of Haiti to the paper's publication and content, see Brigitte Fielder, Cassander Smith, and Derrick R. Spires' Introduction to "*Weekly Anglo-African* and *The Pine and Palm* (1861–1862)," Just Teach One: Early African American Print no. 4 (Spring 2018). http://jtoaa.common-place.org/welcome-to-just-teach-one-african-american/weekly-anglo-african-and-the-pine-and-palm/.

3 Derrick Spires, *The Practice of Citizenship: Black Politics and Print Culture in the Early United States* (Philadelphia: University of Pennsylvania Press, 2019), 32.

4 Spires, *The Practice of Citizenship*, 8.

5 Throughout this essay I will refer to Frances Ellen Watkins Harper as both "Harper," as she is most commonly called, and "Watkins Harper," in order to emphasize the fact of this author's literary production prior to her marriage, after which she did not omit but retained the name Watkins, adding Harper to it. Here I follow scholars such as Carla Peterson, Andréa Williams, and Koritha Mitchell, who similarly use "Watkins Harper" together to emphasize the author's premarital career. Attending to this emphasis is particularly important for Watkins Harper's *Anglo-African* writing, which predated her marriage in 1860.

6 Frances Ellen Watkins (Harper), "The Two Offers," *Anglo-African Magazine* 1 (September 1859): 288–91; 339–45.

7 Frances Ellen Watkins (Harper), "The Triumph of Freedom—a Dream," *Anglo-African Magazine* (January 1860): 21. (This story can also be found in

A Brighter Coming Day: A Frances Ellen Watkins Harper Reader, ed. Frances Smith Foster (New York: Feminist Press, 1990), 114–17.) Page numbers given are from the original publication.

8   Watkins (Harper), "The Triumph of Freedom," 21–2.

9   Watkins (Harper), "The Triumph of Freedom," 22.

10 Watkins (Harper), "The Triumph of Freedom," 22–3.

11 Fittingly, the magazine follows Watkins (Harper)'s story directly with Joseph Murray Wells's poem, "John Brown at Harper's Ferry," *The Anglo-African Magazine* (January 1860): 23–7.

12 Michael Stancliff, *Frances Ellen Watkins Harper: African American Reform and the Rise of a Modern Nation State* (New York: Routledge, 2010), 34–5.

13 Watkins (Harper), "The Triumph of Freedom," 22.

14 Marlene Daut, *Tropics of Haiti: Race and the Literary History of the Haitian Revolution in the Atlantic World, 1789–1865* (Liverpool: Liverpool University Press, 2015), 2.

15 Gabriele Pisarz-Ramirez, "The Darkest Is Before the Break Of Day": Rhetorical Uses of Haiti in the Works of Early African-American Writers" *Atlantic Studies: The French Atlantic* 4, no. 1 (April 2007): 41.

16 Prince Hall, *A charge, delivered to the African Lodge, June 24, 1797, at Menotomy. By the Right Worshipful Prince Hall; Published by the desire of the members of said Lodge* (Boston: Printed by Benjamin Edes, 1797), 11. Evans Early American Imprint Collection: https://quod.lib.umich.edu/e/evans/N24354.0001.001/1:2?rgn=div1;view=fulltext.

17 Maria W. Stewart, "An Address Delivered Before the Afric-American Female Intelligence Society of Boston. By Mrs. Maria W. Stewart." *The Liberator*, 28 April 1832.

18 Maurice Jackson, "'Friends of the Negro! Fly with me, The path is open to the sea'- Remembering the Haitian Revolution in the History, Music, and Culture of the African American People" *Early American Studies* 6, no. 1 (Spring 2008): 59, 59–103.

19 Colleen C. O'Brien, *Race, Romance, and Rebellion: Literatures of the Americas in the Nineteenth Century* (Charlottesville: University of Virginia Press, 2013), ix.

20 Charlton W. Yingling, "'No One Who Reads the History of Hayti Can Doubt the Capacity of Colored Men': Racial Formation and Atlantic Rehabilitation in New York City's Early Black Press, 1827–1841," *Early American Studies* 11, no. 2 (April 2013): 317, 314–48.

21 James Theodore Holly, *A Vindication of the Capacity of the Negro Race for Self-Government and Civilized Progress, as Demonstrated by Historical Events of the Haytian Revolution; and the Subsequent Acts of That People since Their National Independence* (New Haven: W. H. Stanley, Printer, 1857), 6.

22 J. Theodore Holly, "Thoughts on Hayti" Number VII. *Anglo-African Magazine* 2 (January 1860): 18.

23 Holly, "Thoughts on Hayti," 18.

24 See, for example, Laura Sansay's 1808 epistolary novel, *Secret History; or, The Horrors of St. Domingo.*

25 Michel-Rolph Trouillot, "The Odd and the Ordinary: Haiti, the Caribbean, and the World," *Cimarron* 2, no. 3 (1990): 3.

26 Edlie Wong, "In the Shadow of Haiti: The Negro Seamen Act, Counter-Revolutionary St. Domingue, and Black Emigration," in *The Haitian Revolution and the Early United States: Histories, Textualities, Geographies,* ed. Elizabeth Maddock Dillon and Michael Drexler (Philadelphia: University of Pennsylvania Press, 2016), 163.

27 Daut, *Tropics of Haiti*, 3, 4.

28 Frank J. Webb, *The Garies and Their Friends*, ed. Robert Reid-Pharr (Baltimore: Johns Hopkins University Press, 1997), 123.

29 Eric Gardner, "'A Gentleman of Superior Cultivation and Refinement': Recovering the Biography of Frank J. Webb," *African American Review* 35, no. 2 (2001): 1043.

30 Ethiop [William J. Wilson] "Afric-American Picture Gallery—Second Paper," *Anglo-African Magazine* (March 1859): 87.

31 Jean Lee Cole, "Theresa and Blake: Mobility and Resistance in Antebellum African American Serialized Fiction," *Callaloo* 34, no. 1 (2011) 162, 158.

32 Cole, "Theresa And Blake," 159.

33 Colleen O'Brien, *Race, Romance, and Rebellion: Literatures of the Americas in the Nineteenth Century* (Charlottesville: University of Virginia Press, 2013), 3.

34 Carla Peterson, "Reconstructing the Nation: Frances Harper, Charlotte Forten, and the Racial Politics of Periodical Publication," *Proceedings of the American Antiquarian Society* 107.2 (January 1, 1997): 314.

35 Frances Ellen Watkins (Harper) as Jane Rustic, "Fancy Sketches," Number III *Anglo-African Magazine* 2 (January 1860): 11.

36 Peterson "Literary Transnationalism," 205.

37 Frances Ellen Watkins (Harper) as Jane Rustic, "Zombi, or Fancy Sketches," Number IV *Anglo-African Magazine* 2 (February 1860): 36.

38 Watkins (Harper) as Jane Rustic, "Zombi, or Fancy Sketches," 36.

39 Watkins (Harper) as Jane Rustic, "Zombi, or Fancy Sketches," 36.

40 Monique-Adelle Callahan, *Between the Lines: Literary Transnationalism and African American Poetics* (Oxford: Oxford University Press, 2011), 45.

41 Carla Peterson "Literary Transnationalism and Diasporic History: Frances Watkins Harper's 'Fancy Sketches,' 1859–1860," in *Women's Rights and Transatlantic Antislavery in the Era of Emancipation*, ed. Kathryn Kish Sklar and James Brewer Stewart (New Haven: Yale University Press, 2007), 193.

42 Spires, *The Practice of Citizenship*, 211.

43 Frances Ellen Watkins (Harper), "Our Greatest Want," *Anglo-African Magazine* 1 (May 1859): 160.

REVOLUTIONARY RESONANCES 183

44 Watkins (Harper), "Our Greatest Want," 160.

45 Watkins (Harper), "The Triumph of Freedom," 23.

46 C. L. R. James, Preface to the First [1938] Edition, *The Black Jacobins: Toussaint L'Ouverture and the San Domingo Revolution*, 2nd ed., rev. (New York: Vintage Books, 1963), x.

47 Spires, *The Practice of Citizenship*, 242.

48 In a December 1859 letter to Black abolitionist William Still, Harper urges him to assist Stephens by sending him "a box of nice things every week till he dies or is acquitted." Frances Ellen Watkins (Harper), December 12, 1859, letter to William Still. In *A Brighter Coming Day: A Frances Ellen Watkins Harper Reader*, ed. Frances Smith Foster (New York: Feminist Press, 1990), 51.

49 Osborne Perry Anderson, *A Voice from Harper's Ferry; with Incidents Prior and Subsequent to Its Capture by Captain Brown and his Men* (Boston: Printed for the Author, 1861), 5.

50 Anderson, *A Voice from Harper's Ferry*, 5–6.

51 Cole, "Theresa and Blake," 161.

52 John Ernest, *Chaotic Justice: Rethinking African American Literary History* (Chapel Hill: University of North Carolina Press, 2009), 201.

53 Jennifer James, *A Freedom Bought with Blood: African American Literature form the Civil War to World War II* (Chapel Hill: University of North Carolina Press, 2007), 39.

54 James, Preface to the Vintage [1963] Edition, *The Black Jacobins*, vii.

55 James, Preface to the Vintage [1963] Edition, *The Black Jacobins*, vii.

56 Saidiya Hartman, "Venus in Two Acts," *Small Axe* 12, no. 2 (2008): 4.

57 Watkins (Harper) as Jane Rustic, "Zombi, or Fancy Sketches," 36.

58 Frances Ellen Watkins (Harper), "An Appeal for the Philadelphia Rescuers," *Weekly Anglo-African* (June 23, 1860), 1.

59 Watkins (Harper), "An Appeal for the Philadelphia Rescuers," 1.

60 Watkins (Harper), "An Appeal for the Philadelphia Rescuers," 1.

8

Revolutionary Shattering: Emerson on the Haitian Revolution

Branka Arsić

Fear, craft, and avarice cannot rear a state.

—RALPH WALDO EMERSON, "POLITICS"

From the early to later writings Emerson insists on continuity between what is internal to the mind and what surrounds it.[1] *Nature* (1836) famously speaks of it as a continuity that renders the "laws of ethics" translations of the "axioms of physics."[2] This continuity is commonly interpreted as a form of idealism whereby the mind imposes itself on what is natural, *ideating* it, not only denigrating the relevance of the natural but also presuming it to be uninterested in what is external to it. In fact, Emerson means the opposite of that, for in saying that "nature is the vehicle of thought"[3]—and nature in Emerson includes not just "essences unchanged by man," such as "space, the air, the river, the leaf," but also what is cultural and social, "art, all other men and my own body"—he is claiming nothing less than a substantial continuity and even coincidence between the natural, cultural, and the mental. According to his idea, then, trees and paintings do not simply embody thoughts (of Gods or humans); more strangely, thoughts, which are never specified as human, circulate throughout the natural, affecting and so changing it. All matter is alive with a thinking that turns "material objects ... [into] substantial thoughts";[4] and conversely, each perception and thought is more refined matter. Only the "I"—yet not its body and perceptions—is excluded from this meshing of embodied thoughts and thoughtful things, like some spectral gloom gliding through it, unable to mediate it. Thus, even if this "I" is idealistic, its idealism—because of the lack of connection between it and what it ideates—is always a failure.

Not only "Nature" but indeed Emerson's entire oeuvre will be an investigation into the possibility of relinking the "I" with the continuity of phenomena. To answer just how the "I" might heal the gap between itself and its body, other living beings and objects, the essay will explore experiences of self-cancellation—"I am nothing; ... the currents of the Universal Being circulate through me"[5]—similar to "Circles," which talks of self-abandonment, and "Intellect," which proposes relinquishing the will in favor of an attitude of reception through which what is external to the "I" might enter it. Emerson formulated this receptive posture most precisely in "Powers of the Mind," a lecture delivered in March 1858 as the third in a series on the *Natural Method of Mental Philosophy*:[6] "The fundamental fact is ... correspondence and impressionability,—so that every change in [the world] writes a record on the mind. The mind yields ... to the tendencies ... which stream through things ... this obedience is a vital obedience ... as sharing the same blood and destiny."[7] Emerson here expects the "I" to assume a posture of utter exposure and fragility (hence of *unsafety*), in order to allow what is external to it to impress itself on it and so fashion it. For it is only when the "I" is made of, and by, what it is not that it will join the flow of beings and things in the world, affording it the feeling of life while allowing it to share the "blood and destiny" of others.

It is this exposure, frailness, and unsafety of the self that will interest me in what follows, as I seek not just to elucidate Emerson's ontology or psychology but above all to connect it to the question of the political that affects it. The first part of the essay will chart Emerson's theory of two types of self—one appropriative and individuated, the other desired by Emerson but difficult to reach, fragile, and receptive—arguing that Emerson imagined them both as embodying and fashioning two opposing ideas of the political: one generates the world of modern liberalism, obsessed with safety but lacking in liberty; the other wants to move toward a condition of radical unsafety in order to give beings the gift of the unpredictable. In the second part of my essay, I go on to propose that receptive personhood, which Emerson imagines as capable of cancelling self-appropriation—and which he positively formulates through a critique of Locke—was also at the center of his theory of the political. For Emerson, the political as imagined by Locke's liberalism—that is, the political that sees the essence of liberty in a person's right to turn itself into its first and most fundamental property—introduces a fusion between being and having that is transformed, following

Locke, into their confusion, that is, into a gray zone that sanctions the substitution of persons for appropriable things, something that was most disturbingly embodied in the institution of slavery. It is for that reason that I also outline Emerson's critique of liberalist politics. Finally, in the third part of the essay, I discuss in detail Emerson's "An Address on the Emancipation of the Negroes in the British West Indies," arguing that his celebration of the goals and means of the Haitian Revolution advocates revolutionary action not just as an adequate expression of an exposed self, a self released from the fear of its own safety, but also as the way into the new sociality that such a self would create, which blocks any confusion between persons and property. In connecting Emerson's philosophy of the mind to his politics my aim is to demonstrate that his insistence on revolutionary change in general, and his praise of the Haitian Revolution in particular, is no rhetorical accident generated by a particularly heated historical moment, hence something external to his thinking. Instead, I argue that Emerson is the thinker of revolution par excellence.

Revolution is always on Emerson's mind, through its relation to his ontological understanding of beings, his existential interpretation of personhood, and his political conception of the social. His insistence on revolutionary change cuts deep across his essays and addresses, connecting all of them in a single statement of radical opposition to what he sees as the most despicable compromise there is: desiring safety. Thus, when he famously says in "Circles" that "only so far as [people] are unsettled is there any hope for them,"[8] he is not aestheticizing unsafety, offering those who pale at the thought of death some vague reassurance that they are courageous reformers. To the contrary, he is crystallizing the essence of his whole thought, which is traversed by the insistence on revolutionary change. Such radical change is identified there as the happy ("uncommon") moment when all "we reckoned settled shakes and rattles; and literatures, cities, climates, religions, leave their foundations."[9] This unfounding of the world—hence, also of cities (states)—is happy because in shaking everything it also rattles and finally removes the "veil which shroud[s] all things." In other words, revolutionary turmoil undoes relations and meanings that we presume so settled as to be taken for granted, as a result growing insensitive to their shifts until we finally forget them (which is why they are "veiled"). Revolution wakes us out of this oblivion. By reassembling things and relations, it revives the meanings of the world; by making us see everything as if for the first time, revolutionary upsetting leads us to reassess the more general meaning of institutions and laws as well as the sense of what most ordinarily, hence boringly, surrounds us, "the meaning of the very furniture, of cup and saucer, of chair and clock and tester."[10] For Emerson that is happiness. The moment of utmost risk and highest danger—the moment of the revolutionary shattering of established relations—coincides with the instant of recovery, whether of the individual or the world. In fact,

188   HAITI'S LITERARY LEGACIES

the one can't happen without the other: persons can't undergo radical transformation in a world that is not revolutionarily changed, and the world can't be changed, and the political radically revised, if persons inhabiting it are conserved or preserved in their current state. When Emerson also says in "Circles" that only new thought can revolutionize the world by putting "all things at risk," so that everything is as if "a conflagration has broken out in a great city, and no man knows what is safe,"[11] he establishes a clear and precise link between the configuration of a new mind—a new assemblage of thoughts and perceptions—and a radical transformation of the world. What follows reconstructs this link.

1

"Self-Reliance" extrapolates insights regarding the inner workings of the mind into an argument about operations of the collective—what Emerson calls "our society"—moving from the existential to the political and turning discussion of mental phenomena into a call for social reform.

In that essay, as well as in "Intellect" and in the later series *The Natural Method of Mental Philosophy*, Emerson imagines the mind as a set of relations among perceptions and thoughts generated without any interference of the will and intention of the "I": "they [perceptions and thoughts] have a life of their own, and a motion proper to themselves,"[12] which is why "intellections are external to intellect."[13] The relations constituting the mind are volatile, since upon entering it each new perception affects the already existing relations among former perceptions and thoughts. Conceived of as a set of relations that generate themselves as they get affected by other perceptions, the mind in Emerson is less an entity than an activity, a mobile cluster of relays and links "wonderful, again, is their making and relation each to each."[14] But in affecting existing relations, new perceptions also create new thoughts, since thoughts are for Emerson precisely "perceptions of single relations" established among perceptions.[15] That relations are perceptible means, much as will be the case in William James's radical empiricism, that they are posited as phenomena that can be experienced like any other object or affect. Additionally, that thoughts are perceptions means that they can enter into relation with what they perceive, becoming themselves an object of perception for another thought.

Because the perceptions and thoughts constituting the mind assemble themselves without the "I," since the "I" never mediates and subjectivizes them, mental content is for Emerson as objective as any other natural phenomenon. Thus, when he says in "Self-Reliance" that "my perception is as much a fact as the sun"[16] he is not formulating a credo of subjective idealism that will bluntly afford an individual mind the right to render objectivity even less relevant than mental imagery. Rather, Emerson can say

REVOLUTIONARY SHATTERING

that what an "I" sees is as much a fact as is the existence of the sun precisely because that "I" has done nothing to generate what it perceives. Perceptions and thoughts are not derived from an "I" but external to it. Hence his claim that only to "involuntary perceptions a perfect faith is due."[17]

A mind that is always in the process of being generated by ongoing encounters between things and senses implies that each new perception enacted by those encounters can radically rearrange it. That is why in "Self-Reliance" perception is called "not whimsical but fatal";[18] or why in "Intellect" what we perceive is called our "fortune": "All that mass of mental and moral phenomena, which we do not make objects of voluntary thought, came with the power of fortune"[19]; or why in "Powers of the Mind" perception is identified as our "destiny": "A perception ... is there [in my mind] with all its destinies."[20] The mind is never safe within itself, but is instead remarkably vulnerable, disposed to what it encounters, lying "open to the mercy of coming events"[21] in such a way that the encounter can shatter it. This moment of shattering is variously called "abandonment," "rapture," or "revolution." In Emerson's vocabulary those notions suggest neither divination nor a quasi-Romantic elevation enacted by something sublime. Instead, they mean that encounters with things and beings in the world generate new perceptions capable of reassembling the relations among already existing thoughts in such a way as to produce a new mind: "a revolution impends more radical than any whereof we have experience. A perception came into my mind, by no chance, by no illusion; it is there by a fate, the same or much older than that in geology or gravitation."[22]

Emerson outlines two possible reactions of the "I" to this revolutionary reassembling of the mind. One, which he privileges and desires, is affirmative: the "I" weakens or suspends its will and allows itself to be drawn into the "currents of might and mind."[23] Realizing that it has "little control over [its] thoughts,"[24] that it is completely contingent since its will hasn't done anything to make it ("what am I? What has my will done to make me that I am? Nothing,"[25]), the "I" affirms the power of what makes it and lets itself go "into this thought ... this connection of events";[26] it abandons its supposed consciousness of events (something subjective) and turns itself into one relation among them (something objective), susceptible to being revised by other relations that affect it. "Self-Reliance" additionally argues that this "letting go" occurs only if the self stops worrying about its self-gatheredness or consistency. Refraining from trying to bind itself into a continuity that would safeguard its identity, such a self entrusts itself to becoming otherwise, even if in the process it undergoes the horror of complete dissolution, crossing an abyss without reliance, for everything reliable has precisely been shattered. In fact, because the "self"—signifying a stable or reliable identity—has been shattered in this revisionary becoming, Emerson will say that "to talk of reliance is a poor external way of speaking. Speak rather of that which relies, because it works and is."[27] In this process of revolutionary revision the "I" becomes an "it" that "works and is," an "I" dissolved into perceptions and thoughts whose relations are constantly altered; in other words, nothing other than pure becoming. Far from trusting the power of his will, as is so often presumed, the self-reliant man is one who doesn't flee like a "coward ... before a revolution," or sit like a "minor" in a "protected corner"; rather, unprotected, the self entrusts itself to its own revolutionary shattering: "and we are now men ... before a revolution ... advancing on Chaos and the Dark."[28]

Yet, as "Self-Reliance" famously claimed, the world resists the becoming that Emerson welcomes ("this one fact the world hates, that the soul becomes"[29]). Resistance to radical self-transformation is thus a second, negative response to the revolutionary shattering of the self. The self is by nature conservative, desiring to protect its consistency, even when such consistency is inconsistent with the perceptions and thoughts that conjure the mind. Such a position is, moreover, epistemologically fallacious, since to contradict perceptions is to deny the truthfulness of their disorderliness, a denial that Emerson calls thoughtless: "thoughtless people contradict the statement of perceptions."[30] And finally, it is ethically suspect, for it privileges what is only fantasized (the self's continuity and consistency) over what is (the actuality of multiple relations that constitute the mind); it is therefore the characteristic of "little minds, adored by little statesmen and philosophers and divines."[31]

"Self-Reliance" straightforwardly identifies fear as the reactionary emotion that turns us all into thoughtless conservatives who resist becoming. As Emerson specifies in that essay, we are afraid of losing the little that we have—the empty will of an "I" that cannot be trusted[32] but which deludes us into a feeling of self-continuity—in the discontinuity of perceptions and thoughts, just as we are afraid that the new modes of life and mind into which radical transformation might lead us won't be appealing "in the eyes of others."[33] In the core of our identity resides such an angst that, perversely, when we fear losing our identity we in fact fear losing fear. And to safeguard this fear—of being undone, of being left lonely and friendless after a radical transformation—we exchange revolutionary becoming for the safety of continuity: "the other terror that scares us from self-trust"—which would precisely entrust us to incalculable becoming—"is our consistency."[34] Revolutionary revisions are thus quashed by the conservative celebration of the stability of forms (the conservative is, as Emerson puts it in the lecture of the same name, precisely one who doesn't see that "the form is bad.")[35]

Emerson draws a strict parallel between the ways in which the self responds to change and the way it organizes the political. A mind that doesn't fear its own revolutionary shattering and understands also that nature is "not fixed but fluid" but constantly "alters its moulds," will work to enact similar revolutionary transformation in the social; thus, following the mind's transformation, "a correspondent revolution in things will attend,"[36] amounting to the "achievement of a principle, as in religious and political revolutions."[37] As "Self-Reliance" argues, in contrast to the self that welcomes revolutionary change, the self generated by fear of ruptures establishes a society whose very core is constituted by the conservative desire for safety and continuity: "Society is a joint-stock company, in which the members agree, for the better securing of his bread to each shareholder, to surrender the liberty and culture of the eater."[38] In this concise interpretation of the social contract, Emerson claims society to be a corporation that protects the property of its members in exchange not for their partial surrender of rights—as would be the case in Hobbes—but for the complete abrogation of liberty. In its most elemental orientation, such a society—which, I will here maintain, Emerson equates with modern liberal social formations— coincides with the bearings of the fearful self. For just as that self gives up everything (its becoming and transformation) for nothing (protection of its fear), so the society it establishes safeguards the property of its members in exchange for their liberty, and so becomes a "conspiracy against ... every one of its members."[39]

2

The fundamental coincidence that Emerson detects between the formation of (modern) subjectivity and its understanding of the political—which in both cases ends in the cancellation of the very thing it is supposed to protect—forms a basis for his critique of modern liberalism, as well as his thinking about slavery, radical reform, and revolution. That thinking is most clearly formulated in the essay "Politics," published in 1844 only a couple of months after Emerson had delivered "An Address ... on ... the Emancipation of the Negroes in the British West Indies." "Politics" is guided by the premise that the modern form of the political—which also provides the ideological background to the American Revolution—derives from Locke's claim that the task of the state is to protect the life, liberty, and property of persons. This is how Emerson phrases it:

> The theory of politics, which has possessed the mind of men, and which they have expressed the best they could in their laws and in their revolutions, considers persons and property as the two objects for whose protection government exists. Of persons, all have equal rights, in virtue of being identical in nature. This interest, of course, with its whole power demands a democracy. Whilst the rights of all as persons are equal, in virtue of their access to reason, their rights in property are very unequal.[40]

Emerson, always unimpressed by Locke ("Talked last eve. With G. P. B. of Locke who, I maintained, had given me little"),[41] here references the core of

Locke's political philosophy and the source of its most entangled paradoxes, namely, that the equal rights given to all persons on the basis of their capacity to appropriate themselves through self-reflection (what Emerson's paraphrase calls their equal "access to reason"), which thereby becomes their first and "originary" property, are contradicted by their unequal access to other types of property. The element of Locke's theory that Emerson has in mind is famously formulated in chapter five ("Property") of the *Second Treatise on Government*:

> Though the earth, and all inferior creatures, be common to all men, yet every man has a *property* in his own *person*: this no body has any right to but himself. The *labour* of his body, and the *work* of his hands, we may say, are properly his. Whatsoever then he removes out of the state that nature hath provided, and left it in, he hath mixed his *labour* with, and joined to it something that is his own, and thereby makes it his *property*. It being by him removed from the common state nature hath placed it in, it hath by this *labour* something annexed to it, that excludes the common right of other men: for this *labour* being the unquestionable property of the labourer, no man but he can have a right to what that is once joined to, at least where there is enough, and as good, left in common for others.[42]

On Locke's understanding, labor intervenes in the natural by transforming it from what is given in common to all (what anybody can simply pick up from the earth and appropriate) to something exclusive to the laborer, the product of his actions. But the right of labor to appropriate renders obvious the reliance of Locke's political theory on a particular ontology and understanding of personhood. Labor allows appropriation of what it mediates only if the laborer identifies it as an action *belonging* to his body, which in turn belongs to his person ("the work of his hands"). However, for the mind to be able to identify the laboring body and its life as its own, it must first have been able to identify itself as belonging to itself throughout time—it must be able to assert that it continuously coincides with itself— and through this self-identification to apprehend itself, turning itself into its first property. Locke states as much in his *Essay Concerning Human Understanding*: "to find wherein *personal identity* consists, we must consider what *person* stands for; which, I think, is a thinking intelligent being that … can consider itself as itself, the same thinking thing in different times and places; which it does only by that consciousness, which is inseparable from thinking."[43] As Étienne Balibar puts it in his discussion of this passage, in Locke "appropriation is fundamentally the appropriation of *my thoughts* and thus of *myself insofar as I think*," which is why personal identity becomes equivalent to property in oneself.[44] On Balibar's account, Locke dismantles the essentialism of Descartes's substantial soul only in order to replace it with "*another* metaphysical conception, perhaps more originary than that of substance: the conception of the *proper* and of *appropriation*," and so introduces "a remarkable fusion (and not confusion) of the paradigms of *being* and *having*."[45]

Locke's fusions—a concatenation of appropriations, from self-appropriation constitutive of personal identity, via the body as a person's first embodied property, to its action (labor) and its result, which establishes a continuity between mental and material—were read by Emerson precisely as confusions.[46] His central argument in "Politics" is that nineteenth-century political and juridical interpretations of Locke generated an ontological amalgam that enabled modern, but specifically US, democracy, to smuggle things in with minds. As a result, the equal rights of all persons predicated on their capacity to appropriate themselves came to be canceled out by their unequal rights in accessing capital. Such a substitution of things for persons perverted Locke's principle that government should exist to protect the two distinct categories of persons and property into the idea that government should above all protect property, under the pretext that property and appropriation is what affords the existence of persons in the first place. That reasoning came to be enshrined in an American Constitution that sanctioned slavery, as well as the numerous juridical opinions that reasserted it. It was a reasoning that exiled certain persons—most obviously the persons of slaves—into the realm of objects, affording them only the legally murky status of animated and appropriable things. Instead of safeguarding persons, governmental "protection" thus became the means to annul them, promoting a concept of property that was "injurious" to them. Its logic operated much like the core of the self described in "Self-Reliance," seeking to safeguard its continuity and identity—precisely the self that enacts Locke's social contract—but finding in its place only awe and fear. Emerson witnesses those ontological and juridical confusions from the historical vantage that fashions his thinking about politics. Locke's principle of "persons and property as the two objects for whose protection government exists," he argues in "Politics,"

> no longer looks so self-evident as it appeared in former times, partly because doubts have arisen whether too much weight had not been allowed in the laws, to property, and such a structure given to our usages, as allowed the rich to encroach on the poor, and to keep them poor; but mainly, because there is an instinctive sense, however obscure and yet inarticulate, that the whole constitution of property on its present tenures, is injurious, and its influence on persons deteriorating and degrading.[47]

On Emerson's understanding, Locke's requirement that there be two different sets of laws—one attending to "persons" as unappropriable, demanding "a government framed on the ratio of the census"; the other

194 HAITI'S LITERARY LEGACIES

invested in property and things, demanding a "government framed on the ratio of owners and of owning"[48]—is possible only because in describing the distribution of property Locke had in mind a quasi-originary moment of the social when one labors with one's hands, appropriating only what the laborer has himself manufactured, and only as much as he needed. As Emerson puts it, Locke has in mind "the earliest society" in which "the proprietors made their own wealth, and so long as it comes to the owners in the direct way, no other opinion would arise in any equitable community, than that property should make the law for property, and persons the law for persons."[49] But the requirement of an equitable community, which gave rise to Locke's clear distinction between appropriation and existence, things, and persons, was disabled by the very logic of trade and accumulation of capital. Every form—let alone the capitalist form—of trade makes manifest that what Locke claimed can become property only if made by the proprietor, is in fact appropriable by persons not involved in its making. Emerson's explicit examples are institutions such as donation or inheritance: "But property passes through donation or inheritance to those who do not create it. Gift, in one case, makes it as really the new owner's, as labor made it the first owner's: in the other case, of patrimony, the law makes an ownership, which will be valid in each man's view according to the estimate which he sets on the public tranquility."[50] The institutions of gift and inheritance—themselves confusing property and a person's desire by objectivizing that will into a thing donated to another—demonstrate that persons can appropriate what they haven't manufactured, by the same token manifesting that the actions, body, or mind of the laborer that have been embodied in the products of his labor are able to be severed from him. For Emerson, the institution of donation or inheritance that transacts property to those "who do not create it" reveals what is a general logic of capitalism—radically contradicting Locke's fantasy of appropriating only what is made with one's hands—namely, the mixing of persons and property that takes place in every single transaction: "it was not, however, found easy to embody the readily admitted principle, that property should make law for property, and persons for persons: since persons and property mixed themselves in every transaction."[51] In each appropriable or tradable thing— because it embodies the actions and hence minds of others—a personhood is embedded.[52]

The separation of a person from his acts breaks Locke's constitutive chain of personhood, in which, to use Balibar's economical phrasing, the "conscious experience I have of the actions of the body as 'my actions' is equally important as 'my experience ... of the operations of my thought.'"[53] According to the argument Emerson advances in "Politics," the rupture of Locke's concatenation—alienation of what Locke deemed inalienable—enables the generation of a political and legal zone in which there is constant negotiation between what counts as person and what counts as thing available for purchase. The reconfiguration of personhood into a property that so concerns Emerson was, of course, by no means specific to American experience. Yet, presuming that his first responsibility is to critique the political and social environment in which he lives—presuming, that is, that one's most urgent duty is to critique and subvert what is presumed to be "one's own"—Emerson focuses his argument on the contemporary US legal and political institutions that enacted the legal redefinition of some persons into partial persons or even objects, as was the case with the American Constitution's sanctioning of slavery.

According to Emerson, both the Constitution and the Fugitive Slave Law rendered persons, liberties, and things substitutable. His point is that this "metaphysical debility"[54] did not result from any interruption of democracy or violation of laws designed to guarantee personal rights, but was rather based on the politico-juridical system of democracy. For example, he has in mind the perverse reasoning that slavery can't be abolished because slaveholders can't be severed from their constitutionally guaranteed right to possess their property as something inalienable, a property that is therefore constitutive of their personhood. The "wickedness" of such legal reasoning[55] convinced Emerson that laws don't constitute and impose rights and liberties but instead sanction the "metaphysical" and political condition that is already in operation, outside any zone of legality. According to the argument advanced in "Politics," far from being "mystical" in origin— transmitting and safeguarding justice independently of the political, and resisting its injustice—laws come in the wake of political turmoil or war, as a means of justifying its outcome. What is "carried as grievance and bill of rights through conflict and war" will become "triumphant law and establishment for a hundred years, until it gives place, in turn, to new prayers and pictures."[56] "The law is only a memorandum"[57] of what takes place outside it, contradicting it and often violating and interrupting it. Paradoxically, laws legalize the violation of laws.[58]

The same holds for laws designed to protect lives and the "rights of all as persons"[59] irrespective of "rights in property." "Politics" argues that when the unequal distribution of property violates, de facto, equal "personal rights," laws have not only begun to sanction the confusion of persons and property but, furthermore, have begun to give more rights to property than persons: "the property will, year after year, write every statute that respects property. The non-proprietor will be the scribe of the proprietor."[60] A sort of magical transformation occurs, therefore, turning property into a force of law-writing, giving to a dead thing a living legal voice through which it secures its own rights over the rights of persons. As Emerson will later specify, this perversion of the law supposed to protect persons (being) into a law protecting things (having) found its most explicit expression in Daniel Webster's argument that "government exists for the protection of property" above liberty, life, and personal rights, which makes it understandable why, seeing everything as property, "[Webster] looks at the Union as an estate, a large farm," on which there are only things, plants, and animals, all appropriable.[61] If Emerson here uses an agricultural metaphor to reference the state, it is in order to signal that when a major constitutional lawyer turns a state that is predicated on the "rights of all as persons" into a farm, then all life within it becomes subject to transaction, as if it were vegetal or animal only.

As I have already emphasized, the most obvious example of this metaphysical perversion that enacts the concrete legal transformation of humans into things is slavery, enabling as it does the lives of persons to be traded as if they were without personal identity, as if bodies were "lands, money, furniture and the like."[62] But Emerson's "Politics" detects the same logic in a whole series of other instances supported by American democracy. His examples include: the penal system, in which the government appropriates the lives of the incarcerated; capital punishment, "legal cruelties in the penal code," and corporal punishment; blocking the "access of the young and the poor to the sources of wealth and power"; and, finally, exclusion of the "Indian and the immigrant" from the political.[63] All of those effectuate, albeit each time in a different manner, the transformation of persons into forms of life to which mind is denied.[64] Again, Emerson draws an exact parallel between the self and the political. In "Self-Reliance," the self plays a cunning trick on itself: safeguarding its identity, the self gives up the threatening heterogeneity of perceptions and affects, but in the process loses everything, clapping itself into the irons of the empty form of its consciousness.[65] In the juridical and governmental sphere of "Politics," on the other hand, Emerson detects a corresponding "cunningness" that makes of the state "a trick"[66] because it substitutes the safety of things for the life of persons.[67]

By arguing that "the state is a trick," Emerson additionally suggests that neither the juridical nor the political that is generated within the democratic institutions of 1844 will be able to dispel this ontological sleight of hand that morphs persons into property; for the political, as much as the juridical system, merely sanctions it. A long section of "Politics" is dedicated to a detailed critique of both Democratic and Republican parties, claiming that neither can be called "parties of principle"—by which Emerson means parties that work on radical reform—but are instead "parties of circumstance," "perpetually corrupted by personality," "timid," and, like the law and the government, "merely defensive of property."[68] Insofar as they are organized to defend what Emerson wants to cancel altogether—the confusion of being and having—the "two great parties ... have not at heart the ends which give to the name of democracy what hope and virtue are in it," but instead only show that "the spirit of our American radicalism is destructive and aimless."[69]

On March 7, 1854, in his "Fugitive Slave Law" address, Emerson reasserts the argument of "Politics," claiming that "possession is sure to throw its stupid strength for existing power."[70] But he argues on that occasion that in addition to the juridical and the political systems, instances charged with

REVOLUTIONARY SHATTERING 197

generating discursive formations and knowledge, specifically universities, have also come under the spell of property:

> Yet the lovers of liberty may tax with reason the coldness and indifferentism of the scholars and literary men. They are lovers of liberty in Greece, and in Rome, and in the English Commonwealth, but they are very lukewarm lovers of the specific liberty of America in 1854. The universities are not now as in Hobbes's time, the core of rebellion; no, but the seat of whiggery. They have forgotten their allegiance to the muse and grown worldly and political.[71]

Under the pretext that thinking should stay uninvolved in political reality in order to remain scholarly, academics will have chosen to voice their disagreement with our current "domestic slavery" by critiquing Greek or Roman slavery, or by praising the radicalism of the Puritan revolution. But for Emerson, even if all unjust conditions might have something in common, injustice is always a "specific" injury to a particular liberty of a particular body, taking place at a very concrete site, which is why he believes that to critique Roman slave codes is not, in fact, to formulate a sustained critique of the Fugitive Slave Law of 1850. Moreover, in the opinion of Emerson— for whom, ever since "The American Scholar," thinking is not acting ("The preamble of thought ... is action"[72])—scholarly and academic arguments in favor of political radicalism remain far from any enactment of that radicalism. To read affirmatively the radicalism of the Puritan or American revolutions, for instance, is by no means to mobilize a revolutionary uprising against American slavery in 1854 but, to the contrary, to demobilize it, appeasing it by sophisticating it within scholarly arguments. For Emerson, then, to identify thinking about past injustice with acting against the current one only testifies to the fact that "thinking, which was a rage," and coincident with the revolutionary act, has now "become an art."[73] And because this transformation of an act into art only preserves the continuity and safety of institutions even as it claims to destabilize them, in the same way that the political and the juridical do, Emerson will include universities among the forces contriving and maintaining what he calls the "trick" of the State.[74] Indeed, Emerson's primary reproach to democracy is that it devises its institutions in such a way that they cancel democracy's capacity to interrupt itself, or to abandon itself into becoming otherwise. For that reason, no matter how reform-oriented a democracy be, it will always run the risk of conservatism.

3

The discussion in "Politics" is not limited to the ways in which the "corporation" Emerson calls "society" perverts persons into things, creating a "conspiracy" against all its members. Emerson will also ask whether a society that doesn't confuse persons and property, one that doesn't understand personal identity as effectuated by self-appropriation, can be established. In order for the society he has in mind to permit "recognition of higher rights" than "the security of property,"[75] it would have to be predicated on a differently fashioned personhood, precisely the one that "Self-Reliance" describes, a personhood in becoming, exposed to revolutionary transformation. Such a society would not be terrorized by the obsession with safety and continuity. Instead, it would be based on a "fluid" politics, composed of actions capable of radically reorienting the social. "Politics" calls it an "all alterable" society, and in the poem that prefaces the essay Emerson refers to "the perfect State [to] come."[76] It will have no "roots and centers, but any particle may suddenly become the centre of the movement, and compel the system to gyrate round it."[77] Emerson explicitly affirms that, rather than large parties or organizations, instead small groups on the margin, even a "pair of lovers" or a "knot of friends,"[78] would be able, as their ideas gained in intensity, to trigger a "sudden" interruption of its system, taking it by surprise and ushering in a new set of relations.

The radical nature of the interruption of the social that he has in mind when he talks about "renovating the State"[79] is signaled on several occasions in the essay. The epigraphic poem speaks of crumbling everything to dust in order to start from scratch ("Out of dust to build / What is more than dust"[80]), while the end of the essay specifically refers to revolutionary action, stating that the "tendencies of the times" favor it: "The movement in this direction has been very marked in modern history. Much has been blind and discreditable, but the nature of the revolution is not affected by the vices of the revolters; for this is a purely moral force. It was never adopted by any party in history, neither can be. It separates the individual from all party, and unites him, at the same time, to the race."[81] And although "Politics" doesn't give precise examples of such revolutionary action, restricting itself instead to outlining its theory, "An Address ... on ... the Emancipation of the Negroes in the British West Indies" explicitly identifies the Haitian Revolution, arguing that it embodies a "new principle [that] appears ... in race" to reorganize the political according to a "new idea" of it.[82] In this way the two texts elucidate each other and ask to be read together. "Politics" becomes a theory of the revolution whose concrete instantiation is celebrated in the "Address." The pairing of the two texts also makes clear that Emerson's reading of the Haitian Revolution in the "Address" is not an accident, something solicited by the political tension of the time, but rather a concretization of the philosophy of revolution that is inherent to his thinking more generally.

The first part of the "Address" reacts to the conservative obsessions of the American society Emerson critiques, whose members, both in the North and the South, albeit in different ways, feared in 1844 for the safety of their lives, property, and property-in-lives should the emancipation of slaves occur. As Eric Sundquist details, from 1804 to 1850 in the American South, fear was generated precisely by the recirculating story of Haitian revolutionary violence, which served to intensify apprehension regarding potential acts of vengeance by emancipated slaves: "The large number of refugee planters from the island who came to the South in the wake of the revolution spread tales of terror that were reawakened with each newly discovered conspiracy or revolt—most notably ... those of Gabriel Prosser, Denmark Vesey, and Turner—and the history of Haiti and its revolution became deeply ingrained in southern history."[83] Antislavery writers in the North also "hesitated to invoke Haiti as a model of black rule; even those sympathetic to its revolution considered its subsequent history violent and ruinous," as the negative attitude toward a specific revolution merged into a generalized dismissal of revolution as legitimate political action.[84]

If Emerson addresses those fears it is in order to dispel them by documenting an experience of emancipation that did not generate vengeful violence. He focuses on Antigua since it was feared that, because of the ratio of slaveholders to slaves, the emancipation declared by the British Parliament might there generate tensions similar to what had occurred in Haiti: "It was feared that the interest of the master and servant would now produce perpetual discord between them," for "the island of Antigua, contain[ed] 37,000 people, 30,000 being negroes."[85] (Contrary to that fear of violence, which was so intense that "some American captains left the shore and put to sea, anticipating insurrection and general murder,"[86] the reception of the news of emancipation among the slaves was distinguished by non-violence: "equal in nobleness to the deed ... they met everywhere at their churches and chapels ... they cried, they sung, they prayed, they were wild with joy, but there was no riot, no feasting."[87] However, even though Emerson's "Address" praises this effort of the law to overturn by democratic means the regressive institutions it had installed, calling it a "moral revolution"[88]—the emancipation was enacted by a bill of the British Parliament that abolished the system it had previously adopted—he also understands that democratic initiative to have been only partially successful. In contrast to "Lord Aberdeen and Sir George Grey," who "declared to the Parliament, that the system worked well" because "now for ten months, from 1st August, 1834, no injury or violence had been offered to any white, and only one black had been hurt in 800,000 negroes," Emerson argues that "the oppression was not destroyed by the law."[89] Although abolished *de jure* it persevered *de facto*, for the continuity of other state institutions enabled its prolongation, albeit in a different manner, by importing the memory and habit of it into a new social landscape: "the planters were disposed to use their old privileges and overwork the apprentices... and to exert the same licentious despotism as before."[90]

It is because the continuity of state institutions blocks radical reform even when the state and law nominally support it that the second part of the "Address" calls—much like "Politics" does—for abolishing slavery by interrupting the continuity assured to it by laws and political agency: "Virtuous men will not again rely on political agents. They have found out the deleterious effect of political association ... The superstition respecting power and office, is going to the ground ... What great masses of men wish done, will be done [by] energies *other than political*," which we "have now" and "which no man in future can allow himself to disregard."[91] We should read those "other than political" mediating energies as the forces of immediacy—"there is direct conversation and influence,"[92] he writes—that constitute revolution. Slavery is to be abolished only by this "direct influence," which would overthrow the "office" and power of the government, radically shattering social institutions and creating the possibility for a "new and coming civilization." Such a "new principle" is precisely embodied in the Haitian Revolution:

> But if the black man carries in his bosom an indispensable element of a new and coming civilization, for the sake of that element ... he will survive and play his part. So now, the arrival in the world of such men as Toussaint, and the Haytian heroes, or of the leaders of their race in Barbadoes and Jamaica, outweighs in good omen all the English and American humanity. The anti-slavery of the whole world, is dust in the balance before this,—is poor squeamishness and nervousness: the might and the right are here: here is the anti-slave.[93]

In contrast to such a revolution, the anti-slavery movement seeks to abolish slavery while preserving the equilibrium of the state, and hence maintains the institutions that enacted slavery in the first place. It therefore figures not as a radical or revolutionary opposition to oppression but merely middle-class squeamishness, nervousness about the safety of the state. Emerson responds to those anti-slavery initiatives that feared to evoke the Haitian Revolution and considered it "ruinous," as Sundquist put it, by summoning precisely the forces of Caribbean experience as a model for American resistance to domestic slavery. This is not to say that in identifying the Haitian Revolution as a model of resistance to oppression for the world to come Emerson also recommended its vengeance against the oppressor, such as indeed took place in Haiti. To the contrary, as his remarks in "Politics" make clear, he regarded that violence—even if it could be humanly understood in the light of the forms of violence to which slaves had been exposed—as "blind and discreditable."[94] But its blindness is for him historically accidental, that is, subjective, a "blindness" particular to those "revolters"; it does not structurally disqualify revolution as a desirable mode of resistance: "the nature of the revolution is not affected by the vices of the revolters."[95] Thus when Emerson celebrates Louverture as a hero, it is because Louverture embodies a principle that Emerson affirms: as a slave becoming a non-slave and anti-slave, Louverture is the figure par excellence of revolutionary becoming that transforms a person and personhood as it reforms the world. He becomes the figure of the anti-slave because his action is motivated by a desire for emancipation that refrains from calculating and safeguarding, that instead interrupts the existing system to produce a radical instability through which new institutions of equality will be articulated. Not a "political" but an "anti- political" agent, Louverture gave right to the force of the multiple (to "what great masses of men wish done"), and to a sense of justice that proliferates without conceding. And because he makes all things shake and tremble, he becomes the concrete instantiation both of Emerson's desired self—sufficiently unconcerned about the security of life to abandon itself to a multiple and discontinuous world—and of the revolutionary action that such a self enacts, a model candidate for addition to the list of Emerson's representative men.[96]

Notes

1   Eds note: A slightly different version of this essay first appeared in *Telos* 170 (Spring 2015), 109–30. Our thanks to Telos Press for permission to reprint.

2   Ralph Waldo Emerson, "Nature," in *Essays and Poems*, ed. Joel Porte (New York: Library of America, 1996), 24, 25.

3   Emerson, "Nature," 20.

4   Emerson, "Nature," 25.

5   Emerson, "Nature," 10.

6   Ralph Waldo Emerson, "Natural Method of Mental Philosophy," Lecture III: 'Powers of the Mind,' " in *The Later Lectures of Ralph Waldo Emerson, 1843–1871*, vol. 2, ed. Ronald A. Bosco and Joel Myerson (Athens: University of Georgia Press, 2001), editorial note, p. 68.

7   Emerson, "Natural Method," 75

8   Ralph Waldo Emerson, "Circles," in *Essays and Poems*, 413.

9   Emerson, "Circles," 408.

10   Emerson, "Circles," 408.

11   Emerson, "Circles," 407.

12   Emerson, "Natural Method" vol. 2, 78.

13   Emerson, "Natural Method" vol. 2, 77.

14   Emerson, "Natural Method" vol. 2, 78.

15   Emerson, "Natural Method" vol. 2, 77.

16   Ralph Waldo Emerson, "Self-Reliance," in *Essays and Poems*, ed. Joel Porte (New York: Library of America, 1996), 268.

17 Emerson, "Self-Reliance," 269. The "I" only observes the mind external to it, and by means of the "will" that is its core attempts to intervene in it, just as with any other external reality. But because thoughts and perceptions are not its own, it will always act as an imposter; it intervenes too late, the mind having already changed, which is why "my willful actions and acquisitions are but roving" (Emerson, "Self-Reliance," 269).

18 Emerson, "Self-Reliance," 269.

19 Ralph Waldo Emerson, "Intellect," in *Essays and Poems*, ed. Joel Porte (New York: Library of America, 1996), 418.

20 Emerson, "Natural Method" vol. 2, 75.

21 Emerson, "Intellect," 418.

22 Emerson, "Natural Method" vol. 2, 75.

23 Emerson, "Intellect," 418.

24 Emerson, "Intellect," 419.

25 Emerson, "Intellect," 418.

26 Emerson, "Intellect," 419.

27 Emerson, "Self-Reliance," 272.

28 Emerson, "Self-Reliance," 260.

29 Emerson, "Self-Reliance," 271.

30 Emerson, "Self-Reliance," 269.

31 Emerson, "Self-Reliance," 265.

32 Emerson, "Self-Reliance," 265.

33 Emerson, "Self-Reliance," 265.

34 Emerson, "Self-Reliance," 265.

35 Ralph Waldo Emerson, "Conservative," in *Essays and Poems*, 183.

36 Emerson, "Nature," 48.

37 Emerson, "Nature," 47.

38 Emerson, "Self-Reliance," 261.

39 Emerson, "Self-Reliance," 261.

40 Ralph Waldo Emerson, "Politics," in *Essays and Poems*, 560.

41 Ralph Waldo Emerson, *Journals and Miscellaneous Notebooks* (Cambridge, MA: Harvard University Press, 1960–82), 5:57.

42 John Locke, *Second Treatise of Government*, ed. C. B. Macpherson (Indianapolis: Hackett, 1980), § 27, 19 (emphases in original). My argument here cannot possibly do justice to Locke's complex theory of property. I aim to address only that aspect of it that most influenced Emerson, and which served as a basis for his critiques of personhood predicated on appropriation.

43 John Locke, *An Essay Concerning Human Understanding*, ed. Roger Woolhouse (New York: Penguin, 1997), 302.

REVOLUTIONARY SHATTERING 203

44 Étienne Balibar, *Identity and Difference: John Locke and the Invention of Consciousness*, ed. Stella Sandford, trans. Warren Montag (London: Verso, 2013), 99. Balibar argues that personal identity in Locke "rests solely on the continuity of consciousness in time" (Balibar, *Identity and Difference*, 57).

45 Balibar, *Identity and Difference*, 61, 99.

46 As Balibar points out, the appropriation of my body's actions as "my own" is also the source of responsibility in Locke, the core of ethical personhood: "Locke does not say that the conscious experience I have of the actions of the body as 'my actions' is more important than my experience, for example, of the operations of my thought. But having arrived at this stage in his reflection, Locke nevertheless accords it a fundamental importance. This is why the experience of my body's actions belongs at once or indistinctly to the sphere of responsibility and to that of property" (Balibar, *Identity and Difference*, 101).

47 Emerson, "Politics," 561.

48 Emerson, "Politics," 560.

49 Emerson, "Politics," 561.

50 Emerson, "Politics," 561.

51 Emerson, "Politics," 561.

52 Locke himself engaged in a complex discussion that shows that he took into account the appropriation of what is not the laborer's labor. Emerson's references to Locke are, however, oblique, and neither in his journals nor in "Politics" does he discuss Locke's philosophy of appropriation in any detail. It seems that what he finds most interesting in Locke is precisely the latter's description of the "originary" moment of just appropriation. Since my aim here is to reconstruct Emerson's argument, I leave aside Locke's complex elaborations.

53 Balibar, *Identity and Difference*, 101.

54 Ralph Waldo Emerson, "Fugitive Slave Law," in *Emerson's Antislavery Writings*, ed. Len Gougeon and Joel Myerson (New Haven: Yale University Press, 1995), 56.

55 The "wickedness of this American law [the Fugitive Slave Law]" is "not easy to parallel." Ralph Waldo Emerson, "Fugitive Slave Law," in *Emerson's Antislavery Writings*, 87.

56 Emerson, "Politics," 560.

57 Emerson, "Politics," 559.

58 I thank Johannes Voelz for pointing out (in correspondence) that one could instead say here that "positive law legalizes the violation of natural law," in which case the cancelation of one law by another would not be "paradoxical." However, since Emerson's essays do not register this distinction, and since Emerson always talks simply about "the law," I would argue that he thought of the distinction between "natural" and "positive" as fine philosophical sophistry meant to account for the actual weakening of "natural law" and thus the a priori rights of persons.

59 Emerson, "Politics," 560.

60 Emerson, "Politics," 563.

61 Emerson, "Fugitive Slave Law," 66.

62 Emerson, "Politics," 560, 564. As Roberto Esposito clarifies, even if Locke "doesn't always include life among the properties of the subject ... in general he unifies lives, liberties, and estates within the denomination of property, so that he can say that 'civil goods are life, liberty, bodily health and freedom from pain, and the possession of outward things, such as lands, money, furniture, and the like'" (Roberto Esposito, *Bios: Biopolitics and Philosophy*, trans. Timothy Campbell (Minneapolis: University of Minnesota Press, 2008), 64).

63 Emerson, "Politics," 564, 565.

64 Emerson will, of course, never question the exceptional status of the atrocities of slavery. In other words, he will never say that a slave has the status of exploited labor. The complete appropriation of the person of a slave by a slaveholder, and the legal cancellation of the status of the slave as person, remains for Emerson an unparalleled historical crime, which is why he insists that "language must be raked, the secrets of slaughter-houses and infamous holes that cannot front the day must be ransacked, to tell what negro-slavery has been" (Ralph Waldo Emerson, "An Address ... on ... the Emancipation of the Negroes in the British West Indies," in *Emerson's Antislavery Writings*, 9). So, when in "Politics" he talks about the urgency of achieving "universal suffrage, abolition of slavery, ... abolition of capital punishment" (Emerson, "Politics," 564), he does not equate them. Rather he seeks to emphasize that democratic institutions have enacted a whole series of legal crimes that embrace the reality they generate.

65 Emerson, "Self-Reliance," 261.

66 Emerson, "Politics," 563.

67 That substitution is precisely what Emerson means when, in "Self-Reliance," he maintains that the state is a "conspiracy," and society a "company" in which the "liberty of the eater" is sacrificed in order to "better secure" what is eaten (Emerson, "Self-Reliance," 261). We eat our lives when we eat our meals and even enjoy doing so. That we like eating human lives is something that slavery makes obvious for, as Emerson argues in the "Address on the Emancipation," it creates conditions in which the blood of slaves is coated in the beautiful scents of coffee and sugar, seducing the eater's sensorium into enjoyment, thus making the eater—but that means everybody, all well-eating citizens, judges, lawyers and even abolitionists, and not just slaveholders— complicit in the crime of slavery: "If any mention was made of homicide, madness, adultery, and intolerable tortures [of slaves] we would let the church-bells ring louder ... The sugar they raised was excellent: nobody tasted blood in it. The coffee was fragrant; the tobacco was incense; the brandy made nations happy; the cotton clothed the world. What a convenience!" (Emerson, "Address on the Emancipation," 20).

68 Emerson, "Politics," 564, 565.

69 Emerson, "Politics," 564–5.

70 Emerson, "Fugitive Slave Law," 87.

71 Emerson, "Fugitive Slave Law," 87.

72 Ralph Waldo Emerson, "The American Scholar," in *Essays and Poems*, 60.

73 Ralph Waldo Emerson, "Lecture on the Times," in *Essays and Poems*, 165–6.

74 Thus, seventy years after the American Revolution, for which he always had the highest respect—precisely because it represented the force of radical interruption—Emerson voices disappointment with democracy and its institutions, arguing that the existence of slavery, capital punishment, penal cruelties, and the removals of Native Americans make us realize that it does not cancel but rather sanctions atrocious realities we once thought were irreconcilable with it. Because, like other forms of governing concerned with self-continuity, "Politics" will minimize its excellence, claiming that the democratic "form and methods of governing … are not better, but only fitter for us. Born democrats, we are nowise qualified to judge of monarchy, which, to our fathers living in the monarchical idea, was also relatively right. But our institutions, though in coincidence with the spirit of the age, have not any exemption from the practical defects which have discredited other forms. Every actual State is corrupt. Good men must not obey the laws too well" (Emerson, "Politics," 563).

75 Emerson, "Politics," 569.

76 Emerson, "Politics," 557.

77 Emerson, "Politics," 559.

78 Emerson, "Politics," 571.

79 Emerson, "Politics," 570.

80 Emerson, "Politics," 557.

81 Emerson, "Politics," 569.

82 Emerson, "Address on the Emancipation," 31.

83 Eric J. Sundquist, *To Wake the Nations: Race in the Making of American Literature* (Cambridge, MA: Harvard University Press, 1993), 140.

84 Sundquist, *To Wake the Nations*, 146. Sundquist describes this merging as "interweaving Jacobinism, the Inquisition, the terror of liberation and the terror of repression" (146).

85 Emerson, "Address on the Emancipation," 15.

86 Emerson, "Address on the Emancipation," 15.

87 Emerson, "Address on the Emancipation," 15.

88 Emerson, "Address on the Emancipation," 26.

89 Emerson, "Address on the Emancipation," 16–17. Aberdeen and Grey here give numbers referencing the whole British West Indies, not just Antigua.

90 Emerson, "Address on the Emancipation," 17.

91 Emerson, "Address on the Emancipation," 28 (my emphasis).

92 Emerson, "Address on the Emancipation," 28.

93 Emerson, "Address on the Emancipation," 31.

94 Emerson, "Politics," 569.

95 Emerson, "Politics," 569.

96 However, the radical instability that Louverture generates interrupts history only in order for a completely novel historical situation to appear. That new historical moment—which will also radically interrupt the traditions of Western religions and thinking—is imagined by Emerson as the period in which the "civilization of Africa" will shape the political, religious, and philosophical interest of humanity (Emerson, "Address on the Emancipation," 29). In the new world announced by Louverture, the "arts and culture of the negro" (Emerson, "Address on the Emancipation," 29), African fashion, sculpture, glass, ornamentation, and pottery-making, will preoccupy the intellect of all, for they will be expressions of the new political and social arrangement generated by the revolutionary shattering of slavery. They will express the "new element" of modernity (Emerson, "Address on the Emancipation," 29)—Emerson calls it the "talisman of the intellect" (Emerson, "Address on the Emancipation," 31)—destined to become the talisman of all ("who has [the intellect] has the talisman"). The new modernity to come following the Haitian revolutionary shattering of the old world will thus be a becoming African of humanity as a whole.

NOTES ON CONTRIBUTORS

Mary Grace Albanese is Assistant Professor of English at SUNY Binghamton, USA. Her book project, *Prophetic Power: Haiti, the United States and Black Women's Spiritual Labor*, reveals how African American women, including Marie Laveau, Sojourner Truth, Maria Stewart, and Pauline Hopkins, drew on Afro-Caribbean spiritual energies to reclaim their right to their own bodies, minds, and kinship structures. Articles from this project, and others, appear or are forthcoming in *American Literature*, *ESQ*, and *J19*, as well as several edited collections. She has also written reviews and short essays for *Critical Inquiry*, *American Literary History*, *SX Salon*, *Callaloo*, and *Common-Place*.

Branka Arsić is Charles and Lynn Zhang Professor of English and Comparative Literature at Columbia University, USA. She is the author, most recently, of *Bird Relics: Grief and Vitalism in Thoreau* (2016), which was awarded the MLA James Russell Lowell prize for the outstanding book of 2016. She has also written *On Leaving: A Reading in Emerson* (2010), and a book on Melville entitled *Passive Constitutions or 7 1/2 Times Bartleby* (2007). She coedited (with Cary Wolfe) *The Other Emerson: New Approaches, Divergent Paths* (2010) and (with K. L. Evans) *Melville's Philosophies* (2017).

Chris Bongie is Professor of English Language and Literature at Queen's University at Kingston Ontario, Canada. He is the author of *Exotic Memories: Literature, Colonialism and the Fin de Siècle* (1991), *Islands and Exiles: The Creole Identities of Post/Colonial Literature* (1998), and *Friends and Enemies: The Scribal Politics of Post/Colonial Literature* (2008). He has produced critical editions of several Romantic-era novels about the Haitian Revolution (including Victor Hugo's *Bug-Jargal* and Jean-Baptiste Picquenard's *Adonis*), as well as a translation of Baron de Vastey's seminal contribution to Haitian anticolonialism, *The Colonial System Unveiled* (1814; 2014).

Brigitte Fielder is Associate Professor at the University of Wisconsin-Madison, USA. She is the author of *Relative Races: Genealogies of Interracial Kinship in Nineteenth-Century America* (2020) and a coeditor of *Against a Sharp White Background: Infrastructures of African American Print* (2019). She is currently writing a book about racialized human–animal relationships in the long nineteenth century, which shows how childhood becomes a key site for (often simultaneous) humanization and racialization.

Theresa M. Kelley is Marjorie and Lorin Tiefenthaler Professor Emerita of English at the University of Wisconsin-Madison, USA. She is the author of *Clandestine Marriage; Botany and Romantic Culture* (2012), *Reinventing Allegory* (1997), and *Wordsworth's Revisionary Aesthetics* (1988). Her essays include contributions to *Studies in Romanticism, ELH* and essay collections, among them *Lessons of Romanticism, Rhetorical Traditions and British Romantic Literature, Keats and History*, and several companion volumes on Romanticism. She has edited special issues for scholarly journals and coedits the Romantic Circles Gallery. She is writing two books: "Reading for the Future" and "Color Trouble."

Kir Kuiken is Associate Professor of English at SUNY Albany, USA, and the author of *Imagined Sovereignties: Towards a New Political Romanticism* (2014). He has published essays on Romanticism and critical theory in a range of journals including *Oxford Literary Review, Essays in Romanticism, Comparative Literature, Keats-Shelley Journal, SubStance*, and *Research in Phenomenology*.

Brian McGrath is Associate Professor of English at Clemson University, USA. He is the author of *The Poetics of Unremembered Acts: Reading, Lyric, Pedagogy* (2013) and has published essays on Romanticism and literary theory in a range of journals including *Studies in Romanticism, Diacritics, New Literary History, Eighteenth-Century Fiction*, and *Studies in English Literature*.

Deborah Elise White is Associate Professor of English and Comparative Literature at Emory University, USA. She is the author of *Romantic Returns: Superstition, Imagination, History* (2000) and the editor of the Romantic Praxis series volume: *Irony and Clerisy* (1998). She has also published essays on Romanticism, revolution, and literary theory in a range of journals including *Comparative Literature Yearbook, Studies in Romanticism, European Romantic Review, MLN*, and *Romance Studies*.

INDEX

abolitionism 4, 9, 16, 17, 19, 163, 164, 165–7, 168, 169, 177, 179, 200
aesthetic education 77–8
affects 64, 186, 188, 196
Agamben, Giorgio 116 n.49, 161 n.56
agency/agent 15–16, 147, 148, 156
  and personification 111
  political or erotic agency 142, 144, 147, 153, 157 n.6, 200
Alexander, M. Jacqui 60
Allegory 34, 163, 165, 167, 174–8
Allewaert, Monique 62–3
Alvarez, Joseph 34
Anderson, Osborne Perry 176–7
Anglo-African Magazine 163, 164, 168, 169, 171, 180 n.2
Angress, Ruth 137 n.7
anthropomorphism 96, 103, 105, 107–8
Antigua 199
apostrophe, usage in poems 96, 103, 105–6, 107–8, 110
Apter, Emily 9, 22 n.33
Aravamudan, Srinivas 103, 104
Ardouin, Beaubrun
  Études sur l'histoire d'Haïti 30–1
Arendt, Hannah 21 n.22
assemblage 42
Austen, Jane 67 n.16
Austin, J. L. 120, 138 n.18

Badiou, Alain 5, 19 n.16, 78–9
  chance 78–9
  subject theory 78–9
Balfour, Ian 90 n.4
Balibar, Étienne 192, 194, 203 n.44, 203 n.46
Bataille, Georges 119–20

Beauvais, Louis-Jacques 38
Behn, Aphra 153, 159 n.28
Bell, Caryn Cossé 51
Benjamin, Walter 117, 136 n.1, 139 n.36, 156, 161 n.56
Bewell, Alan 53, 54, 55
Bigger 6 Collective 100
bio-politics 121
Black
  abolitionism (*see* abolitionism)
  diaspora 63, 167, 169, 170, 172, 174, 176–7
  emancipation 16, 135, 164–5, 168, 169–70, 172, 174, 175–6, 177, 178, 179, 199
  peasant traditions 51
  as a racial designation 5, 8
#BlackLivesMatter movement 12
Blackness 82, 85–6, 94 n.52, 152–3
Black press *see* African American press
Black Spartacus 14, 82–5
Black Studies 27, 41, 42
Blake, William 79
Blanchot, Maurice 119
Bois Caïman (BwaKayiman) 31, 17
Boisrond-Tonnerre, Louis 32
brotherhood, *see* fraternity
Brown, John 163, 176
  raid on Harper's Ferry 163, 167, 174–5, 178
Buck-Morss, Susan 11, 23 n.43, 167
Burke, Edmund 102
Byron, Lord 54, 72

calenda 13, 49, 58
  etymology of 58–60
  and Haitian Romanticism 51
  prohibition of 61

210 INDEX

spiritual and political dimensions of 63
and Vodou practices 61
calenda/calenture, indeterminacy of 51, 64
calenture 13, 49, 55–6, 64
  as calentura (fever) 52, 56, 58
  comparison with calenda 64
  conceptual instability of 50
  as contagion 58
  as gendered 56, 57, 60
  as hallucination 49–50
  origins of 54
  in the Romantic tradition 50
  and slavery 52
  as symptomatic of colonial expansion 53
Callahan, Monique-Adelle 173–4
Cameau, Jacques 30
Carpentier, Alejo 63
Chander, Manu Samriti 100, 113 n.20
Chanlatte, Antoine 38
Chanlatte, Juste 12–13, 28–31, 37, 38, 39–40, 44 n.16
Chavannes, Jean-Baptiste 31
Cheshire, Paul 55
Christian Recorder 171, 172
Christophe, Henri 169
citizenship 5, 8, 164, 168, 175
Civil Commissioners 38, 39
civil war
  between Louverture and Rigaud forces (1799-1800) 28
  US Civil War 177, 178
Clemanson plantation, and planter's deposition 25–6, 37, 42, 43
Code Noir 61, 91
Cole, Jean Lee 171, 177
Coleridge, Samuel Taylor 54
Collins, Julia C. 171
Collins, Lauren 6
colonialism 10, 27, 28–9, 55, 64, 154
Colored American 168
community 118
  community of lovers 15, 118–21, 135, 138 n.19
  equitable community 194

maroon communities 2–3, 4, 81, 173, 174
  as opposed to state 119, 125, 128–9, 131–2
Constituent Assembly (France) 31, 34
contingency 76, 77, 79, 89, 90
Copeland, John Anthony, Jr. 176
Creole (Kreyòl) 7, 49, 51, 74, 81, 86, 88, 171
Culler, Jonathan 106

Dames, Nicholas 66, 67 n.16
dance, see calenda
Dante
  Inferno 150, 159 n.36
Darwin, Erasmus 53, 57, 67 n.16
  Zoonomia; or the Laws of Organic Life 53
Dash, J. Michael 51
Daut, Marlene 1, 9, 22 n.32, 84, 158 n.8, 163, 168, 170
D'Avallon, Cousin 84
Dayan, Colin 49, 167
Defoe, Daniel 52, 56
Delany, Martin 163, 171
Derrida, Jacques 23 n.36, 23 n.39
Dessalines, Jean-Jacques 7, 27–9, 44 n.16, 104, 112, 121, 169
  1806 coup against 39–40
  and Pétion 41
diaspora 63, 167, 169, 170, 172, 174, 176–7
Dillon, Elizabeth Maddock 167
divine violence 156
Douglass, Sarah Mapps 163
Drexler, Michael 168
Dubois, Laurent 5, 18–19 n.5, 29, 64
Dubroca, Louis 84

ego 78, see also "I"; self
emancipation 16, 135, 164–5, 168, 169–70, 172, 174, 175–6, 177, 178, 179, 199
Emerson, Ralph Waldo 16–17, 185–201, 204–5 n.67, 204 n.64
  "An Address on the Emancipation of the Negroes in the British

INDEX

West Indies" 187, 198–9, 200, 204–5 n.67
"Circles" 186, 187
"Fugitive Slave Law" 196
insistence on revolutionary change 187–8
"Intellect" 186, 188, 189
on mind 188
The Natural Method of Mental Philosophy 188
"Politics" 191, 193, 194, 196, 197, 205 n.74
on possible reactions of the "I" 189
"Powers of the Mind" 186, 189
"Property" 192–3
Second Treatise on Government 192–3
"Self-Reliance" 188–9, 190–1, 193, 196, 198, 202 n.17
on society 191
Enlightenment 14, 36, 74, 97
Enlightenment history 11
European Enlightenment 7, 8
Ernest, John 177
Esposito, Roberto 204 n.62
European literary periodizations 9–10

Ferrer, Ada 1
fetishism 8, 144
Fick, Carolyn 2, 3, 19 n.6
figurative vs literal 95–6
Fischer, Sibylle 9, 160 n.46
Floyd, George 12
folklores 51, 63
Foreman, P. Gabrielle 165
Forsdick, Charles 104
Foster, Frances Smith 165
Foucault, Michel 116 n.49
fraternity 7, 118, 127, 135, 155
free colored insurrection (1791) 12, 149, 156
freedom 2–3, 71, 79, 87, 118
individual freedom 78, 121
political freedom 76, 77, 78, 89
right to 4, 10–11, 169
struggles for 55
Freedom's Journal 168, 170, 171

free people of color *(gens de couleur libres)* 25, 31, 33, 41, 43
insurrection of 1791 26, 28, 37, 38, 41, 43
political imaginary 26, 30, 33–4, 36
struggle for recognition 26–7, 33, 35, 41–2
French Revolution 6, 15, 31, 67 n.16, 117, 156
Convention 4, 122, 144
declaration of rights 35, 85, 87
and Haitian Revolution 2, 4–5
impact on Romantic writing 9
Jacobinism, Jacobin 16, 153–4, 161 n.53
Legislative Assembly 35, 38
National Assembly 32, 35, 36, 37
sansculottes 154–5
Freneau, Philip 56, 57
"The House of Night" 56
friend/enemy distinction 121–3, 130–2, 135
Fugitive Slave Law 195, 197
futurity 14, 60, 75, 76, 83, 86–8, 178

Gailus, Andreas 117–18, 121, 122, 135
Garraway, Doris 94 n.52
Gatereau, Louis 47 n.60
Geffard, Fabre-Nicolas 169
Geggus, David 91 n.9, 103
Genovese, Eugene 2
genre, literary genre 7, 56, 164, 167–71, 172, 173, 174–5, 177
Gilbert, William 54–5
Fragment by a West Indian 54
"The Hurricane: A Theosophical and Western Eclogue" 54, 55
Gilman, Sander 118
Girard, Philippe 73, 90 n.6
Girod-Chantrans, Justin 97–8
Gold, Joshua 118, 130
Goodman, Kevis 53–4
Gothic 33, 49, 56, 171
Gray, Thomas 108–9, 110
Green, Shields 176
Grüner, Eduardo 3, 4, 5, 8
Guyer, Sara 113 n.7

INDEX

Haiti, *see also* Haitian Constitution; Haitian Revolution
  exceptionalism 8–9
  literary field 11, 12, 27, 32, 33, 51
  sovereignty 156
  topography of 80–1
Haitian Constitution
  Article Fourteen 5, 8, 21 n.27
  rights of Man 5
Haitian Declaration of Independence (1804) 12–13, 15, 27, 28, 38, 39, 40, 112
Haitian Revolution 1–5, 15, 41, 54–5, 75, 96, 99, 103, 111–12, 151, 155, 156, 163, 169–70, 187, 200
  and counter modernity 4–5
  and Enlightenment (*see* Enlightenment)
  forgetting of 5–9, 18 n.3
  and French Revolution 2, 4–5
  in the African American Press 16, 161–4, 168–73, 179
  and rethinking of literary-historical boundaries 9–11
  shock effect of 117, 118, 135, 136 n.1
  unprecedented character of 2, 5, 6, 8
  unthinkability 5–9, 142
Hall, Prince 168
Hallward, Peter 137 n.6
Hamilton, Thomas 163, 179
Harper, Frances Watkins 16, 163–4, 165, 171, 178, 180 n.5
  "Death of Zombi, the Chief of a Negro Kingdom in Latin America" 173–4
  letter to Still 183 n.48
  Minnie's Sacrifice 171–2
  other "revolutionary" 164
  "Our Greatest Want" 175
  "The Triumph of Freedom—A Dream" 163
  "The Two Offers" 165
  "Zombi, and the Negro Kingdom" 173

  "Zombi, or Fancy Sketches" 172, 175
Harper's Ferry Raid 163, 167, 174–5, 178
Hartman, Saidiya 98, 178
Henry, William "Jerry" 101, 179
Hickman, Jared 157 n.4
Hoermann, Raphael 33, 46 n.39
Hofer, Johannes 67 n.15
Hölderlin, Friedrich 78
Holly, James Theodore 163, 168–9
Horner, Moses 179
hospitality 125, 133
Hugo, Victor 141–56
  Bug-Jargal 15–16, 141–56

"I" 186, 188, 189, 190, 202 n.17, *see also* self
  affirmative reactions of 189–90
  and perspectives and thoughts 188–9
  resistance to radical self-transformation 190
identity 27
  collective identity 30, 60, 61, 78–9
  performative structure of 61
imagined memorializations 170–1
individuated self 186
insurgency 26, 118, 137 n.7
intertextuality, *see* Voltaire
irony 35–6, 146, 148

Jackson, Maurice 168
Jacobinism 154 *see* French Revolution
James, C. L. R. 75, 84, 95–6, 112, 137 n.6, 176, 177
  The Black Jacobins 4, 14, 31, 95, 99, 101, 103, 107, 111, 177
  on Haitian Revolution's uniqueness 2
  on history 99
  "How I Would Rewrite The Black Jacobins" 97–8
  on power of Romanticism 114 n.25
  Toussaint Louverture 26, 104, 111
  and Wordsworth 103
James, Jennifer 177
James, William 188

INDEX

Jameson, Fredric 108
Jenson, Deborah 7, 21 n.26, 29, 44–5
  n.16, 85, 87, 112
Johnson, Barbara 97, 106, 114 n.37
Johnson, Samuel 52–3, 56
Josué, Erol 64
Jumécourt, Hanus de 34

Kant, Immanuel 15, 135, 136 n.2
Keats, John 74
  "Ode to a Nightingale" 100, 101
kinship 60, 127, 128
Kleist, Heinrich von 15, 117–36
  The Battle of Hermann 118, 119
  The Betrothal in San Domingo
  117–136
  Earthquake in Chili 122
Koretsky, Deanna 22 n.34, 151
Korngold, Ralph 80

Labat, Père 59–60, 61, 63
Labuissonnière, Pierre 31–2, 34,
  38, 39, 41
Lacan, Jacques 78
Lacroix, Pamphile de 84, 90 n.6, 149,
  159 n.31
Lapointe, Jean-Baptiste 30
Lattre, Philippe-Albert de 58
Laveaux, Étienne 84
Leary, Lewis Sheridon 176
Legislative Assembly (France) 35, 38
Léogâne Journal 31–2, 34, 36, 37
liberalism 14, 74, 186–7, 191
Locke, John 17, 191, 192–3, 203 n.52
  fusions of 193
  liberalism 186–7
  political philosophy of 192, 193
Louis XIV 61
Louverture, Toussaint (L'Ouverture,
  Toussaint) 6, 7, 13–15, 16, 17,
  71–6, 96, 80–90, 104–10, 153,
  154, 157 n.6, 160 n.49, 170, 171,
  172, 174, 175, 176, 177, 200–1,
  206 n. 96
  and civil war (1799-1800) 28
  on political freedom 89
  private life and early history 73–4
  as a public subject 74, 78, 81

Raynal's prediction 82–5
  and Sonthonax 86–8
  and a white woman, dialogue
    between 85–6
Lovejoy, Arthur 11, 22–3 n.35
Luhmann, Niklas 76, 78, 79, 87
Lupton, Christina 76

Mabee, Frank 55
Mahlis, Kristen 110
Makandal, François 62–3
Man, Paul de 77
Mannoni, Octave 144
maroon communities 2–3, 81, 173,
  174
  guerilla warfare 3
  marronage 2–3, 4
Martin, James 129, 131, 132
Marx, Karl 75, 101
Mathes, Carmen Faye 106
Matthews, Patricia 100
May 1968 120
Mbembe, Achille 141, 143
McCallam, David 102
McKittrick, Katherine 51–2
melancholy 10, 141, 151–2
Melville, Herman 56, 57
  Moby Dick: or the Whale 57
Mercier, Louis-Sébastien 83–4
Métraux, Alfred 61
Miller, Christopher 6, 18 n.3
mind 185, 186, 187, 188–9, 190,
  192
Mirabeau 159 n.31
Le Moniteur 84, 85
Morning Post 103, 106, 107
Moten, Fred 101
"mulattoes" (*les mulâtres*) 4, 26
mythologization 163, 164, 165, 168,
  169–70, 173, 177–8

Naimou, Angela 97
Nancy, Jean-Luc 138 n.19
Napoleon 4, 5, 72, 74, 81, 87–8, 104,
  123, 175
nature 185, 190, 198, 200
Nesbitt, Nick 4, 20 n.20, 45 n.22
New Yorker, The 6

nostalgia 53, 67 n.15, 67 n.16, 152
  and calenture in Romantic
    literature 57
  and epidemics suffered by French
    soldiers in Saint Domingue 58
Novalis 77
  "Pollen" 77
  Zufälle (accidents) 77–8

oaths 124–5, 127–8, 130–1, 132
O'Brien, Colleen 168, 171
Ogé, Vincent 31
Olson, Kevin 26, 36
Osbey, Brenda Marie 50–1
(the other) 1791 12–13, 27, 40, 43
  and founding documents of
    postindependence Haitian
    literature 27
  political imaginary of 41

Pace, Joel 11, 22 n.34
pastoral 53, 54, 55, 64, 105
penal system 123, 196, 205 n.74
performative displays 8, 15, 26, 28,
  131, 132
Perraudin, Michael 119, 137 n.11
personifications 14–15, 96, 97, 101,
  102, 105, 110
persons/personhood 13, 14, 15, 17, 77,
  96, 97, 103, 105, 194, 198
  becoming a 76–7, 78
  and property 187, 191–7, 199
Peterson, Carla 165, 167, 171–2,
  174
Pétion, Alexandre 41
petits blancs 34
Pierrot, Grégory 71, 157 n.6
Pinchinat, Pierre 34, 37
The Pine and Palm 172, 180 n.2
Pisarz-Ramirez, Gabriele 168
Poe, Edgar Allan
  *The Narrative of the Life of Arthur
    Gordon Pym of Nantucket* 56–7
politics of recognition 26–7, 33,
  35, 41–2
Polverel, Étienne 38
Popkin, Jeremy 163
Port-au-Prince 25, 31, 34–5, 121

print culture 71, 73, 74, 80, 88
proclamation of 1804, *see*
  Haitian Declaration of
  Independence (1804)
property
  institution of donation or
    inheritance 194
  and persons 187, 191–7, 199
  protection of 191
  right in 195
  and self, confusion between 17
Provincial Freeman 176

Quincy, John 53

race
  "ci-devant" racism 154, 155
  racial hierarchies 3, 8, 121, 123,
    126, 135
  racist imaginary 27, 33–4, 36,
    38, 152
Raimond, Julien 31
Rainsford, Marcus 44 n.7, 71
Raynal, Abbé Guillaume-
    Thomas 14, 72
  History of the two Indies 82–3
  prediction of a Black Spartacus
    82–5
recognition, politics of 26–7, 33,
  35, 41–2
Redpath, James 180 n.2
representative men 30, 201
republicanism, republic 41, 58,
  167, 196
revolution, revolutionary history,
  see French Revolution; Haitian
  Revolution
revolutionary abolition, *see*
  abolitionism
Rigaud, André 28
rights of Man 5
risk 42, 75, 88, 153, 187–8, 197
Roger, Jacques-François 18 n.3
romance 7, 145, 153
Romantic ideology 100
Romanticism 1–2, 9–12, 30, 40, 43,
  49, 50, 51, 57
  Black Romanticism 1, 11

INDEX

British Romanticism 49–50, 57
definitions and rethinking of
9–11
European Romanticism 51
French Romanticism 51
Haitian Romanticism 51
and Romantic heroes 11, 72, 89
Romantic historicism 41
and Romantic subjects 71, 72,
75–80, 89
US Romanticism 51
transhistorical transmissions 11

Saint-Domingue 1, 2, 3, 4, 6, 7, 11, 15,
16, 25, 26, 30, 31, 33, 36, 37, 40,
56, 57–8, 142, 143–4, 146, 147,
148, 151, 154
Sala-Molins, Louis 69–70 n.48
San Domingo revolution, *see* Haitian
Revolution
Savary, Jean 35, 38, 39
Schiller, J. C. Friedrich von 76, 77,
78, 79, 90
*Letters on Aesthetic
Education* 76, 77
Schmitt, Carl 120, 137–8 n.12
Scott, David 69–70 n.48, 99, 111
Seebacher, Jacques 159 n.36
self 69–70 n.48, 189, 196, *see also* "I"
appropriative and individuated
186
modern self 75, 90
and political 186–7, 190, 196–7
and property, confusion
between 17
self-transformation 190
as trick of the state 196, 197
understanding of 64
self-abandonment 186
Sepinwall, Alyssa 18 n.4
Serres, Michel 81–2, 93 n.36
Sharpe, Christina 55, 98
Shelley, Mary 80
Shelley, Percy Bysshe 10, 23 n.39,
80
A Defense of Poetry 10
"Ode to the West Wind" 106
Revolt of Islam 80

*Silencing the Past: Power and the
Production of History* 1, 18 n.4,
137 n.6, 142, 155
slavery 3, 4, 12, 17, 72, 82, 104,
118, 172
abolition of (*see* abolitionism)
American Constitution sanctioning
of 193, 195
domestic slavery 197–200
as a modern capitalist institution 99
violence of 169, 199–200
Smith, Gerrit 179
Smith, James McCune 163
social contract 119, 120, 121
Sonthonax, Léger-Félicité 38, 72,
82, 86–8
sovereignty 16, 117, 118, 151,
153, 156
speech acts 88, 107, 120, 128
Spillers, Hortense 98
Spires, Derrick 164, 167, 174, 175,
176
Stain Méry, Médéric-Louis-Élie
Moreau de 61–2, 62–3, 94 n.52
Stancliff, Michael 167
Stanley, Joshua 105
Stephens, Aaron Dwight 176
Stewart, Maria 168
Still, William 183 n.48
Strongman, Roberto 60
stupefaction, stupeur 142–4, 147,
148–9, 151, 154–5
subject(s)
Absolute subject 77, 78
Badiou's theory of 77–8
contingency and futurity 75
and ego 78
public subjects 73, 78–9, 81
Romantic subjects 14, 72, 76, 77–
8, 79, 89
in social systems 40, 79
as stable identity 78–9
what makes (or breaks) 71, 74–5,
76, 78, 81, 89, 90
and world 78
Sundquist, Eric 199
Swift, Jonathan 52, 56
"Upon the South-Sea Project" 52–3

216 INDEX

Taylor, Charles 75, 90
teleology 31, 155, 156
Temple, Crystal 163
Thoreau, Henry David 56
Tinsley, Omise'eke Natasha 60
tranquility 99, 100
Trotsky, Leon 102
Trouillot, Hénock 47–8 n.65
Trouillot, Michel-Rolph 5–6, 8, 137
 n.6, 142, 157 n.4, 167, 170

universalism, universal humanity 8, 4,
 16, 161 n.53
universality 128, 133, 135
unthinkability/the unthinkable 1, 2,
 5–9, 12, 142, 155, 170
US Constitution 193, 195

Vastey, Baron de 32
vengeance 27–8, 33, 121–2, 127
 divine vengeance 130
Victor, Pierre (Baron de
 Malouet) 57, 58
Vodou, Vodun 3, 31, 49, 50, 62
 cosmologies, gender and sexuality
 60
 as a form of resistance 3–4
 Louisiana voodoo 51
 "Sou lanmè" (song) 64
 transcorporeality 63
 Vodou songs 51, 64
volcano, metaphor of revolutions
 as 102–3
Voltaire, François Marie Arouet de
 12–13, 26–7, 32–3, 35, 43
 Alzire 28, 29
 Dessalines' familiarity with 27, 29
 Eriphile 33–4, 36, 46 n.38, 46 n.46
 *Le fanatisme, ou Mahomet le
 prophète* 35–6
 shadowy presence in Proclamation
 of 1804 28–9, 30, 40, 42

Zaïre 29, 41
vow, avowal 118, 119, 120, 121, 130,
 133, 135

Walsh, John 90 n.6
Wang, Orrin 11
Webb, Frank 170
Webster, Daniel 195–6
Weekly Anglo-African 164, 179,
 180 n.2
Weheliye, Alexander 27, 42, 109,
 116 n.49
 Habeas Viscus 41
whiteness 61, 86, 149
white supremacy/supremacist 27, 42,
 51–2, 63
Wilderson, Frank 152–3
Wilson, William J. 163, 170
Wong, Edlie 170
Wordsworth, William 55, 57, 64,
 96–7, 104–5
 "The Brothers, a Pastoral
 Poem" 54–5
 personification by 108–9
 Poems, in Two Volumes 103
 on poetry 99
 preface to *Lyrical Ballads* 96, 101,
 105, 109, 111
 The Prelude 4, 75, 105
 responses to his poem 103–4
 "To Toussaint L'Ouverture" 13–14,
 96, 105, 106, 108–9, 110
Wynter, Sylvia 69–70 n.48, 109

Yingling, Charlton 168
Yoruba 3
Youngquist, Paul 1, 11, 22 n.34,
 71, 109
Yusoff, Kathryn 81

Zustand (state or condition) 77–8,
 196, 197

Printed in the USA
CPSIA information can be obtained
at www.ICGtesting.com
LVHW010354060124
768264LV00003B/150